MASTERPIECES OF
MODERN SPANISH DRAMA

MASTERPIECES OF
MODERN SPANISH DRAMA

THE GREAT GALEOTO
THE DUCHESS OF SAN QUENTIN
DANIELA

TRANSLATED FROM THE SPANISH AND CATALAN

EDITED, WITH A PREFACE BY
BARRETT H. CLARK

D. APPLETON AND COMPANY
NEW YORK :: MCMXXVIII :: LONDON

KRAUS REPRINT CO.
New York
1969

CONTENTS

PREFACE

THE drama of Spain, early and modern, has in English-speaking countries been sadly neglected. It is a regrettable fact that one of the most gorgeous and passionate outbursts of national dramatic genius has received but scant attention from English readers. Cervantes' name is at least not unknown to the great mass of readers in every language, but to the majority of English and Americans, Lope de Vega, Tirso de Molina, and Calderon—to mention only the greatest of dozens of dramatists of the time—are a closed book. About fifteen Calderon plays are available in some form in English translation or adaptation, only two or three of Lope and, to my knowledge, not one of Tirso. Of the eighteenth century lesser lights I should venture to say that there is in English no translation. The case is the same with the dramatists of the early nineteenth century, if we except one or two notable translations and studies, like that recently issued by the Hispanic Society (a translation of *Un nuevo drama*). And yet this period saw a rebirth of the national spirit in the drama unequalled in any other country save France.

The modern drama in Spain is somewhat better known, and bids fair to receive even better treatment than it has already received. Echegaray is represented by six or seven of his most typical plays, the translations of which range from very bad to excellent; Galdós by three; Guimerá by two; Benavente by two—though a volume of five has been announced.[1] There remains, however, a vast field as yet

[1] Translated by John Garrett Underhill and published by Charles Scribner's Sons.

untouched. Surely there are many plays of the dramatists already mentioned which ought to be translated, while Dicenta, Linares Rivas, Martiñez Sierra, and Rusiñol, cannot be neglected.

The present volume will, it is hoped, encourage the publication of further contemporary Spanish plays. The work is as yet scarcely begun. Of the plays here presented to English readers, two have never before been translated, and the other—*El gran galeoto*—in a literal and rather stiff version, in a free adaptation and modernization, and in a good translation recently published but little known. No excuse is therefore needed for the inclusion of this masterpiece in a volume whose function it is to present three varied aspects of the dramatic genius of modern Spain.

The three dramatists whose work is here represented exemplify three widely different branches of recent Spanish drama. Echegaray, who is in spirit a typical Spaniard in his fondness for melodramatic and, to the Anglo-Saxon mind, exaggerated situations, is by far the most European, I had almost said, eclectic, of the group. His wide education and many-sided interests and activities, his acquaintance with foreign languages and literatures, have resulted at times in an unhappy fusion of many manners. As has been pointed out by Miss Elizabeth Wallace in her article on Modern Spanish Drama, the main currents of contemporary drama have for the most part failed to interest the Spaniards. She says: "The northern realistic drama has also been doomed to unsuccess in Spain. Aside from the enigmatical character of some episodes and the puerility of some of the allegories, the dramas of Ibsen have interested the reading classes because of the vitality, not so much passional as intellectual, of their subjects. But the harsh individualism, the intimate and subtle sentiments of self-centered men cannot be understood by the Spanish public. Such types as are found in

PREFACE

Ibsen, Björnson, and Sudermann are unknown in Spain."
Attempts were made—Echegaray's own *El Hijo de Don Juan*
is a case in question—to treat subjects that were basically
foreign to the Spanish temperament, but these seem to lack
the spontaneity of the true indigenous play. It is a curious
fact that Spain is the only country whose drama is funda-
mentally at its best when it follows the best traditions of
its Golden Age. This does not mean that Galdós writes
like Lope de Vega. Galdós has ideas of his own on the subject of technic, but it is incontestable that *El Abuelo* is part
and parcel of the spirit that produced *La Estrella de Sevilla*,
and that *Terra Baixa* (*Marta of the Lowlands*) thrills with the
passion of Calderon. Giacosa in Italy, Hauptmann in Germany, Becque in France, were each of them able to adopt the
new manner and produce works of significance and value;
Echegaray and Galdós at best could only assimilate a few
technical points. It is their glory that they remained truly
Spanish.

Galdós won international fame with his novels, but not
until the nineties did he return to the drama, from the
pursuit of which an early failure had discouraged him. It
would be matter for surprise if an author, after writing
novels for twenty years, should turn to the drama, and find
himself endowed with a dramatic technic ready to hand.
Galdós' technic is not the technic of Echegaray, nor of Scribe,
nor of Ibsen; it is rather a technic derived from the earlier
Spanish drama, and partly evolved out of the author's own
novelistic methods. He says: "There are some who aver
that there is a natural antagonism between the means and
ends of these two forms [the novel and the drama]; they
start, however, at the same source, and are two fraternal
rivers, each intermingling with the other." *Electra*, and more
especially *Realidad*, are novelistic; *El Abuelo* combines
many of the excellences of the novel, but not one of these

plays is primarily important for its inherent dramatic or theatrical qualities. It may well be doubted whether *El Abuelo,* strong and beautiful as it is, would not have been stronger and still more beautiful had it been written as a novel. The canvas is too large, the ideas too general. The play-form requires a rigid adherence to a set of tested rules, and while these rules may be, and are questioned, and once in a while found wanting and changed, it seems rather a pity that men with great ideas should sacrifice themselves to the work of pure technical innovation.

Guimerá is the central figure in the rebirth of Catalan nationalism in literature, art, and politics. His native language is the Catalan, which, according to John Garrett Underhill, is "one of the Romance family to which the neighboring French and Spanish also belong. Like them it derives from the Latin, but its closest affinity is with the Provençal. The medieval troubadours overran Catalonia and Valencia quite as they did their own Provence, and Catalan attained its greatest development shortly afterward." All his plays are written in Catalan and acted at the *Teatre Catala.* Guimerá in his best plays is a dramatist of the front rank; he has studied, imitated the technic of others, but has finally adopted one of his own, which is economical, tense, and compelling.

And yet, despite their differences, Echegaray, Galdós, and Guimerá are essentially Spanish. The first exemplifies nationalism and internationalism, nationalism in subject-matter, and internationalism in the manner of its presentation; the second, the tendency to depict soberly, skilfully, deeply, the life of the Spaniard of today; the third, nationalism of a particular section. As may be seen after a cursory reading of the three plays contained in this little collection, the Spanish drama of today cannot easily be summed up in a few words; the attempt here made is largely with a view

PREFACE

to showing something of the genius of a nation whose dramatic products have as yet scarcely begun to receive the attention they so well deserve.

BARRETT H. CLARK.

PREFACE TO THE NEW EDITION

The publication of *Masterpieces of Modern Spanish Drama* in 1917 marked the close of an epoch: two of the three dramatists whose work was chosen to represent that epoch had practically ceased writing; one of them (Echegaray) was dead, and one of them (Galdós) ill and infirm. Galdós has since died, and Guimerà has, I believe, written no plays during the past few years.

The epoch which in 1917 was drawing to a close is now, or may by us who are not too close to the day-by-day developments in Spain be considered an epoch of the past. Younger dramatists have taken the place of the recognized "masters" and are in their turn designated by the same word, and I fancy that in Madrid Echegaray and Galdós are among the writers whose work is periodically resuscitated much as we celebrate literary centenaries. Certainly Echegaray seems old-fashioned compared with Benavente; and Galdós, as a dramatist, is woefully Mid-Victorian —or whatever the Spanish say when they mean that. As for Guimerà, the Catalan Nationalists may still revere him as a great political figure, but I know that his best plays are often referred to as outmoded.

Ought I, then, to delete the "Modern" from the title of this collection? I think not; or at least, retaining it, I am willing to grow old along with the Moderns of a few years ago. I am

PREFACE

willing to admit that Echegaray and Galdós have given way
to Benavente and *his* juniors, but while admitting the merits of
the younger men I beg leave to perpetuate, so far as I am able,
with the coöperation of my publisher, the memory of three dramatic artists who carried on, not without honor both at home and
abroad, the best traditions of the Spanish stage. If my trio
have suffered a little by the advent of the younger generation, we
must remember how bravely they took up arms in that great
dramatic "movement" throughout Europe that followed close
upon the heels of Ibsen and that today seems like a page out of
ancient history. Echegaray and Galdós and Guimerà are not
doomed to oblivion, for they were men of vision and men of
passion, and their art is still alive, even though it is not the out-
growth of the latest discoveries of scientists and historians.

BARRETT H. CLARK.

NOTE

Thanks to the courtesy and interest of Mr. John Garrett
Underhill, I am able to furnish information regarding the
life of Guimerá and publish authoritative references and lists
of plays of all the dramatists represented in this volume,
which would otherwise have been either very difficult or
else impossible to obtain.

JOSÉ ECHEGARAY

JOSÉ ECHEGARAY was born at Madrid in 1832. Always
an apt pupil, at an early age he showed marked propensities
for mathematics and the exact sciences, but although he
has never lost his interest in these pursuits, he became interested in literature and the theater, and in later years made an
extensive study of the drama of modern Europe. He was
graduated in 1853 from the Escuela de Caminos, with high
honors, and became a tutor in mathematics. Not long afterward, he was appointed to a professorship in that subject in
the same school from which he graduated. From that time
on, his interests widened; he studied political economy, philosophy, geology, and politics. He was likewise engaged in
engineering and chemical work, and became a recognized
authority. At the age of thirty-two he wrote a play, but laid
it aside, deeming it unworthy; but his interest in the theater
was rapidly increasing. He was appointed Minister for the
Colonies under the government following the Revolution of
1868, and his political duties prevented further development
of his dramatic talent. Five years later he was proscribed,
forced to leave the country and go to France, where he wrote
his first play to be produced, "El Libro Talonario." On
his return to Spain in 1874, it was presented, but did not
attract widespread attention. His first success was "En
el Puño de la Espada" (1875), which was followed by a
long series of tragedies, comedies, and thesis plays.

Echegaray died in the summer of 1916.

CHRONOLOGICAL LIST OF THE PLAYS OF JOSÉ ECHEGARAY

O locura ó santidad is translated as *Folly or Saintliness* by Hannah Lynch (John Lane Co.), London, 1895, and as *Madman or Saint*, by Ruth Lansing (Poet Lore, 1912); *El gran Galeoto* as *The Great Galeoto*, by Hannah Lynch (John Lane

Co., 1895), and later reprinted by Doubleday, Page & Co. in the Drama League Series of Plays); also as *The Great Galeoto*, translated by Jacob S. Fassett (Badger, Boston, 1914); *El Hijo de Don Juan* as *The Son of Don Juan* by James Graham (Roberts Bros., Boston, 1895); *Mariana* by the same, and by Fredico Sarda and Carlos D. S. Wuppermann (Moods, New York, 1909), *El hombre negro* as *The Man in Black* by Ellen Watson (Universal Anthology); and *El loco Dios* as *The Madman Divine*, by Elizabeth Howard West (Poet Lore, 1908); *Siempre en Ridículo* as *Always Ridiculous*, by T. Walter Gilkyson (Poet Lore, 1916).

References: The introductions to the Lynch and Graham translations above referred to; Bernard Shaw, *Dramatic Opinions and Essays* (Brentano); C. F. Nirdlinger, *Masks and Mummers* (De Witt, New York); Manuel Bueno, *Teatro Español contemporáneo* (Madrid, 1909); Luis Antón del Olmet y Arturo García Carraffa, *Echegaray* (Madrid, 1912); Barrett H. Clark, *The Continental Drama of Today* (Henry Holt & Co.); Atlantic Monthly, vol. cii, p. 357; Poet Lore, vol. xii, p. 405; Contemporary Review, vol. lxiv, p. 576; Review of Reviews, vol. xxxi, p. 613.

THE GREAT GALEOTO
(*El Gran Galeoto*)

A PLAY IN THREE ACTS AND A PROLOGUE
BY JOSÉ ECHEGARAY

TRANSLATED FROM THE SPANISH BY
ELEANOR BONTECOU

———————

Produced, for the first time, in Madrid, at the Teatro Español, March 19, 18--

CHARACTERS

TEODORA
DON JULIAN, *her husband*
DOÑA MERCEDES
DON SEVERO, *her husband*
PEPITO, *her son*
ERNESTO
A BYSTANDER
A SERVANT
ANOTHER SERVANT

THE GREAT GALEOTO

PROLOGUE

ERNESTO'S *study. To the left, a French window; to the right, a door.—Nearly in the center, a table on which are books, papers, and a lighted lamp.—To the right is a sofa. It is evening.* ERNESTO *is seated at the table, as though about to write.*

ERN. There's no use. I can't do it. It is impossible. I am simply contending with the impossible. The idea is here; it is stirring in my brain; I can feel it. Sometimes a light from within illumines it and I see it with its shifting form and vague contours, and suddenly there sound in the hidden depths voices that give it life; cries of grief, sighs of love, sardonic, mocking laughter—a whole world of living, struggling passions. They break from me, and spread out, and fill the air all about me! Then, then, I say to myself, the moment has come, and I take up my pen, and with eyes gazing into space, with straining ears, with fast-beating heart, I bend over my paper.—But oh, the irony of impotence! The contours become blurred, the vision disappears, the shouts and sighs die away, and nothingness, nothingness surrounds me! The desolation of empty space, of meaningless thought, of deadly weariness! More than all that, the desolation of an idle pen and a barren page—a page bereft of all life-giving thought. Ah, how many forms has nothingness, and how it mocks, dark and silent, at creatures of my sort! Many, many

7

forms:—the colorless canvas, the shapeless piece of marble, the discordant sound, but none more irritating, more mocking, more blighting than this worthless pen and this blank paper. Ah, I cannot cover you, but I can destroy you, vile accomplice in my wrecked ambitions and my everlasting humiliation!—So, so,—smaller, still smaller. [*Tearing the paper—then, a pause*] Well, it's fortunate that no one saw me, for at best such ranting is foolish, and it's all wrong. No—I will not give in; I will think harder, harder, until I conquer or blow up in a thousand pieces. No, I will never admit I am beaten. Come, let's see whether now—

> *Enter* DON JULIAN, *right, wearing a frock coat and carrying his overcoat on his arm. He looks in at the door but doesn't come in.*

JUL. Hello, Ernesto!

ERN. Don Julian!

JUL. Still working? Am I disturbing you?

ERN. Disturbing me? Indeed, no. Come in, come in, Don Julian. Where's Teodora?

JUL. We've just come from the opera. She went up to the third floor with my brother and his wife to see some purchases of Mercedes, and I was on my way to my own room, when I saw a light in yours and looked in to say good-night.

ERN. Were there many people there?

JUL. A good many—as usual. All my friends were asking for you. They were surprised at your not going.

ERN. How kind of them!

JUL. Not so very, considering all that you deserve. But how about you? Have you made good use of these three hours of solitude and inspiration?

ERN. Solitude, yes; inspiration, no. That would not come to me, though I called upon it desperately and with passion.

JUL. It wouldn't obey the summons?

ERN. No, and this was not the first time. But I did make a profitable discovery, though I accomplished nothing.

JUL. What?

ERN. Simply this—that I am a poor good-for-nothing.

JUL. Good-for-nothing! Well, that's a profitable discovery, indeed.

ERN. Precisely.

JUL. And why so disgusted with yourself? Isn't the play you told about the other day going well?

ERN. I'm the one who is going—out of my mind!

JUL. And what is all this trouble that inspiration and the play together are making for my Ernesto?

ERN. The trouble is this; when I conceived it I thought the idea a good one; but when I give it form and dress it out in the proper stage trappings the result is extraordinary; contrary to all laws of the drama; utterly impossible.

JUL. But why impossible? Come, tell me about it. I am curious.

ERN. Imagine, then, that the principal character, the one who creates the drama, who develops, who animates it, who brings about the catastrophe, and who thrives upon that catastrophe and revels in it—that person cannot appear on the stage.

JUL. Is he so ugly? Or so repulsive? Or so wicked?

ERN. It's not that. He is no uglier than any one else—than you or I. Nor is he bad. Neither bad nor good. Repulsive? No indeed. I am not such a sceptic, nor such a misanthrope, nor so at odds with the world that I would say such a thing or commit such an injustice.

JUL. Well, then, what is the reason?

ERN. Don Julian, the reason is that there probably wouldn't be room on the stage for the character in question.

JUL. Good heavens, listen to the man! Is this a mythological play, then, and do Titans appear on the stage?

ERN. They are Titans; but a modern variety.

JUL. In short?

ERN. In short this character is—*Everybody*.

JUL. *Everybody!* Well, you are right! There's not room in the theater for everybody. That is an indisputable fact that has often been demonstrated.

ERN. Now you see how right I was.

JUL. Not altogether. *Everybody* can be condensed into a certain number of types, or characters. I don't understand these things myself, but I have heard that authors have done it more than once.

ERN. Yes, but in my case, that is, in my play, it can't be done.

JUL. Why not?

ERN. For many reasons that it would take too long to explain; especially at this time of night.

JUL. Never mind, let's have some of them.

ERN. Well then, each part of this vast whole, each head of this thousand-headed monster, of this Titan of today whom I call *Everybody*, takes part in my play only for the briefest instant, speaks one word and no more, gives one glance; perhaps his entire action consists in the suggestion of one smile; he appears for a moment and goes away again; he works without passion, without guile, without malice, indifferently, and absently—often *by* his very abstraction.

JUL. And what then?

ERN. From those words, from those fleeting glances, from those indifferent smiles, from all those little whispers, from all those peccadilloes; from all these things that we might call insignificant rays of dramatic light, when brought to a focus in one family, result the spark and the explosion, the struggle and the victims. If I represent the whole of mankind by a given number of types or symbolic characters, I have to ascribe to each one that which is really distributed among many, with the result that a certain number of characters must appear who are made repulsive by vices that lack verisimilitude, whose crimes have no object. And, as an additional result, there is the danger that people will believe I am trying to paint society as evil, corrupt, and cruel, when I only want to show that not even the most insignificant acts are really insignificant or impotent for good or evil; for, gathered together by the mysterious agencies of modern life, they may succeed in producing tremendous results.

JUL. Come, stop, stop! That is all dreadfully metaphysical. I get a glimmering, but the clouds are pretty thick. In fact, you understand more than I do about these things. Now, if it were a question of drafts, of notes, of letters of credit, of discount, it would be another matter.

ERN. Oh, no, you have common-sense, which is the main thing.

JUL. Thanks, Ernesto, you are very kind.

ERN. But are you convinced?

JUL. No, I'm not. There must be some way of getting round the difficulty.

ERN. If only there were!

JUL. Is there something more?

ERN. I should say so! Tell me, what is the moving force of the drama?

JUL. I don't know exactly what you mean by the moving force of the drama, but I will say that I don't find any pleasure in plays in which there are no love-affairs; preferably unhappy love-affairs, for I have plenty of happy love-making in my own house with my Teodora.

ERN. Good. Splendid! Well, in my play there is hardly any love-making at all.

JUL. Bad, very bad indeed, I say. Listen, I don't know

what your play is about, but I am afraid that it won't interest anybody.

ERN. That's just what I told you. Still, love-making might be put in, and even a little jealousy.

JUL. Well, with that, with an interesting and well-developed intrigue, with some really striking situation. . . .

ERN. No, señor, certainly not that. Everything must be quite commonplace, almost vulgar. This drama can have no outward manifestation. It goes on in the hearts and minds of the characters; it progresses slowly; today it is a question of a thought; tomorrow of a heartbeat; gradually the will is undermined. . . .

JUL. But how is all this shown? How are these inner struggles expressed? Who tells the audience about them? Where are they seen? Are we to spend the whole evening in pursuit of a glance, a sigh, a gesture, a word? My dear boy, that is no sort of amusement. When a man wants to meddle with such abstractions he studies philosophy.

ERN. That's it, exactly. You repeat my thoughts like an echo.

JUL. I don't want to discourage you, however. You probably know what you are doing. And, even though the play may be a little colorless, even though it may seem a bit heavy and uninteresting, so long as it has a fine climax and the catastrophe. . . . eh?

ERN. Catastrophe—climax! They have hardly come when the curtain falls.

JUL. You mean that the play begins when the play ends?

ERN. I'm afraid so—though, of course, I shall try to put a little warmth into it.

JUL. Come now, what you ought to do is write the second play, the one that begins when the first ends; for the first, judging by what you say, isn't worth the trouble—and plenty of trouble it's bound to give you.

ERN. I was convinced of that.

JUL. And now we both are—thanks to your cleverness and the force of your logic. What is the title?

ERN. Title! Why, that's another thing. It has no title.

JUL. What! What did you say? No title, either?

ERN. No, señor.

JUL. Well, Ernesto, you must have been asleep when I came in—you were having a nightmare and now you are telling me your dreams.

ERN. Dreaming? Yes. A nightmare? Perhaps. And I am telling you my dreams, good and bad. You have common - sense, and you always guess right in everything.

JUL. It didn't take much penetration to guess right in this case. A play in which the principal character doesn't appear, in which there is almost no love-making, in which nothing happens that doesn't happen every day, which begins as the curtain falls on the last act, and which has no title.—Well, I don't see how it can be written, how it can be acted, or how any one can be found to listen to it,—or, indeed, how it is a play at all.

ERN. Ah, but it is a play. The only trouble is that I must give it form, and *that* I don't know how to do.

JUL. Do you want my advice?

ERN. Your advice? The advice of my friend, my benefactor, my second father! Oh, Don Julian!

JUL. Come, come, Ernesto, let us not have a little sentimental play of our own here in place of yours which we have pronounced impossible. I only asked you whether you wanted to know my advice.

ERN. And I said, Yes.

JUL. Well, forget all about plays—go to bed—go to sleep—go shooting with me tomorrow, kill any number of partridges instead of killing two characters, and perhaps having the audience kill you—and when all is said and done, you'll be thankful to me.

ERN. That can't be: I must write the play.

JUL. But, my dear fellow, you must have thought of it by way of penance for your sins.

ERN. I don't know why it happened, but think of it I did. I feel it stirring in my mind, it begs for life in the outer world, and I am bound to give it that.

JUL. Can't you find some other plot?

ERN. But what about this idea?

JUL. Let the devil take care of it.

ERN. Ah, Don Julian, do you think that when an idea has been hammered out in our minds, we can destroy it and bring it to naught whenever we choose? I should like to think of another play, but this accursed one won't let me until it has been born into the world.

JUL. There's no use talking, then. I only hope you get some light on the subject.

ERN. That is the question, as Hamlet says.

JUL. [*In a low voice, with mock mystery*] Couldn't you put it in the literary orphanage for anonymous works?

ERN. Don Julian, I am a man of conscience. My children, good or bad, are legitimate, and shall bear my name.

JUL. I'll say no more. It must be—it is written.

ERN. I only wish it were. Unfortunately it is not written; but no matter, if I don't write it, someone else will.

JUL. Well, to work! Good luck, and don't let any one get ahead of you.

TEO. [*Without*] Julian! Julian!

JUL. There's Teodora!

TEO. Are you here, Julian?

JUL. Yes, here I am. Come in!

    Enter TEODORA.

TEO. Good-evening, Ernesto.

ERN. Good-evening, Teodora. Did they sing well?

TEO. As usual. Have you done a lot of work?

ERN. As usual; nothing.

TEO. Why, you might better have gone with us. All my friends were asking for you.

ERN. It seems that everybody is taking an interest in me.

JUL. I should say so; since you are going to make *Everybody* the principal character in your play, naturally it is to his interest to have you for his friend.

TEO. A play?

JUL. Hush, it's a great mystery; you mustn't ask anything about it. It has no title, no actors, no action, no catastrophe! Oh, how sublime! Good-night, Ernesto.— Come, Teodora.

ERN. Good-bye, Julian.

TEO. Until tomorrow.

ERN. Good-night.

TEO. [*To* JULIAN] How preoccupied Mercedes seemed!

JUL. And Severo was in a rage.

TEO. I wonder why.

JUL. I'm sure I don't know. Pepito, on the other hand, was lively enough for both.

TEO. He always is,—and speaking ill of every one.

JUL. A character for Ernesto's play.

TEODORA *and* JULIAN *go out, right.*

ERN. Let Julian say what he likes, I am not going to give up my undertaking. It would be rank cowardice. No, I will not retreat. Forward! [*He rises and walks up and down in agitation. Then he goes over to the French window*] Night, lend me your protection, for against your blackness the luminous outlines of my inspiration are defined more clearly than against the blue cloak of day. Lift up your roofs, ye thousands of houses in this mighty city; for surely you should do as much for a poet in distress as for that crooked devil who mischievously lifted your tops off. Let me see the men and women coming back to your rooms to rest after the busy hours of pleasure-seeking. As my ears become more sensitive, let them distinguish the many words of those who were asking Julian and Teodora about me; and as a great light is made from scattered rays when they are gathered into a crystal lens, as the mountains are formed from grains of sand and the sea from drops of water, so from your chance words, your stray smiles, your idle glances, from a thousand trivial thoughts which you have left scattered in cafés, in theaters, in ball-rooms, and which are now floating in the air, I shall shape my drama, and the crystal of my mind shall be the lens that brings to a focus the lights and shadows, so that from them shall result the dramatic spark and the tragic explosion. My drama is taking shape. Now it has a title, for there in the lamplight I see the work of the immortal Florentine poet, and in Italian it has given me the name which it would be madness or folly to write or speak in plain Spanish. Paolo and Francesca, may your love help me! [*Sitting down at the table and beginning to write*] The play! the play begins! The first page is no longer blank [*writing*]. Now it has a title. [*Writes madly*] *The Great Galeoto!*

Curtain.

ACT I

A room in DON JULIAN'S *house. At the back a large door. Beyond it, a little passage, at the very end of which is the dining-room door. This door is closed until the end of the act. To the left of the audience, towards the front, a French window. To the right, two doors. In front, at the right, a sofa. To the left a small table and an arm-chair. Everything is expensive and luxurious. It is late afternoon.* TEODORA *is looking out of the French window.* JULIAN *sits on the sofa, lost in thought.*

TEO. What a beautiful sunset! Such glorious colors, such clouds! If the future is printed on those azure pages, as poets say and our fathers believed; if the mysterious secret of human destiny is written on the sapphire sphere in stars of fire, and if this glorious sky is the page that tells of our fate, what joys await us, how the future smiles upon us! But what are you thinking of? Come, Julian, look out here. Why don't you say something?

JUL. [*Absent-mindedly*] What is it?

TEO. [*Going to him*] Weren't you listening to me?

JUL. My heart is always with you, for you are its goal and its loadstone; but sometimes my mind is distracted by importunate cares, by business affairs—

TEO. Which I detest, since they rob me of my husband's attention, if not of his affection. But what is it, Julian? Something is worrying you, and it must be serious, because you have been sitting there for a long time, sadly, without speaking. Are you in trouble, Julian dear? Then my heart

17

demands a share in it, for if my joys are yours I want your sorrows to be mine.

JUL. In trouble? When you are happy! Sorrows? When in my Teodora I have the sum of all joys? While your cheeks show those two roses and your eyes that fire which is the light of the soul, shining in twin heavens, while I know that I alone am master of your heart, what sorrows or troubles or afflictions could keep me from being the happiest man in the whole world?

TEO. And you have no business worries, either?

JUL. Money has never yet made me lose sleep or appetite. Though I have no aversion to it, I've always been perfectly indifferent, so it has always come running into my coffers as meek as a lamb. I've always been rich and I am rich now, and until I die of old age, thanks to God and his own good fortune, Don Julian de Garagarza will have the best credit, though perhaps not the largest fortune, of any banker in Madrid, Cadiz, or El Puerto.

TEO. Well, then, why were you so preoccupied a few minutes ago?

JUL. I was thinking—thinking of something nice.

TEO. That's not strange, Julian, since the thought was yours.

JUL. Flatterer, don't try to wheedle me!

TEO. But tell me what it was.

JUL. I wanted to close up a promising little deal.

TEO. Something about the new works?

JUL. Oh, it's not a question of works of stone and iron.

TEO. Of what, then?

JUL. Of works of charity and good-will in connection with a sacred debt of long standing.

TEO. [*With natural and spontaneous joy*] Oh, I know!

JUL. Really?

TEO. You were thinking of Ernesto.

JUL. You have guessed right.

TEO. Poor lad, you do well to think of him. He is so good, so noble, so generous!

JUL. Exactly like his father, the very pattern of honor and chivalry!

TEO. So he is! And so talented! Twenty-six years old . . . and so scholarly! He knows everything! Why, he is an absolute prodigy!

JUL. A scholar, you say? Well, that doesn't help much. Indeed, that's just the trouble, for I'm afraid that as he goes about with his head in the clouds, he'll never learn to get on in this world, which is prosaic and treacherous, and never pays any tribute to genius until some three hundred years after it has hounded it to death.

TEO. But with you for a guide . . . for surely, Julian, you are not thinking of deserting him?

JUL. Desert him! I should be ungrateful indeed if I could forget what I owe his father. For my sake Don Juan de Acedo risked name, fortune, even honor. If this young man wants the blood in my veins he need only ask for it, for it is ever ready to pay my debt of honor.

TEO. Bravo, Julian! Spoken like yourself!

JUL. You yourself saw how it was. When they told me about a year ago that Don Juan was dead and that his son was left in poverty, I couldn't take the Gerona train fast enough. I fairly dragged him away by main force, brought him here with me, led him into the middle of the room, and said to him, "Everything I own is at your disposal, for it is really yours. I owe it all to your father. If you like, you shall be master of this house. At least, look upon me as a second father. Though I can't equal the first in goodness, I shall strive to be a close second, and as for loving you. . . . Well, we shall see who is best at that!"

TEO. It's true! . . . Those were your very words; and the

poor boy—he is so good—burst out crying like a child, and threw his arms about your neck.

JUL. You're right, he is a child. And we must think of him and of his future. And now you know why you saw me looking grave and preoccupied a while ago. I was trying to think of some way to do for him all I should like to, while you were chattering to me about a beautiful view and a glorious sky and a red sun, for which I have no use at all, since two far brighter suns shine for me in our own heaven.

TEO. But I don't understand? What would you like to do for Ernesto?

JUL. That's what I said.

TEO. But how can you possibly do more than you have done? For a year now he has been living here with us like one of the family. Why, if he were your own son you couldn't show greater love for him, nor could I feel more affection for him if he were my own brother.

JUL. That's all very well, but it's not enough.

TEO. Not enough? Why, I believe . . .

JUL. You are thinking of the present, and I of the future.

TEO. The future.—Oh, I can arrange that very easily.— Listen! He will live in this house as long as he likes—oh, for years—just as though it were his own. That's quite simple. Then, in due course, as is right and natural, he will fall in love and marry. Then, honorably discharging your debts, you will hand over to him a large part of your fortune. From the church, *he* and *she* will go to his own house—for, as the saying goes, "To be head of a household one needs a house." But we shall not forget him, nor shall we love him any the less because he doesn't live here. And now everything is quite clear. Of course, they are happy; we are more so.—They have children—undoubtedly—we have more. At any rate we have a daughter. She and Ernesto's son fall in love with each other.—They get married. . . .

JUL. [*Laughing*] But, good heavens, where does all this end?

TEO. You were talking about the future, and this is the future that I offer you. If you have any other, Julian, I don't like it, and I won't accept it.

JUL. Oh, mine is like yours, Teodora, but . . .

TEO. Mercy on us, here's a *but* already . . .

JUL. Listen, Teodora; in taking care of this unfortunate young man we are paying our debts as we should—and to the duty we owe the son of Acedo are added the demands of the affection we feel for him for his own sake. But complications enter into every act of man. There are always two points of view; the shield always has a reverse. By which I mean, Teodora, that in this case, giving help and receiving it are not simply opposites, but are entirely different things, and that I am afraid in the end he may consider my gifts a humiliation. He is high-minded, and he is extremely proud. We must find some way out of the situation for him, Teodora. We must do still more for him and pretend that we are doing less.

TEO. How?

JUL. You shall see. But here he comes.

TEO. Not a word!

ERNESTO *enters and stands at the back.*

JUL. Welcome!

ERN. Don Julian—Teodora.

He greets them absent-mindedly and sits down by the table, lost in thought.

JUL. [*Going up to him*] What's the matter?

ERN. Nothing.

JUL. I see something in your eyes, and your uneasiness betrays you. Are you unhappy?

ERN. Nonsense.

JUL. Are you worried about something?

ERN. Not at all.

JUL. Perhaps I am importunate?

ERN. You importunate! Good gracious! [*Rising and going up to him. Effusively*] No indeed, your affection moves you, your friendship gives you the right, and you read my very heart when you look into my eyes. Yes, señor, there is something wrong. But I will tell you all about it. Don Julian, forgive me, and you, too, I beg of you—[*to* TEODORA]. I'm foolish and childish and ungrateful. Indeed, I don't deserve your kindness, I don't deserve your affection. I ought to be happy with such a father and such a sister, and not think of the morrow—and yet I must think of it. This explanation makes me blush; but don't you both understand? Yes, yes, you must understand that my position here is a false one [*Vehemently*], that I am living here on charity.

TEO. That word . . .

ERN. Teodora!

TEO. Is displeasing to us.

ERN. Yes, señora, I have spoken awkwardly, but it is the truth.

JUL. And I tell you, it is not true. If any one in this house lives on charity, and no mean charity at that, it is not you, but I.

ERN. I know, señor, the story of two loyal friends, and of a great fortune of which I have no recollection. That noble act did honor to my father, but I should stain that honor if I demanded payment for his kindness. I am a young man, Don Julian, and although I am not good for much, I can certainly do something to earn my bread. Is this pride or madness? I don't know, and I have lost the ability to judge— but I have not forgotten that my father used to say to me, "What you can do yourself, entrust to no man; for what you can earn yourself, be indebted to no one."

JUL. So my favors humiliate you and are a burden to you—your friends seem importunate creditors?

TEO. Your argument is fallacious. You know a great deal, Ernesto, but in this case the heart knows more.

JUL. My father didn't show any such haughty disdain for yours. . . .

TEO. Friendship, it seems, was a different thing in those days.

ERN. Teodora!

TEO. [*To* JULIAN] It's his idealism.

ERN. It's true. I am ungracious. . . . I know it. And foolish, too. Forgive me, Don Julian. [*Deeply moved*]

JUL. [*To* TEODORA] He's raving mad.

TEO. Why, he doesn't live on this earth at all.

JUL. You're right, wise man and philosopher though he may be. . . . And he is drowning himself in a puddle of water.

ERN. You say I know nothing of the world and can't make my way in it. It's true. But I can see that way dimly, and I tremble, I know not why. I'm drowning in the puddles of life as though in the deep sea! They frighten me more, I don't deny it, much more than the vast ocean. The sea stretches out to the boundaries set for it by the wide sands; the puddle sends its emanations throughout all space. Strong arms may struggle against the waves of the sea; there is no way to struggle against treacherous infections. And if I am destined to be defeated, I pray only that in the end, defeat may not dishonor me. I ask only to see before me— and this shall suffice—the sea that is waiting to engulf me, the sword that shall pierce me, or the rock that shall crush me; to recognize my enemy, to realize his strength and his fury, and to scorn him as I fall, to scorn him as I die. Let me not gradually breathe in from the atmosphere all about me the poison that shall slowly destroy me.

JUL. Didn't I tell you? He's out of his senses.

TEO. But, Ernesto, what does all this mean?

JUL. What has all this to do with the subject we were discussing?

ERN. It means, señor, that I believe that when people see me living here under your protection, they think the same things about me that I have been thinking about myself, when I ride with you in the park, when I go out with Teodora or Mercedes in the morning, when I sit in your box at the opera, when I hunt in your coverts, when, day after day, I take the same place at your table. The fact is, señor—though your goodness may not let you believe it—that people say to each other, "Who is this man? Some relation of his? Not at all. His secretary, then? No, not that, either. His companion—He doesn't add much to the company." That is what they are whispering.

JUL. Nobody thinks that. You are dreaming.

ERN. Pardon me . . .

JUL. Well, let's have a name, then.

ERN. Señor . . .

JUL. I'll be satisfied with just one.

ERN. Then there is some one near at hand. The man lives in the third floor.

JUL. And his name is?

ERN. Don Severo.

JUL. My brother?

ERN. Exactly, your brother. If that isn't enough, Doña Mercedes, his wife. Another? Pepito. And now what have you to say?

JUL. Then I say—and I stick to it, and make no mistake about it—that Severo is a martinet; that she doesn't know what she is talking about; and that the boy is a puppy.

ERN. They only repeat what they hear.

JUL. Enough, these are foolish scruples. Where there are honest intentions, upright people need pay little heed to what the world may say. The louder the whispering the more deep-seated the scorn.

ERN. That is honorable, and that is how every generous man would feel. But I have learned that what people say, either with or without malice, begins by being false and ends by being true. Does spreading gossip reveal to us hidden sin, and is it a reflection of the past, or does it invent the evil and lay a foundation for it? Does it brand with the seal of shame the fault which already exists, or does it engender vice and give opportunity for crime? Are gossiping tongues infamous, or avenging? Are they accomplices, or heralds? Executioners, or tempters? Do they strike down, or do they cause us to stumble? Do they wound in malice, or in sorrow? Do they condemn justly, or wantonly? I don't know, Don Julian. Perhaps they are two-edged. But time and opportunity and the event will show.

JUL. See here, I don't understand a word of that. It's all philosophy, or madness rather, with which you smother your natural good sense. But, to be brief, I don't want to distress or annoy you. You want, Ernesto, to earn for yourself, independently and by your own efforts, an honorable position. Isn't that it?

ERN. Don Julian—

JUL. Answer me.

ERN [*Joyfully*] Yes.

JUL. Then you have succeeded already. I happen to be without a secretary. I have been negotiating for one from London, [*in a tone of affectionate reproach*] but I don't want any one but an eccentric person who would rather have poverty, hard work, and a fixed salary like every one else, than be the son of a man who loves him as if he were his own child.

ERN. Don Julian . . .

JUL. [*In a tone of mock severity*] But I am exacting and

very business-like, and I don't pay good wages to people for nothing. I shall get all I can out of you, and in my house you will have to earn your salt. You will be at your desk ten hours a day. I wake up at daybreak, and I am going to be sterner with you than Severo. [*Unable to control himself any longer, and changing his tone and opening his arms*] That's how we shall be before the world, you the victim of my self-ishness.—But, Ernesto, in the bottom of my heart, I shall feel the same love for you!

ERN. Don Julian—

JUL. Do you accept the offer?

ERN. Yes. Do what you like with me.

TEO. At last you have tamed the wild beast.

ERN. I will do anything for you.

JUL. That's right. That's the way I like to see you. Now I shall write to my kind correspondent. I shall thank him and tell him that I realize the unusual merits of the English-man he recommends, but that he is too late, as I already have a secretary. [*Turning towards the first door to the right*] This will do for the present—later we shall see! [*Turning around and pretending to be very mysterious*] Perhaps a companion —then!

TEO. For pity's sake, be still. Don't you see that you are frightening him!

> *Exit* DON JULIAN, *right, laughing and looking good-*
> *naturedly at* ERNESTO. *During the scene, daylight*
> *has been gradually dying away, so that by now the*
> *room is quite dark.*

ERN. His kindness overwhelms me! How can I ever re-pay him?

> *He sinks down on the sofa, deeply moved.* TEODORA
> *goes and stands beside him.*

TEO. By resolutely putting aside all waywardness and distrust; by being reasonable and realizing that we really love you, and that we are not going to change. In short, Ernesto, by understanding that Julian does not make empty promises, but that he keeps his word, with the result that you have in him a father, and in me a sister.

> Doña Mercedes *and* Don Severo *appear in the background, and remain there. The room is quite dark, except for a little light from the French window, to which* Teodora *and* Ernesto *go.*

Ern. Ah, how good you both are!

Teo. And what a child you are! After today you must never be unhappy again.

Ern. Never.

Mer. [*In low tone*] How dark it is!

Sev. Come, Mercedes.

Mer. There is no one here. [*Coming forward*]

Sev. [*Stopping her*] There *is* some one there.

> *They both stand at the back, watching.*

Ern. Teodora, I would gladly give my life, and more, too, in return for the benefits I have received from you. You must think that I am unfeeling. I don't like to make protestations of affection, but I can love, and I can hate, too. Every one may find in my heart a reflection of the emotion he chooses to arouse there.

Mer. What are they saying?

Sev. Strange things.—I can't hear very well.

> Teodora *and* Ernesto *remain at the window, talking in low tones.*

Mer. It certainly is Ernesto.

Sev. And she! It is she, of course.

Mer. Teodora!

Sev. The same tricks, and always together! I have no patience with it! And those words . . . Why do I wait?

Mer. You're right. Come, Severo, it has become a matter of duty. Everybody is saying . . .

SEV. [*Coming forward*] I must speak plainly to Julian today.

MER. Poor girl, she is such a child. I'll speak to her myself.

TEO. Go to some other house? No! Leave us? A fine idea, indeed! Julian would never consent to it.

SEV. Nor I, by heaven. [*To* MERCEDES—*aloud*] Oh, Teodora, didn't you see me? Is this the way you receive people?

TEO. [*Coming away from the window*] Don Severo, how glad I am to see you!

MER. Not at dinner? Isn't it time yet?

TEO. Ah, Mercedes.

SEV. [*Aside*] How well she acts.

TEO. I'll ring for lights. [*Touching a bell on the table*]

SEV. Good, one likes to be able to see something.

SERVANT [*Appearing in the doorway*] Señora.

TEO. Lights, Genero.   [*The servant goes out.*

SEV. Those who tread the narrow path of duty and honor, and are always what they seem, need never be afraid or ashamed of any amount of light.

> *Servants come in with lights; the room is brilliantly illuminated.*

TEO. [*After a little pause, laughs and speaks quite naturally*] That applies to me and to some one else. [*Going to* MERCEDES]

MER. Of course.

SEV. Hello, hello, Don Ernesto. [*Meaningly*] So you were here with Teodora when I came in?

ERN. [*Coldly*] As you see—apparently.

SEV. No, indeed, not apparently, for in the darkness one couldn't see you. [*Going up to him, taking his hand, and looking at him fixedly.* TEODORA *and* MERCEDES *talk aside.* SEVERO *says to himself*] He is flushed and seems to have been weeping. Only children and lovers weep in this world. [*Aloud*] And where is Julian?

Teo. He went off to write a letter.

Sev. [*Aside*] Be as patient as I may, this man upsets me. [*Aloud*] I am going to speak to him. [*To* Teodora] Is there time before dinner?

Teo. Plenty of time.

Sev. [*Aside, rubbing his hands and looking at* Ernesto *and* Teodora] Good. To work, then. [*Aloud*] Au revoir.

Teo. Au revoir.

Sev. [*Aside, looking at them angrily as he goes out the door*] Upon my word!

> Mercedes *and* Teodora *remain. They are seated on the sofa.* Ernesto *is standing.*

Mer. [*To* Ernesto] You haven't been to see us today.

Ern. No.

Mer. Nor Pepito, either.

Ern. No, señora.

Mer. He is all alone up there.

Ern. [*Aside*] Let him stay so!

Mer. [*To* Teodora, *gravely and mysteriously*] I wish he'd go away. I want to speak to you.

Teo. You?

Mer. [*In the same tone*] Yes, on a very grave matter.

Teo. Speak then.

Mer. If this man doesn't go . . .

Teo. [*In a low tone*] I don't understand?

Mer. Courage! [*Takes her hand and strokes it affectionately.* Teodora *looks at her in astonishment, not understanding at all*] Get rid of him quickly.

Teo. Since you insist. [*Aloud*] Ernesto, will you do me a favor?

Ern. I'd love to.

Mer. [*Aside*] Ah, there's too much love about it.

Teo. Then go upstairs to Pepito—but perhaps I am bothering you with this errand?

ERN. Indeed, no.

MER. How affectionate they are!

TEO. Ask him . . . if he renewed the subscription for our box at the opera as I told him to. He knows about it.

ERN. With pleasure.—I'll go at once.

TEO. Thanks, Ernesto. I appreciate—

ERN. Not at all.

TEO. Good-bye. [ERNESTO *goes out.*] A grave matter? You frighten me, Mercedes. This tone, this mysterious air! What is it?

MER. Something very serious.

TEO. But whom is it about?

MER. About all of you.

TEO. About us?

MER. About Julian and Ernesto and you. Now you understand.

TEO. About all three?

MER. Yes, you three.

TEO. [*Looks at* MERCEDES *in astonishment. A short pause*] But tell me quickly.

MER. [*Aside*] I dislike doing it, but I mustn't falter. It's an ugly business. [*Aloud*] Listen, Teodora: after all, my husband and yours are brothers, and we have all become one family, so that in life and in death, for better, for worse, we ought to support and aid and advise each other. So I gladly offer you my protection, and tomorrow, if need should arise, I should not be ashamed to ask help of you.

TEO. And you might count upon us, Mercedes. But, quick, tell me—

MER. Until now I was unwilling to take this step, Teodora, but today Severo said to me, "I cannot suffer this any longer. I value my brother's honor as highly as any one, and when I see certain things, I groan with shame and sorrow. Always making sly allusions, always watching for meaningful smiles, always lowering their eyes, always shunning other people! These disgraceful actions must end, for I cannot endure the things that are being said in Madrid."

Teo. Go on, go on.

Mer. Listen, then.

A pause.   Mercedes *looks fixedly at* Teodora.

Teo. Tell us; what do they say?

Mer. Where there is smoke, there is fire—

Teo. I don't know anything about smoke or anything about fire. I only know that I am going mad.

Mer. [*Aside*] Poor child, it grieves me! [*Aloud*] But don't you understand, then?

Teo. I? No.

Mer. [*Aside*] She's dull, too. [*Aloud—emphatically*] He is a laughing-stock!

Teo. Who?

Mer. Who would it be? Your husband.

Teo. [*Rising, impetuously*] Julian? It's a lie. The person who said that was a scoundrel. Ah, if only Julian were face to face with him!

Mer. [*Soothing her and making her sit down beside her again*] He would have to face a great many people, for unless rumor is mistaken, every one is of the same opinion.

Teo. But tell me, then, what is this scandal? This great mystery? What is the world saying?

Mer. So it makes you angry?

Teo. Makes me angry! But what is it?

Mer. Listen, Teodora. You are very young. At your age one does many thoughtless things, without meaning any harm. . . and then later come many tears. Come, don't you understand me yet?

Teo. No. Why should I understand you, unless this story is about me?

Mer. It is the story of a wretch, and it is the story of a lady.

TEO. [*Anxiously*] And her name?

MER. Her name is . . .

TEO. [*Stopping her*] What difference does it make what her name is?

> TEODORA *moves away from* MERCEDES *without getting up from the sofa.* MERCEDES *draws nearer to her as she speaks. The contrast between* TEODORA'S *movement of repulsion and* MERCEDES' *of protection and insistence is very marked.*

MER. Some men are worthless and treacherous, and in return for one hour of pleasure they condemn a woman to a life of sorrow. To her are left only the dishonor of her husband, the destruction of her family, and the seal of shame beneath which her head is bowed; the scorn of others is the penance imposed by society, and God's still greater punishment: the voice of conscience. [*Now they are at opposite ends of the sofa.* TEODORA *leans back and covers her face with her hands, understanding at last*] Come to me, Teodora. [*Aside*] Poor little girl, I pity her! [*Aloud*] This man doesn't deserve you.

TEO. Where is your blind folly leading you, señora? I feel neither fear nor horror. There are no tears in my eyes, only blazing anger. About whom did you hear what I have just heard? Who is this man? He is—? It is—?

MER. Ernesto.

TEO. Ah! [*A pause*] And I am the woman? [MERCEDES *makes a sign of assent, and* TEODORA *rises*] Then listen to me, even though I make you angry. I don't know which is more vile, the world that invented this story, or you who repeat it to me. A curse on the slanderous tongue that first gave form to such a thought, and a curse on the knave or the fool who believes it! So vile, so deadly is it that whether I blot it from my memory, or whether I keep it there, I become guilty. Good heavens, I wouldn't have thought it! I never would have believed it! I saw him so unhappy that I loved him as a brother. Julian played Providence to him. And he is so generous, so noble . . . [*Checking herself, watching* MERCEDES, *and turning her head—Aside*] How she looks at me! I mustn't praise him before her. So now I must play a part! [*Visibly trying to control herself*]

MER. Come, be calm.

TEO. [*Aloud*] I feel such anguish, such sorrow, such coldness in my very soul. To think that my honor should be stained by public gossip. Oh, mother, dear mother! Oh, Julian, dearest.

> *She sinks, sobbing, into the chair at the left.* MER-CEDES *tries to console her.*

MER. I didn't suppose . . . Oh, forgive me . . . don't cry! I didn't believe there was anything serious. Of course, I knew your past exonerated you. But even so, you yourself must admit that every one might say with justice that you and Julian are very imprudent in letting people think the worst. You, a young girl of twenty, and Julian in the forties, and Ernesto with his head full of fantastic ideas; your husband wrapped up in his business, and the other man in his dreams. You with nothing to occupy your mind; every day a thousand opportunities for meeting. . . . The people who see you in the park, in the theater, have evil minds to think such evil, but, Teodora, to be just, I believe that in all that has happened, the world is in the wrong, but you have given it the opportunity. Let me tell you that the sin that modern society punishes most relentlessly and cruelly and with the greatest ingenuity—in man or in woman—is—don't be frightened, Teodora—rash confidence—indiscretion.

TEO [*Turning to* MERCEDES, *but paying no attention to what she is saying*] And you say that Julian—

MER. Yes, he is the laughing-stock of the city. And you—

TEO. Oh, never mind about me. But Julian . . . he is so good, and so sensitive! When he knows—

MER. He probably does know. Severo is doubtless talking to him this very minute.

TEO. What!

JUL. [*Without*] Enough!

TEO. Good heavens!

JUL. Leave me alone!

TEO. Oh, dear, let's go out quickly.

MER. [*After looking out through the first door to the right*] Yes, quickly! He's beside himself.

TEODORA *and* MERCEDES *go toward the left.*

TEO. [*Stopping*] But what for? It will seem as though I am guilty. This vile slander does more than soil, it debases one. So deadly, so treacherous is it, that in spite of all evidence against it, it works its way into one's consciousness with its tang of guilt. Why should I be paralyzed in the deadly bonds of a senseless terror? [*At this moment*, DON JULIAN *appears in the doorway to the right, with* DON SEVERO *behind him*] Julian!

JUL. Teodora! [*She runs to him and he presses her to his heart, passionately*] Come to me! . . . This is your post of honor. [*To* SEVERO] Come in; but, by heaven, be careful not to go too far. I swear, and I mean it, that if any one stains this cheek with tears again, he shall never more cross my threshold, even if he is my own brother!

A pause. DON JULIAN *caresses and comforts* TEODORA.

SEV. I only repeat what people are saying about you, Julian.

JUL. Libel!

SEV. Maybe—

JUL. It is!

SEV. But at least let me tell you what every one knows

JUL. Slanders, lies, filth!

SEV. I simply wanted to tell you.

JUL. There can be no need for doing so.   [*A short pause.*

SEV. You are wrong.

JUL. Right, and to spare! Would you track the mud of the streets into my salon?

SEV. It may be necessary.

JUL. Well, then, it must not be necessary.

SEV. My name is the same as yours.

JUL. No more!

SEV. And your honor—

JUL. Remember that you are in the presence of my wife.
A pause.

SEV. [*To* JULIAN, *in an undertone*] If our father could see you!

JUL. What! Severo,—what do you mean?

MER. Hush! Ernesto is coming.

TEO. [*Aside*] How dreadful! If he should know.
    TEODORA *turns away and hangs her head.* JULIAN
    looks at her fixedly.

ERN. [*Looking at* TEODORA *and* DON JULIAN *for a minute. Aside*] He and she.—This can't be all imagination! If what I feared should happen? Then what I have just heard from this fool [*Looking at* PEPITO, *who enters at this moment*] wasn't all made up by him.

PEP. [*Looking in surprise from one side to the other*] Greeting, and a good appetite to you. It's almost dinner-time. Here's the ticket, Teodora—Don Julian!

TEO. [*Mechanically taking the ticket*] Thanks, Pepito.

ERN. [*In an undertone to* DON JULIAN] What's the matter with Teodora?

JUL. Nothing.

ERN. [*As before*] She's pale, and she's been crying.

JUL. [*Unable to control himself*] Don't worry about my wife.

A pause. DON JULIAN *and* ERNESTO *look at each other.*

ERN. [*Aside*] Poor souls, this has quite upset them.

PEP. [*To his mother, aside, pointing to* ERNESTO] Mad as a hatter just because I joked about Teodora with him. My! My! He wanted to kill me on the spot!

ERN. [*Aloud. Sadly, but resolutely*] Don Julian, I have been thinking over your generous offer, and although I have an awkward tongue that stumbles and blunders, and I know that I am imposing upon your kindness.—In short, señor, I must refuse the position you offered me.

JUL. Why?

ERN. Because I am made that way. I am a poet, a dreamer. My father never could make a success of me, señor. I must travel. I am restless and rebellious. I can't settle down like other people to vegetate in one spot. I am filled with the spirit of adventure; I see myself as some new Columbus. In short, let Don Severo say whether I am right or not.

SEV. You speak like a man of understanding, like the very fount of wisdom. I have been thinking the same thing for a long, long time.

JUL. And so you feel a craving for travel, seeing the world? So you want to leave us? But how about the necessary funds?

SEV. He—is going away—to some place that will be more to his liking. Of course, for the rest he must depend upon you. Anything that he wants. I don't suppose he has saved any money at all?

ERN. [*To* DON SEVERO] I neither spread scandal nor receive alms! [*A pause*] But indeed this must be. And as the parting must be sad—since perhaps I may never see you again—we had better embrace now . . . and break this bond . . . and—forgive my selfishness. [*Deeply moved*]

SEV. [*Aside*] How strangely they both look at me!

TEO. [*Aside*] How fine he is!

ERN. Don Julian, why hesitate? This is a last farewell.
He goes to DON JULIAN *with open arms.* DON JULIAN
takes him in his arms and they embrace tenderly.

JUL. No, all things considered, it is neither the last nor
the first. It is simply the sincere embrace of two honorable
men. I don't want to hear anything more about this foolish
plan.

SEV. But isn't he going away?

JUL. Never. I don't change with every wind, nor do I
give up my cherished plans for the whim of a boy or the ravings of a madman. It would be a still greater blot on my
honor to regulate my conduct by the foolish gossip of this
most high-minded city!

SEV. Julian!

JUL. Enough. Dinner is ready—

ERN. My dear father! I can't—

JUL. But I trust that you can. Or is my authority burden-
some to you?

ERN. I beg you!

JUL. Come, then, it is time to go. Give Teodora your arm
and take her in to dinner.

ERN. Teodora! [*Looking at her and drawing back*]

JUL. Yes—as usual. [*A movement of doubt and hesitation
from both. Finally* ERNESTO *goes up to* TEODORA *and she
leans on his arm, but they do not look at each other, and seem
agitated. To* PEPITO] Give your mother your arm. [PEPITO
offers his arm to MERCEDES] And, Severo, my dear brother,
you come with me [*Leaning on his arm for a minute*] Now we
shall dine *en famille,* and our cup of happiness will overflow.
You say people are whispering about us? All right. Let them
whisper, or let them shout. I don't care a fig what they say.
I wish I lived in a palace with glass walls, so that all those
who are making free with our names might look in and see

Ernesto and Teodora, so that they might realize how much importance I attach to their vile calumnies. Let every man go his own way.

> *A servant appears in conventional dress.*

SERVANT. Dinner is served.

> *He opens the dining-room door. One can see the table, chairs, chandeliers, etc. Everything is very luxurious.*

JUL. Well, let's attend to the things of this life and leave them to see to our funeral. Come. [*Urging them to go in*]

TEO. Mercedes.

MER. Teodora.

TEO. You—

MER. You first.

TEO. No, go first, Mercedes.

> MERCEDES *and* PEPITO *go ahead and walk slowly toward the dining-room.* TEODORA *and* ERNESTO *stand still, as though lost in thought.* ERNESTO *fixes his eyes on her.*

JUL. [*Aside*] He is looking at her, and she is weeping. [*They slowly follow* MERCEDES. TEODORA *hesitates, tries to pull herself together and control her tears.—Aside to* SEVERO] Are they whispering to each other?

SEV. I don't know; I suppose so.

> ERNESTO *and* TEODORA *stop and look around furtively, then proceed.*

JUL. Why do they both look back? Why—?

SEV. Now you are coming to your senses.

JUL. Say, rather, I am catching your madness. Ah, scandal has a sure aim! It goes straight to the heart.

> *He and* SEVERO *go into the dining-room.*

Curtain.

ACT II

A small room furnished with extreme simplicity; it is almost poverty-stricken. At the back, a door; to the right of the audience, another door; to the left, a French window. A little pine bookcase with a few books in it, a table, an arm-chair. The table is at the left. On it is a framed picture of DON JULIAN. *On the other end, a frame, like the first, but without a picture. Both are rather small. There are also on the table, an unlighted lamp, a copy of Dante's "Divine Comedy," opened at the incident of Francesca, and a half-burned piece of paper; in addition, some loose papers and the manuscript of a play. A few chairs. This is all the furniture.* DON JULIAN, DON SEVERO, *and a servant enter at the back.*

SEV. Isn't your master in?

SERVANT. No, señor. He went out very early.

SEV. Never mind, we'll wait. I suppose Don Ernesto is sure to return soon?

SERVANT. Probably. The master is most punctual and exact.

SEV. Good. You may go.

SERVANT. Yes, señor. If you want anything, I'll be at hand. [*The servant goes out at the back.*

SEV. [*Looking about the room*] What simplicity!

JUL. What poverty, you'd better say!

SEV. [*Looking through the door at the right, then through the one at the back*] Well, this is a splendid apartment! A little alcove, the anteroom, this study, and there you have it all.

39

Jul. And the devil has all he wants of human ingratitude and unworthy thoughts, of despicable passion, of base calumny. A nice little pile it is.

Sev. It was simply chance that brought it about.

Jul. That's not the right name, brother. It was brought about by . . . Well, I know whom—

Sev. Who was it, then? I, perhaps?

Jul. Partly you. And before you, the idle fools who gossiped shamelessly about my honor and my wife. And then I myself who, like a coward, a jealous fool, a low scoundrel, let this young man leave my house after he had proved himself as noble as I was base—base and ungrateful! Think of the splendor and luxury in which I live, the magnificence of my salon, my stable, the credit of my firm, the wealth I enjoy. Well, do you know where every bit of it came from?

Sev. I have quite forgotten.

Jul. There you have it. Forgetfulness—the reward of mankind for every generous act, for every great sacrifice that one man makes for another, if he do it modestly, with no blare of trumpets and shouting of heralds—simply out of love and respect.

Sev. You are unjust to yourself. Your gratitude carried you to such lengths that you almost sacrificed honor, and even happiness to it. What more could any one ask? What more could a saint do? There is a limit to all things, good and bad. He is proud; he insisted, though you opposed him. Of course, he is his own master. He controls his own person and his own acts; and one fine morning he left the palace in which you live because he wanted to; and in despair he betook himself to this garret. It is all very sad; but, my dear fellow, who could help it?

Jul. Everybody, if everybody had attended to his own affairs instead of throwing mud at other people, wagging his tongue, and gossiping about them, and pointing at them! Tell

me, what business of theirs was it that, performing a sacred
duty, I looked upon Ernesto as a son, and she regarded him as
a brother? If they once see a beautiful girl and a handsome
young man together at my table, or out walking, or at the
opera, do they immediately think vile thoughts and imagine
scandals? Are we to suppose that in this world an impure
love is the one sure bond between men and women? Are
there no such things as friendship, gratitude, sympathy,
and are we so made that youth and beauty can meet
only in the mud? And suppose even that what they
thought were true, why should the fools feel called upon
to avenge my wrongs? I have eyes to see with, and
I have a sword, a heart, and hands to guard my own
interests, and to avenge insults.

SEV. Well, granted that perhaps the people who went
about gossiping were in the wrong, should I, who am your
own flesh and blood, who bear your name—should I have
been silent?

JUL. No, by heaven! but you should have been careful.
You should have spoken cautiously to me alone, and not have
kindled a volcano in my household.

SEV. I sinned through excess of affection. But if I acknowl-
edge my guilt; if I admit that the world and I have done the
harm—it, by inventing the slander, I, by stupidly lending
ear to the thousand echoes of gossip, you, at least, Julian,
are pure and free from sin. So dismiss your scruples and
be light-hearted.

JUL. I can't be light-hearted, for in my heart I have shel-
tered the very thing that my reason and my lips repudiate.
I reject indignantly the slanders of the world. "They lie,"
I cry aloud, and under my breath I repeat, "But what if
they do not lie, but are right, after all!" So, in the struggle
between two conflicting impulses, I am at the same time judge
and accomplice. And so I am distracted; I am fighting with

myself. Suspicion grows and spreads; my wounded heart cries out in anger; a blood-red mist spreads about me.

SEV. You are raving.

JUL. No, I am not raving. I am laying bare my soul to you, brother. Do you by any chance think that Ernesto would have left my house if I had stood in his way with the firm intention of intervening and preventing him? He went away because in the depths of my troubled soul a treacherous voice was sounding, saying to me: "Leave the door open that he may pass out freely, and then close it tightly after him. In the fortress of honor the trusting man is a poor steward." One wish was in my heart and another on my lips. Aloud, I said, "Come back, Ernesto," and under my breath, "Don't come back." When I seemed to be frank with him, I was a hypocrite and a coward, a knave and an ingrate. No, Severo, that was not the action of an honorable man.

He sinks into the arm-chair, near the table, greatly moved.

SEV. It was the action of a man who was protecting a young, high-spirited, and radiantly beautiful wife.

JUL. Don't speak so of Teodora. She is a mirror that we sully with our breath when we rashly try to come too near it. She reflected the sunlight, until the thousand viper-heads of the angry world came near to look at her. Now they seem to be swarming in the crystal inside the divine frame. But they are fleshless spectres. A wave of my hand will surely drive them away and you will see again the clear-blue sky.

SEV. So much the better.

JUL. No.

SEV. What's the trouble?

JUL. Trouble enough. I tell you, this inner struggle I described to you has warped my character. Now my wife always finds me sad and morose. I am not as I used to be.

I try in vain to seem so. And as she notices this change she is bound to ask herself, "Where is Julian? Where is my dear husband? What have I done to lose his confidence? What evil thoughts preoccupy him and keep him from my arms? And so, a shadow is coming between us which divides us and, slowly, step by step, drives us farther apart. We have no more sweet confidences, no more quiet talks. Our smiles are frozen; our tones bitter. I harbor unjust suspicion; she is in tears. I am wounded in my love; she is wounded—and by me—in her womanly dignity and her affection. That's how we stand.

SEV. Then you're on the road to destruction. If you see so clearly what's wrong, why don't you find a remedy?

JUL. I've tried in vain. I know I am wrong to doubt her. More than that, I don't doubt her for the present. But in the end as, little by little I lose ground, and little by little he gains, who can be sure that what we call a lie today may not be true tomorrow? [*Seizing* DON SEVERO *by the arm and speaking to him with restrained passion and ill-concealed eagerness*] I, jealous, morose, unjust; I, the tyrant; and he, noble, great-hearted, always gentle and resigned! With the halo of martyrdom which in every woman's eyes becomes so well a handsome and gallant young man, it's clear that he gets the better part in this unjust assignment of rôles; that he gains what I lose, while I am powerless to help. This is the truth; and the result is that meanwhile the world with its idle talk plays traitor to them both, while now they are saying quite truthfully, "But indeed, we're not in love with each other," and as the latter words re-echo they may become reality.

SEV. Look here, Julian, if you feel this way, I think the wisest thing to do is to let Ernesto carry out his plans.

JUL. But that's what I've come here to prevent.

SEV. Then you're mad. Isn't he thinking of going to

Buenos Ayres? Then why worry about it? Just wish him fair winds and a full sail.

Jul. Do you want me to seem cruel and mean and jealous in Teodora's eyes? Don't you know, my dear brother, that a woman may despise a man and still want him for a lover; but never for a husband? Do you want my wife to follow this unhappy exile across the seas with sad memories? Don't you know that if I saw so much as the trace of a tear on her cheek, and thought that it was a tear for Ernesto, I would strangle her with my own hands? [*With concentrated fury*]

Sev. What are we to do then?

Jul. Suffer. The world must find a dénouement for this drama, which it created simply by looking at us—so potent is its glance for good and evil.

Sev. [*Going back*] I think some one is coming.

Servant [*Without*] My master can't be long now.

     Enter Pepito.

Sev. You here?

Pep. [*Aside*] Phew, they've found it out already. I've overreached myself. [*Aloud*] So we're all here. Good-day, Uncle. Good-day, Papa. [*Aside*] There's no use. They know what's up. [*Aloud*] And so you— I suppose, of course, you've come to look for Ernesto?

Sev. For whom else in this house?

Jul. And I suppose you know all that this madman is planning?

Pep. All what? Oh, of course,—a little— I know—what every one knows.

Sev. And is it tomorrow that—?

Pep. No. Tomorrow he's going away, so he has to settle this today.

Jul. [*With amazement*] What did you say?

Pep. I? What Pepe Ucedo told me last night at the casino door. And he is the Viscount Nebreda's second, so if he doesn't know— But how queer you look! Is it possible you don't know?

JUL. We know everything. [*Resolutely forestalling a movement on his brother's part*]

SEV. We—

JUL. [*Aside*] Be quiet, Severo. [*Aloud*] We heard that he is going away tomorrow—and that today he stakes his life. And we came, naturally, to prevent the duel and the departure.

> *Throughout this scene* DON JULIAN *pretends that he has been informed of the affair, so as to learn the facts from* PEPITO, *though it is evident that he came only on account of* ERNESTO'S *voyage.*

SEV. [*Aside to* JULIAN] What is this duel?

JUL. [*Aside to* SEVERO] I don't know, but we'll find out.

PEP. [*Aside*] Come, I wasn't such a fool after all.

JUL. I know that a viscount—

PEP. Exactly.

JUL. Is to fight a duel with Ernesto. Some one who knew about it at the time told us. They say it's a very serious affair— [*Sign of assent from* PEPITO] a scandalous quarrel; a great many people standing about.—"You lie!" "You say that I lie!" Then words, thick and fast.

PEP. [*Interrupting with the eagerness and pleasure of one who knows more*] Words! A blow that would fell an ox.

SEV. Who struck whom?

PEP. Ernesto struck the other man.

JUL. Ernesto. Didn't you hear about it? This viscount exhausted his patience completely—put him in a perfect passion. Well, the poor boy broke loose—

PEP. Exactly.

JUL. I told you we knew all about it. And is the affair very serious?

PEP. Very serious. I'm sorry to have to say so, but I might as well be frank with you.

JUL What are the conditions?

PEP. It's to the death. And the viscount isn't afraid, and doesn't shrink. He's a wonderful swordsman.

JUL. And the quarrel? What was it about? They blame it on Nebreda?

PEP. Why, it wasn't exactly a quarrel. I'll tell you how it happened. Ernesto was planning to leave Madrid to-morrow so as to reach Cadiz in time to sail in the "Cid," and Luis Alcaraz had promised him a letter of introduction, which he said would serve as a good recommendation. So the poor boy went to the café to get it, with the best intentions in the world. The other man wasn't there; he waited for him. No one then recognized him and they go on with their pleasant game of tearing people to pieces, without noticing his threatening face and set teeth. One by one people are mentioned, and one by one they fall. A heavy hand and a sharp tongue. Every poor dog in the city passes in re-view. And right there in that miserable tavern, belching out more smoke than a train, in the midst of wine-glasses and cigar ashes, and scattered lumps of sugar, they set up a dissecting-table. With each draught of fine old wine, a wo-man's reputation gone. At every cutting lash, a roar of laughter. With four slashes of the scissors those fellows left reputations in tatters, women torn to pieces. But, after all, what does that sort of thing amount to? Echoes of society at the café table. I don't say this myself, and of course I don't think so, but that's what Ernesto said when he told me about it all.

JUL. Go on. Will you never get to the point?

PEP. Finally, in the midst of all these names, some one mentioned a certain man, and Ernesto couldn't control him-self any longer. "Who dares besmirch the name of an hon-

orable man?" he cries out, and they answer, "The lady."
With flashing eyes he throws himself upon Nebreda. The
poor viscount is completely bowled over; the public room becomes a field of argument. There you have a synopsis of
the first act. Today comes the duel with swords in some
salon—I don't know where.

JUL. [*Furiously seizing his arm*] And the man was I?

PEP. Señor—

JUL. And Teodora the woman? And they have dragged
her and my name and my love to such depths?

SEV. [*Aside to* PEPITO] Fool, what have you done?

PEP. Didn't he say he knew about it? Why I— Of
course—I thought.

JUL. Disgraced, disgraced!

SEV. [*Going up to him, affectionately*] Julian!

JUL. True. I know I must be calm. But oh, if I lose
faith, I lose heart. Great heavens! why should they slander
us so? What right have they to turn upon us and throw
mud at us? No matter. I know how to act as befits a gentleman. Can I count on you, Severo?

SEV. Count on me? To the death!   [*They clasp hands.*

JUL. [*To* PEPITO] The duel?

PEP. At three.

JUL. [*Aside*] I'm going to kill him. Yes, I shall kill him.
[*To* SEVERO] Let's be going.

SEV. Where?

JUL. To find this viscount.

SEV. Are you going to—?

JUL. I am going to do what I can to avenge the insult
to my honor and to save the life of Juan Acedo's son. [*To*
PEPITO] Who are the seconds?

PEP. Two—Alcaras and Ruedo.

JUL. I know them. [*Pointing to* PEPITO] He can stay here
in case of emergency. And if Ernesto should come back—

Sev. I understand.

Jul. Try, without arousing suspicion, to find out where the duel is to be.

Sev. You hear?

Jul. Come!

Sev. Julian, what possesses you?

Jul. Joy such as I have not known for a long time.

Sev. What the devil, are you mad?   Joy?

Jul. At the prospect of meeting this young man.

Sev. Nebreda?

Jul. Yes.   Remember.   Until now, calumny was intangible and I could not see its face.   And now at last I know where it is hiding.   At last it has taken human form, and is visibly before me in the guise of a viscount.   For three months I have been eating gall and wormwood.   And now, just think, I am face to face with him.

[Severo *and* Julian *go out.*

Pep. Well, here's a mess; and a useless mess, too.   Just the same, no matter what my uncle may say, it was sheer madness to have a young girl as beautiful as the sun under the same roof, in almost continual contact with Ernesto, who is a handsome fellow with a soul all of fire, and a head full of romance.   He swears there is nothing between them but the purest sort of friendship, that he loves her like a sister, and that my uncle is a father to him.   But I'm pretty sharp, and though I am young, I know a thing or two about this world, and I don't put much faith in this brother-and-sister business; particularly where the brother is so young, and the relationship fictitious.   But suppose this affection is all they say it is, how are other people to know that?   Have they signed any pledge always to think well of every one?   Don't they see them together all the time—in the theater—in the park?   Well, the person who saw them, saw them, and when he saw them, he told about it.   Ernesto swore

to me, "*No*." They had *almost never* gone about in that way.
Did he go once? Well, that's enough. If a hundred people
saw them that day, they might as well have appeared in
public not once, but a hundred different times. Are people
bound to examine their witnesses and compare their dates
to find out whether it was many times or only once that they
went out together, she with her innocent sympathy, and he
with his brotherly affection? Such a demand would be un-
dignified and unjust—altogether ridiculous. They all tell
what they've seen, and they're not lying when they tell it.
"I saw them once. I saw them as well." One and one make
two. There's no way out. "And I saw them, too." There
you have three already. And this man, four; and that one,
five. And so, adding up in all good faith, you go on indefi-
nitely. And they saw because they looked. In short, because naturally one uses one's senses and doesn't stop to ask
permission. So let him look after himself and remember
that nowadays he who avoids the appearance of evil, avoids
the slander and the danger. [*A little pause*] And notice, I
am admitting the purity of their affection; and that is a very
important point; for, between ourselves, I must admit that
to be near Teodora and not to love her, one must be as
steady as a rock. He may be a scholar, and a philosopher,
and a mathematician, and a physicist; but he's human,
and she's divine; and that's enough. If only these
walls could speak. If Ernesto's private thought scattered
about here could only take visible form! Let's see.
That frame, for example, is empty, while in the other is
Don Julian's face. Teodora used to be there as a mate to
my uncle. I wonder why her photograph has disappeared?
To avoid temptation? If that's the reason, it's pretty bad!
But it's still worse if she's left the frame for a better place;
to find shelter near his heart! Let's see, make out your
case against him, little devils who fly through the air,

spinning invisible webs! Have no pity on this mystic, this philosopher! [*Looking at the table and seeing Dante's "Inferno"*] And here's another sign. I've never been to see Ernesto that I haven't found this beautiful book open on his table. [*Reading*] Dante's "*Divine Comedy,*" his favorite poem. And apparently he never gets beyond this passage about Francesca. There are two possible explanations for this. Either Ernesto never reads, or else he always reads the same thing. But here's a spot; just as if a tear had fallen. What mystery, what deep secret have we here! How hard it must be for a married man to live in peace— A paper burned to ashes? [*Taking it up from the table*] No, there are still some traces of writing left.

> *Gets up and goes to the window, trying to read what is written on the paper. At this moment* ERNESTO *enters and, seeing him, stops.*

ERN. What are you looking at?

PEP. Ah, Ernesto. Why, a piece of paper that was lying here. The breeze was blowing it about.

ERN. [*Taking it and returning it to him after a minute's inspection*] I don't remember what this is.

PEP. They were verses. You probably know about it. [*Reading with difficulty*] "I am prey to a consuming fire." [*Aside*] Ah, the next line rhymes with Teodora.

ERN. Oh, some trifle.

PEP. [*Stops reading*] Yes, that's all.

ERN. This worthless paper is symbolic of our lives. A few cries of pain, a few flakes of ash.

PEP. Then they were verses?

ERN. Yes, sometimes I don't know what I'm doing; I let my pen run on. And last night I wrote those.

PEP. And to help this divine afflatus, and to get yourself in the right spirit you were seeking inspiration in the book of the Master?

ERN. It seems to me—

PEP. Oh, you needn't say anything.   It's a marvelous work. [*Pointing at the book*] The episode of Francesca—

ERN. [*Ironically and impatiently*] It seems you've turned detective today?

PEP. Oh, I'm not entirely successful at it.   Here, where the book's open, it says something I don't understand and that you must explain to me.   It says that, reading a tale of love by way of pastime, Paolo and Francesca came to the place where the author, showing himself no fool, tells so freely of the love of Lancelot and Queen Guinevere.   That was like flint striking fire. He pressed a kiss upon the book, and she, mad with love, kissed him upon the lips.   And at this point the Florentine poet says, oddly enough, but with masterly conciseness, these words which are written here, and which I cannot understand: "The book they read was Galeoto, and they read nothing else."   They read nothing else? Of course, that's simple enough.   But this Galeoto, tell me, where did he come from and who was he? [*Pointing at some papers that are supposedly the play*] You certainly ought to know.   It's the title of the play you've written that is to make you so famous.   Come, let's see.

[*Takes up the play and examines it.*

ERN. Galeoto was the go-between for Lancelot and the queen.   And in all love-affairs the third person may be called Galeoto by way of pseudonym.   Especially if it is desirable to avoid a more unpleasant name that brings trouble in its wake.

PEP. All right.   I see that.   But isn't there any appropriate and convenient Spanish name?

ERN. Very appropriate and very expressive.   This business which turns men's lusts into ready money, which plays upon men's passions and grows fat on their amours has a name and I know it; but I would shackle myself if I were to say in so many words what, after all, I am not going to say. [*He snatches the book from* PEPITO *and scatters its pages over the table*] In each particular case I find a particular person, but sometimes Galeoto is all society. Then he works without any realization of the office he is fulfilling, but such cunning has he in undermining honor and virtue, that a greater Galeoto never has been seen, and never will be. A man and woman are living happily and peacefully, doing their duty with all their hearts. No one pays any attention to them and everything is as it should be. But, by heaven, in this great city such a state of affairs doesn't last long. Some fine morning some one looks squarely at them, and from that time, either through stupidity or through malice, all men cling to the belief that they are concealing an impure love. Then there is nothing more to say; the matter is settled. No reasoning can convince them, nor does the man exist who can make them waver. The most upright man finds his reputation of no avail. And the most horrible part of it all is that in the beginning, people had no just grounds, and in the end perhaps they have. So impenetrable an atmosphere surrounds the poor victims, such a torrent sweeps in upon them, such pressure is brought to bear, that without realizing it, they are forced upon one another, against their will. They are drawn together, in their fall they become one and, dying, they adore each other. The world has been the battering-ram that breaks down virtue; it has prepared the way for sin; it has been Galeoto and—[*aside*] Away, away, devilish thought—your fire consumes me!

PEP. [*Aside*] If Teodora reasons this way, heaven help Don Julian! [*Aloud*] And perhaps your verses last night were on this subject?

ERN. Exactly.

PEP. Is it possible that any man can calmly waste his time and be like this—so serene, so unconcerned, when he is about to cross swords with Nebreda, who, with a foil in his hand, is a match for any man?   Wouldn't it be more sensible and more profitable for you to be practising a straight thrust or a parry, instead of wearing out your brain with halting verses of rebel heroics?   Now, really, don't you think it rather a serious matter to be meeting the viscount?

ERN. No; and I have good grounds for my opinion.   If I kill him, the world profits; if he kills me, the profit is mine.

PEP. Good.   That's better.

ERN. Let us not talk any more about it.

PEP. [*Aside*] Now, I'll be very clever about pumping him. [*Going up to him, in a lower tone*] Will it take place today?

ERN. Yes, today.

PEP. Will it be out of doors?

ERN. No.   That wouldn't be possible at such an hour.   An affair that every one knows about.

PEP. In some house?

ERN. That's what I proposed.

PEP. Where?

ERN. Upstairs.   [*Coldly and indifferently*] There's an empty apartment with a large salon, where the light comes in from the side.   For a handful of silver we get a far better place for this business than any mountain-side, and no one will be any the wiser.

PEP. So now the only thing necessary—?

ERN. A sword.

PEP. [*Going back*] There are voices outside.   Some one is coming.   The seconds?

ERN. Perhaps.

PEP. It sounds like a woman's voice.   [*Looking out of the door*]

ERN. But why doesn't he show them in?   [*A servant enters.*

SERVANT. [*Mysteriously*] Some one wants to see the master.

PEP. Who is it?

SERVANT. A lady.

ERN. That's strange.

PEP. [*In a low voice, to the servant*] Is she very insistent?

SERVANT. She's crying.

PEP. Is she young?

SERVANT. Well, I can't exactly say. The anteroom is very dark, and the lady is trying to cover her face, so that it certainly is hard to see her. And she speaks so softly, oh, so softly, I can hardly hear her.

ERN. Who can it be?

PEP. Some one who wants to see you.

ERN. I can't imagine—

PEP. [*Aside*] He seems perplexed. [*Aloud*] See here; I'll go and leave you to yourself. Good-bye, and good luck to you. [*Kissing him, and taking his hat. To the* SERVANT] What are you waiting for, stupid?

SERVANT. For the master to tell me to show her in.

PEP. In affairs of this sort you should divine his intentions; then, until the mysterious lady has gone, don't dare to open the door for any one, though the heavens fall.

SERVANT. Shall I tell her to come in, then?

ERN. [*To* PEPITO, *who is still in the doorway*] Good-bye.

PEP. Good-bye, Ernesto.

[PEPITO *and the servant go out at the back.*

ERN. A lady? Upon what pretext or for what reason? [*A pause.* TEODORA *appears in the doorway, and stops, covering her face with her veil*] Here she is. [TEODORA *remains at the back, not daring to come forward. He is in front, facing her*] You wished to speak to me? If you will be so kind, señora? [*Inviting her to come in*]

TEO. [*Raising her veil*] Forgive me, Ernesto.

ERN. Teodora!

TEO. I am doing wrong, I suppose.

ERN. [*Abruptly, stammering*] I—don't know. For I don't

know to what I owe so great an honor. But what am I saying? Why, in my house you are bound to meet with such respect as could be surpassed nowhere. Why, señora, should you fear there might be any harm in it?

Teo. There's no reason why. And there was a time, Ernesto,—it has gone forever,—when I would neither have doubted nor feared; when any woman you know might have come into your room without a blush, without fear; when, if you were going away from here, as they say you are going to America tomorrow—I myself—yes, since those who go away may never come back, and since it is so sad to lose a friend—before Julian—before all the world— would have given you a parting embrace without any thought of harm.

Ern. [*Makes a movement, then checks himself*] Ah, Teodora!

Teo. But now—I suppose it is not the same. There is a gulf between us.

Ern. You're right, señora. Now we cannot love each other, not even as brother and sister. Now our hands are stained if they touch when we meet. The past is over. We must conquer ourselves; we must hate each other.

Teo. [*Ingenuously*] Hate each other? Why?

Ern. I hate you? Did I say that to you, poor child?

Teo. Yes.

Ern. Never mind what I say. If the occasion arises, if you need my life, ask for it, Teodora, [*Passionately*] To give my life for you would be [*Controlling himself and changing his tone*] simply to do my duty. [*A slight pause*] Hate! If my lips spoke such a word it was because I was thinking of the wrong. I was thinking of the injury I have involuntarily done to one who has been so good to me. You, Teodora, ought to hate me—I—no—

Teo. [*Sadly*] Ah, they have made me weep much. You are right about that. [*Very sweetly*] But you—you, Ernesto.

I cannot accuse you. Nor would any one blame you who was not blinded by passion. How are you to blame for the whisperings and spite of an evil-minded world, or for poor Julian's black mood; for the anger that tortures him, for his tones that wound me, for the agony that is killing him because he doubts my love?

ERN. That I cannot understand; in him, least of all. [*With profound anger*] The thing that puts one in a fury, that deserves no mercy, for which there is no possible excuse, is that any man should doubt a woman like you.

TEO. My poor Julian is paying dear for his cruel doubt.

ERN. [*Frightened at having accused* JULIAN *before* TEODORA] What am I saying? [*Hastening to exculpate* JULIAN *and to kill the effect of what he has said*] Do I blame him? No. He doubted as any one would doubt. As every one who loves, doubts. There is no such thing as love without jealousy. Why, there are people who even doubt the good God, Teodora. It's our earthly egotism. The owner of a treasure guards his gold just because it is gold, and he fears for it. I myself, if by some superhuman effort I succeeded in making a woman mine, *I* would be jealous. I would be suspicious even of my own brother! [*He speaks with increasing exultation. Suddenly he stops, seeing that he is about to fall again from another side into the abyss from which he has just escaped.* TEODORA *hears voices in the direction of the door at the back, and goes toward it.—Aside*] Where are you leading me, my heart? What are my inmost feelings? You say the world speaks base slanders and then you justify them!

TEO. Listen, some one is coming.

ERN. Hardly two o'clock. I wonder who it is?

TEO. [*With a certain terror*] That's Julian's voice. He's probably coming in.

ERN. No. He's stopping.

TEO. [*All in the same tone, as if questioning* ERNESTO] If it is Julian—

> *Makes a movement in the direction of the door on the right.* ERNESTO *detains her, respectfully but firmly.*

ERN. If it is he, stay here. Our innocence protects us. If it is—those suspicious people, go in there. [*Pointing to the door at the right.—Listening*] It's nothing, nothing.

TEO. How my heart beats!

ERN. You needn't be afraid. Whoever wanted to come in has gone away,—or else it was an illusion. [*Coming forward*] Teodora!

TEO. I had to speak to you, Ernesto, and the time is going so fast!

ERN. Teodora, forgive me—but—perhaps it's not wise. If any one should come—and some one probably is coming—

TEO. That's just why I came—to prevent it.

ERN. You mean—?

TEO. I mean that I know all. And the thought of the blood that you want to shed for me terrifies me. It sets my own blood on fire. I feel it rising—here. [*Putting her hand on her heart*]

ERN. Because it is outraged by the shame and disgrace you must suffer until I have taken the viscount's life with my own hand. He wanted mud. Let him have the mud made by his own blood.

TEO. [*Frightened*] Is it to the death?

ERN. Yes. [*Checking a gesture of supplication from* TEODORA] You can lead me where you will, you can do anything with me, anything with one exception. May the time never come when, remembering that insult, I can have compassion on Nebreda.

TEO. [*Tearful and supplicating*] And on me?

ERN. On you?

TEO. Yes. It will be a terrible scandal.

ERN. Perhaps.

TEO. Perhaps? You say it like that and don't try to prevent it, even when I myself plead with you?

ERN. I can't prevent it, but I can make him pay for it. This is what I think, and this is what I say; this is what keeps running through my mind. Others have sought the affront, but I shall seek the punishment.

TEO. [*Going up to him, and speaking in an undertone, as if afraid of her words*] And Julian?

ERN. Julian? Well?

TEO. If he should know?

ERN. He probably does know.

TEO. And what will he say?

ERN. What will he say?

TEO. That in my defence, who should show his courage except my husband who loves me?

ERN. In defence of a woman? Any man of honor, without knowing her, without being relation, friend, or lover! It's enough to hear a woman insulted. You ask why I am going to fight this duel, why I defend her? Because I heard the slander and I am the man I am. Who would refuse to take up the cudgel in such a cause, or who would give up his right to do so? Wasn't I there? Then I was simply the first man on the spot.

TEO. [*Who has listened to him attentively, as though dominated by his vigor, approaches him and presses his hand with great emotion*] That is honorable, noble, and worthy of you, Ernesto. [*Checks herself, goes away from* ERNESTO, *and says sadly*] But this is humiliating to my poor Julian!

ERN. Humiliating?

TEO. Yes, indeed.

ERN. Why?

TEO. Because . . .

ERN. Who says so?

TEO. Every one will think so.

ERN. But why?

TEO. When people hear that I have been insulted, and that it was not my husband who chastised the offender, and that [*Lowering her voice, hanging her head, and avoiding* ERNESTO's *eyes*] it was you who took his place, scandal will be heaped upon scandal.

ERN. [*Convinced, but protesting*] Good heavens, if we have to think what people are going to say about everything that we do, life isn't worth living at all.

TEO. But I am right.

ERN. You're right.   But it's horrible.

TEO. You yield, then?

ERN. Impossible.

TEO. I beg you!

ERN. No.   It is more important than ever, Teodora, that I meet Nebreda, come what may.   The truth is that the viscount makes up for his lack of honor by his skill in swordsmanship.

TEO. [*Somewhat hurt by the rather humiliating protection that* ERNESTO *is offering to* DON JULIAN] My husband is brave, too.

ERN. The deuce!   Either I don't make myself very clear, or you are very slow of understanding: I realize his courage. But when one man has foully insulted the name or honor of another and satisfaction is sought, no one can guess what will happen: which will kill, which be killed.   If this man, therefore, is to win in the deadly combat there can be no doubt as to whether it is better for him to have Don Julian or Ernesto for an opponent.   [*Sincerely but sadly*]

TEO. [*In real distress*] You?   Oh, no.   Not that.

ERN. Why not?   If that is my fate, my death will be no loss to any one, and I myself will lose but little.

TEO. [*Hardly able to restrain her tears*] Don't say that.

ERN. Well, what do I leave behind in the world? What friendship? What love? What woman will follow my body weeping tears of love?

TEO. [*Unable to control her tears*] All last night I was praying for you. And you say that no one— Oh, I don't want you to die!

ERN. Ah, a woman may pray for any one— [*Passionately*] but she weeps for one man only!

TEO. [*Strangely*] Ernesto!

ERN. [*Frightened at his own words*] Yes?

TEO. [*Drawing away from him*] Nothing.

ERN. [*Timidly. Hanging his head and avoiding* TEODORA's *eyes*] If I spoke as I did a little while ago— I am beside myself. Pay no heed to me.

> *A pause. They stand, silent, thinking, at a distance*
> *from each other, and not daring to look at each other.*

TEO. [*Pointing to the back*] Again!

ERN. Some one has come.

TEO. [*Going back and listening*] And they want to come in.

ERN. It must be they. In there, Teodora. [*Pointing to the room*]

TEO. My innocence protects me.

ERN. But this is not your husband.

TEO. It's not Julian!

ERN. No. [*Leading her to the right*]

TEO. I hoped— [*Stopping near the door, beseechingly*] Oh, give up this duel.

ERN. Good heavens! Why, I struck him in the face!

TEO. [*Despairing, but realizing that any settlement is impossible*] I didn't know that. Then flee—

ERN. I flee?

TEO. For my sake—for his. In heaven's name—

ERN. I can bear to be hated, but not to be despised.

TEO. Just one more thing. Are they coming for you?

ERN. It's not time yet.

TEO. You swear it?

ERN. Yes, Teodora.   Do you hate me?

TEO. Never!

PEP. [*Without*] It's no use.   I must see him.

ERN. Quick.

TEO. Yes.   [*Goes out, right.*

PEP. No one shall stop me.

ERN. Ah, slander justifies itself and makes the sin come true!

Enter PEPITO *at the back, hatless, and much excited.*

PEP. To the devil with you!   I will go in.   Ernesto, Ernesto!

ERN. What's the matter?

PEP. I don't know how to tell you about it, but I must.

ERN. Speak, man!

PEP. My head's in a whirl.   Dear me, dear me!   Who would have thought—!

ERN. Quick!   What has happened?

PEP. What has happened?   A terrible calamity.   Don Julian found out about the duel.   He came here to look for you.   You weren't here.   He went to see your seconds.   They all met at the viscount's house—

ERN. At Nebreda's?   But how?

PEP. Don Julian arranged it.   He was like a whirlwind sweeping all before him, plans, conventions, everything, everything.

ERN. Go on.   What happened?

PEP. They're coming up now.

ERN. Who?

PEP. Why, they.   They are carrying him in their arms.

ERN. You frighten me.   Go on—quick. [*Seizing him violently and dragging him forward*]

PEP. He forced Nebreda to fight with him; would listen to

no excuse. So the viscount said, "With both, then." Don
Julian came up here. Your servant barred the door and
swore you were engaged with a lady and that no one was to
come in; no one—

ERN. And then?

PEP. Don Julian came down, saying, "So much the better.
I'll manage the whole affair." And he, Nebreda, the seconds,
my father, and I, who arrived after them all.—Well, the rest
is plain.

ERN. They fought?

PEP. Madly, furiously. Like two men striving to fix upon
the sword's point a heart that they hated.

ERN. And Don Julian? No, it's a lie!

PEP. They're here already.

ERN. Hush! Hush! Tell me who it is—and speak softly.

PEP. See there.

> DON JULIAN, DON SEVERO, *and* RUEDA *appear at the*
> *back.* *They are carrying* DON JULIAN, *who is badly*
> *wounded.*

ERN. God help me! Don Julian, my benefactor, my friend,
my father! *[Rushes to him, weeping.*

JUL. [*In a weak voice*] Ernesto.

ERN. What a wretch I am!

SEV. Come, be quick.

ERN. Father!

SEV. The pain is killing him.

ERN. You did this for my sake. Forgive me.

> *Taking* JULIAN'S *right hand, kneeling beside him, and*
> *leaning over him.*

JUL. There's no need. You did your duty. I have done
mine.

SEV. A bed!

> *He releases* JULIAN, *and* PEPITO *takes his place.*

PEP. Let's go in there. [*Pointing to the door at the right*]

ERN. [*In a terrible voice*] Nebreda—

SEV. No more of this folly. Do you want to finish killing him?

ERN. [*In a frenzy*] Folly! We shall see. Oh, let them both come.

PEP. We'll put him in your bed in the alcove.

[ERNESTO *stops, terrified.*

ERN. Where?

SEV. In there.

PEP. Yes!

ERN. No.

> He rushes up and stands in front of the door. The group, leading the half-fainting JULIAN, stops in astonishment.

SEV. You refuse to let him?

PEP. You are mad!

SEV. Stand aside! Don't you see he's dying?

JUL. What does he mean? He doesn't want me?

> Pulling himself together and looking at ERNESTO with mingled horror and astonishment.

RUEDA. I don't understand.

PEP. Nor I.

ERN. He is dying, and he beseeches me and he doubts me. Father!

SEV. We must.   [*The door opens.* TEODORA *appears.*

ERN. Good God!

SEV. ⎰
PEP. ⎱ She!

RUEDA. A woman!

TEO. [*Rushing up to* JULIAN *and embracing him*] Julian!

JUL. [*Drawing away to look at her, rising by a violent effort, rejecting all help*] Who is it? Teodora!

[*He falls to the floor, unconscious*
    Curtain.

ACT III

The same setting as Act I, except there is a settle instead of a sofa. It is evening. A lighted lamp is on the table.

PEP. At last the crisis is over; at least I can't hear anything. Poor Don Julian. Very serious, very serious. His life is in the balance. On the one side death awaits him; on the other, another death. Two gulfs deeper than a hopeless love. The devil! With all these tragedies going on in the house I'm turning more romantic than *he* with his rhymes and his plots. Why, my head's a regular kaleidescope of scandals, duels, deaths, treachery and infamy! Heavens, what a day and what a night! And the worst is yet to come. [*A little pause*] It was rank imprudence to pick him up and carry him off in such a condition. But, the deuce! Who can oppose my uncle when he sets his jaws, and frowns like that? And you must admit that he was right. No honorable man, so long as there was a breath of life in him, would have stayed in that house in such a situation. And he's a proud and sensitive man. [*Going back*] Who's coming? Why, it's my mother.

Enter MERCEDES.

MER. How is Severo?

PEP. He won't leave his brother for a single instant. I knew he was devoted to him, but I had no idea he loved him as much as all this. I only hope that things won't turn out as I fear.

MER. And your uncle?

PEP. He suffers in silence. Sometimes he cries out "Teodora" in a harsh and anguished tone. At other times

64

he cries, "Ernesto," and clutches the sheet between his fingers. Then he lies motionless as a statue, gazing fixedly into empty space, and the cold sweat of death bathes his brow. Suddenly fever gives him strength; he raises himself up in his bed, and listens eagerly, and says that *he* and *she* are waiting for him. He gets up and wants to go out, and my father resorts to tears and supplications to calm his anxiety. Calm it? He can't do it. His burning blood is carrying the anger of his heart and the tears of his soul through all his veins. Let's go, mother, it's heart-rending to see the bitter distortion of his mouth, to see his hands drawn up like two claws, his hair all in disorder, and his distended pupils eagerly searching every shadow flickering in the room.

MER. And when your father sees him?

PEP. He groans and swears that he will be avenged; and he, too, says "Teodora"; he, too, cries "Ernesto." Heaven forbid that he should meet them, for if he does, nothing can appease his anger, nothing can control his fury.

MER. Your father is very good.

PEP. Yes, with a temper—phew!

MER. It's true. He very seldom gets angry; but when he does—

PEP. With all due respect, he is as fierce as a tiger.

MER. He always has just cause.

PEP. I don't know about that, but he undoubtedly has plenty of reason this time. But how is Teodora?

MER. She's upstairs. She wanted to come down.---And she was weeping. A veritable Magdalen.

PEP. Of course. Repentant or sinning?

MER. Don't talk that way. Why, she's only a child.

PEP. Who, innocent, spotless, sweet, pure, gentle little thing that she is, has killed Don Julian. If you're right and she is only a child, and she does such things when she's hardly out of the cradle, heaven help us a few years from now!

MER. She is hardly to blame. Your fine friend with his play—the poet, the dreamer—has been the cause of all this.

PEP. Well, I don't deny it.

MER. What does he gain by it?

PEP. Well, at present Ernesto is walking the streets fleeing from his conscience, which he can't escape.

MER. Has he any?

PEP. He may have.

MER. How sad it is!

PEP. A terrible misfortune.

MER. How we have been deceived!

PEP. Cruelly!

MER. What treachery!

PEP. Staggering.

MER. What a scandal!

PEP. Unequalled!

MER. Poor Julian!

PEP. A bitter blow!

    Enter a SERVANT.

SERVANT. Don Ernesto.

MER. How dare he!

PEP. What audacity!

SERVANT. I thought—

PEP. You thought wrong.

SERVANT. He is just stopping in on his way. He said to the coachman, "I'll be right out. Wait here." So—

PEP. [*Consulting his mother*] What shall we do?

MER. Let him come in.   [*The* SERVANT *goes out.*

PEP. I'll get rid of him.

MER. Be tactful.

    MERCEDES *sits on the settle;* PEPITO *stands on the other*
    side of the stage. Neither turns to greet ERNESTO,
    who enters through second wing.

ERN. [*Aside*] Scorn, unfriendly silence! It bodes ill. From now on I shall be a monster of wickedness and insolence, even though I am entirely blameless. Every one thinks so; they all despise me.

PEP. [*Turning to him, and speaking in harsh tones*] Look here, Ernesto.

ERN. What is it?

PEP. I want to tell you—

ERN. To get out of here?

PEP. [*Changing his tone*] Goodness, what an idea! It was— I just wanted to ask—if it is true— [*As if hunting for his words*] that afterwards, the viscount—

ERN. [*Gloomily, hanging his head*] Yes.

PEP. With your own hands?

ERN. When I went out of the house I was beside myself. They were coming down.—I stopped them.—We went up again.—I shut the door. Two men, two witnesses,—two swords,—then—I don't know how—two blades crossing.— A cry—a blow—a sob—blood flowing—a murderer standing there—and a man lying on the ground.

PEP. The devil! You have a good aim. Did you hear, mother?

MER. Still more blood!

PEP. Nebreda deserved it!

ERN. Mercedes, I beg of you—just one word! Don Julian? Don Julian? If you only realized my anxiety, my grief. What do they say?

MER. That his wound is mortal, and that it grows more dangerous the nearer you come to his bed of death and sorrow. Leave this house.

ERN. I want to see him.

MER. Go at once!

ERN. No!

PEP. Such insolence!

ERN. Is quite worthy of me! [*To* MERCEDES, *respectfully*] Forgive me, señora, I am what others make me.

MER. For heaven's sake, Ernesto!

ERN. Listen, Mercedes. When a man like me is trampled upon and is called infamous without reason, and is forced and dragged into sin, the struggle that results is dangerous— for all, but not for me; for in this fierce struggle with invisible beings, I have lost honor, affection, love, and there is nothing left for me to lose but the sad tatters of an insipid and monotonous existence. I came only to find out if there is any hope—that's all. Well, why do you deny me that consolation? [*Beseeching* MERCEDES] Just one word!

MER. Well—they say—that he is better.

ERN. But the truth? They're not deceiving me? It's true? They're sure of it? Ah, you are compassionate! You are good! Can it be true? Good God! can it be true? O Lord, save him! Don't let him die! Let him be happy once more! Let him forgive me! Let him embrace me again! Let me live to see it!

> *He sinks into the chair nearest to the table and hides his face in his hands, sobbing.* MERCEDES *and* PEPITO *go over to* ERNESTO.

MER. If your father hears—if your father comes—! [*To* ERNESTO] Courage!

PEP. A man crying! [*Aside*] These nervous people are terrible. One minute they weep, and the next they kill some one.

ERN. If I cry, if my throat is torn by hysterical sobs, if I am as weak as a woman or a child, don't think it's for my own sake. It's for him, for her, for their lost happiness; for their good name, stained forever; for the injury I have done them in return for their love and their favors! I don't weep for my misfortunes, for *my* dark lot! And, by heaven! if the sad past could be wiped out with tears, I'd turn all my blood into tears and not leave a drop in my veins!

MER. Be still, for pity's sake!

PEP. We'll talk of tears and sorrow later.

ERN. If every one else is talking now, why shouldn't we talk, too? The whole town is a seething, boiling whirlpool that sucks in and absorbs and devours and utterly destroys the honor, the good name, the very being of three people, and carries them away on the spray of laughter through the canal of human misery to the social abyss of shame, and there drowns forever the future, the fair name, and the memory, of these unhappy beings.

MER. Speak lower, Ernesto.

ERN. No; they aren't whispering; they're shouting aloud. Why, the air fairly resounds! There isn't a person who doesn't know the tragic story, but every one tells it his own way. Wonder of wonders, people always know everything; but, sad to say, never the truth. [ERNESTO *is standing up now, and* MERCEDES *and* PEPITO *are listening eagerly to hear what is being said in the town*] Some say that Teodora was surprised by her husband in my house, and that I rushed at him, blind with fury, and plunged my cowardly dagger into his breast; *others,* my friends apparently, give me a higher rank than that of a vulgar assassin: I killed him, but in an honorable fight, a properly arranged duel. There *are* some, of course, who know more of the details, and *they* say that Julian took my place in the affair that had been arranged with Nebreda. . . . I arrived too late . . . on purpose, or through cowardice, or because I was in the arms of . . . No, the vile words burn my lips; my brain is on fire! Think of the filthiest, the lowest, vilest, most infamous thing imaginable: dregs of the heart, ashes of the soul, evil scourings of unclean minds; cast it to the breezes blowing through the streets, salt all lips and tongues with it, and you'll have the story, and you will learn then what remains of two honorable men and a woman, when their reputations are bandied about the town!

MER. I don't deny that it's all most unfortunate. But perhaps we can't altogether blame these people for the conclusions they draw.

PEP. Teodora went to your house . . . she was there—

ERN. To prevent the duel with Nebreda.

PEP. Then why did she hide?

ERN. Because we were afraid her presence there would look suspicious.

PEP. The explanation is easy and simple enough. The difficulty, Ernesto, is to make people believe it. There's another one that is still easier, and simpler—

ERN. And more shameful!—so that is the best one.

PEP. Grant at least that Teodora was indiscreet, though she was not guilty.

ERN. Guilt is wily and cautious. On the other hand, how rash is innocence!

PEP. That's all very well for saints and angels, but when you apply that rule to every one—

ERN. Oh, well, you're right. Of what value or importance are such calumnies? Why worry about them? The horrible part is that one's very thoughts are tainted by the fatal contact with this fatal idea! If one ever thinks of crime, it becomes familiar to one's consciousness. One looks on it with fear and loathing—*but one looks on it*—at night, in the darkness! That's how it is! [*Aside*] But what's the matter? Why do they look at me so strangely as they listen? [*Aloud*] You know me; I bear an honorable name! . . . If I killed Nebreda simply because he lied, what would I not do if by my own guilt I turned his slanders into truth!

PEP. [*Aside to* MERCEDES] And he denied it! It's plain as day!

MER. This is madness!

PEP. The one thing that's plain is that he confesses!

MER. [*Aloud*] Leave us, Ernesto.

ERN. Impossible. If I were far from his bed tonight I should go mad.

MER. But if Severo comes and sees you?

ERN. What difference will that make to me? He's an honorable man. All the better! Let him come. He who fears runs away, and he fears who has deceived, so it's not likely that I shall either run from him or fear him.

PEP. [*Listening*] Some one is coming.

MER. It's he.

PEP. It's not he. Teodora!

ERN. It's Teodora! . . . Teodora! . . . I want to see her!

MER. [*Sternly*] Ernesto!

PEP. Ernesto!

ERN. Yes, to ask her to forgive me.

MER. You don't realize—

ERN. I realize everything, and I understand. We two together? Oh, no— Enough! You needn't be afraid. I may give my blood for her, give my life, my future, my honor, and my conscience. . . . But see each other! Never . . . It's no longer possible—a blood-red cloud separates us!

[*He goes out, left.*

MER. Leave me alone with her. Go in with your father. I want to search the very bottom of her heart. I know too well that my words will be like daggers to her.

PEP. Well, I leave you together.

MER. Good-bye.

PEP. Good-bye.   [*He goes out, right.*

MER. Now, to work! [TEODORA *enters timidly, and stops by* JULIAN'S *door. She listens anxiously, stifling her sobs with her handkerchief*] Teodora . . .

TEO. Is that you?

MER. Courage! What good will it do to weep?

TEO. How is he? How is he? The truth!

MER. Much better.

TEO. Will he recover?

MER. I think so.

TEO. O God, take my life for his!

MER. [*Brings her forward affectionately*] And then . . . then I trust in your judgment, for I see by your tears and your anxiety that you are repentant.

TEO. Yes. [MERCEDES *sits down and watches her suspiciously*] It's quite true I did very wrong to go and see him. [MERCEDES, *seeing that this is not the kind of repentance that she meant, shows her disapproval*] But last night you told me about the insult and the duel. . . . I'm grateful for your kindness, though you can't realize, and I wouldn't know how to explain to you the harm you have done me. What a night! Groaning and raving! Dear Julian's anger! the scandal! the insult! . . . the blood! . . . the terrible struggle! . . . It all passed before my eyes! And poor Ernesto, too, perhaps dying for me. . . . Why do you look at me that way? What harm is there in that? Don't you believe me? Do you think as the rest do?

MER. [*Drily*] I think you needn't have feared for this young man's life.

TEO. No? Nebreda is a famous swordsman! You see— my Julian—

MER. In brief, your Julian is avenged and the duellist is iaid low with a wound in his heart, so your doubts and fears were unfounded. [*Coldly and meaningly*]

TEO. [*With interest*] Did Ernesto do it?

MER. Yes, Ernesto.

TEO. He met the viscount?

MER. Face to face!

TEO. [*Unable to control herself*] Ah, how brave and noble!

MER. Teodora!

TEO. What is it? Tell me.

MER. I can read your thoughts.

TEO. My thoughts?

MER. Yes.

TEO. What thoughts?

MER. You know very well!

TEO. I did wrong to show my happiness at seeing Julian avenged; but it was an impulse from my heart that I couldn't control.

MER. That's not what you were thinking.

TEO. Then you must know more about it than I do?

MER. [*Meaningly*] Listen, when the heart admires greatly it is on the road to love.

TEO. You say I admire something?

MER. This young man's courage.

TEO. His goodness.

MER. It's all one, that is the beginning.

TEO. These are the ravings of madness.

MER. It is madness . . . on your part.

TEO. Will you never understand! . . . Always this terrible idea? Why, I feel only infinite pity!

MER. For whom?

TEO. For whom would it be? For Julian!

MER. Have you never heard that pity and forgetfulness go hand in hand in women!

TEO. Be still, for mercy's sake!

MER. I want to awaken your conscience with the voice of my experience and the light of truth. [*A pause.*

TEO. I am listening to you, and as I listen you seem to me not like a mother, a sister, or a friend; your words sound to me as though Satan were counselling you and inspiring you and speaking through your lips. Why do you want to convince me that my love for my husband is a lie—a lie of the soul—and that a rival love is foully growing there, whose flame consumes and defiles? Why, I love him as I have always loved him. I would give the very last drop of the blood that runs through my veins and sets me on fire, for a single instant of life for that man from whom they separate me. I would go in there this very minute if your husband would let me. And I would clasp Julian in my arms and would bathe him with my tears, with such tender love and such passion that his doubts would be consumed by the fire of our souls. But just because I adore Julian, must I be so ungrateful as to hate the noble and generous man who risked his life for me? And if I don't hate him, must I love him? Heaven help me! The world thinks such things. I hear such strange stories, I see such sad things happen, I have such slanders heaped upon me, that sometimes I begin to doubt myself and I ask myself in horror: Am I, perhaps, what they all say I am? Do I nourish an unlawful passion in the very depths of my being, consuming me without my knowledge, and will the evil flame break out some sad and ill-omened hour and overpower my will and my senses?

MER. Are you telling me the truth?

TEO. The absolute truth.

MER. You don't love him?

TEO. Listen, Mercedes. I don't know how to convince you. Any other time such a question would make my blood boil; yet now, as you see, I am calmly discussing the question whether or not I am an honest woman. Can that mean that I really am one? At the bottom of my heart? No; to endure the humiliation is to deserve the shame.

She hides her face in her hands and sinks down on the settle.

MER. Don't cry. Come, I believe you. Don't cry, Teodora. Enough. No more of this. Just one word more, Teodora, and then I have finished. Ernesto is not what you think him: he doesn't deserve your confidence.

TEO. He is good, Mercedes.

MER. No.

TEO. He loves Julian.

MER. He is deceiving him.

TEO. Again! Good heavens!

MER. I don't say that you would listen to his declarations.
I only say . . . I only say that *he loves you.*

TEO. [*In horror, rising*] He loves me?

MER. Every one knows it. A little while ago in this very
room, before me, before my son . . . now, you see.

TEO. [*Anxiously*] Well, go on. What was it?

MER. He confessed it openly, and in impassioned words
swore that for you he would give life, honor, conscience,
and soul. And when you came he wanted to see you,
and it was only by urgent insistence that I persuaded
him to go in there. I am on pins and needles now for
fear Severo may find him, and his anger break out! Now
what do you say?

TEO. [*In spite of herself she has followed this speech with a
strange, indefinable mixture of interest, horror, and fear*] Good
heavens! Can such infamy be? And I grieved for him! I
professed such sincere affection for him!

MER. Are you crying again?

TEO. Can the soul help weeping at the disillusionments of
this unhappy life? A man so noble, so pure . . . to see him
fallen and defiled! You say he is in there! He! Ernesto!
Holy Virgin! Listen, Mercedes—Mercedes—he must leave
this house!

MER. [*With real joy*] That is what I want. Your vehem-
ence delights me. Forgive me. Now I believe you.

TEO. But you didn't before?

MER. Hush! Be still! He is coming!

TEO. [*Impatiently*] I won't see him! You tell him. . . .
Julian is waiting for me. [*Turning to the right*]

MER. Impossible. . . . You know it now. . . . And he won't
obey me. Now that I fully understand your feelings, I

want him to see in you the scorn which he met with before in
my words.

TEO. Let me go.

Enter ERNESTO.

ERN. [*Stopping at the entrance*] Teodora!

MER. [*Aside to* TEODORA] It's too late. Do your duty
and that will be enough. [*Aloud to* ERNESTO] Teodora, as
mistress of this house, is going to repeat to you the command
that you heard from my lips a little while ago.

TEO. [*In a low voice to* MERCEDES] Don't leave me.

MER. Are you afraid of something?

TEO. I afraid! I fear nothing!

[*Signs to her to go. She goes out, right.*

ERN. The command was . . . that I should go away. [*A
pause. They are both silent and do not dare look at each other*]
And you . . . do you repeat it now? [TEODORA *makes a sign
of assent, but does not meet his eye*] Then don't be afraid,
Teodora. I obey, I respect your commands. [*Sadly and respectfully*] The others sha'n't make me obey, little as it pleases
them. [*Harshly*] But from you—even though you hurt—
from you I can suffer all things.

TEO. Hurt you, Ernesto! No. Do you think that I . . . ?

ERN. I don't think so.   [*Another pause.*

TEO. [*Without turning round or looking at him*] Good-bye.
I wish you all happiness.

ERN. Good-bye, Teodora. [*He pauses a moment, but she does
not turn, or look at him, or put out her hand. Finally he starts
to go. Then he turns and goes up to her.* TEODORA *feels
him coming, but does not turn her eyes toward him*] If I could
wipe out now by my death all the harm I have done you in
spite of myself, because of my unhappy fate, I give you my
word of honor that soon not even a shadow of the past
would remain, not a sigh of agony, nor that sad pallor,
[TEODORA *raises her head and looks at him in terror*] nor that

look that frightens me, not a sob in your throat, [TEODORA *does indeed stifle a sob*] not a tear on your cheek.

TEO. [*Aside, drawing away from* ERNESTO] Mercedes told the truth, and I, blind, heedless—

ERN. Give me just one word of farewell—just one, I beg.

TEO. Good-bye. Yes. . . . I forgive the wrong you have done us.

ERN. That I have done, I, Teodora!

TEO. Yes.

ERN. That look, that tone!

TEO. No more, Ernesto, please!

ERN. What have I done to deserve this?

TEO. It is as though I had never existed. All is over between us.

ERN. These scornful words!

TEO. [*Hoarsely, pointing to the door*] Go!

ERN. You tell me to go—like that!

TEO. My husband is dying in there . . . and I am dying here, too.

> She totters, and has to support herself by the arm of the chair so as not to fall.

ERN. [*Hurrying to help her*] Teodora!

TEO. [*Repulsing him violently*] Don't touch me. Leave me alone! [*A pause*] Oh, my heart is breaking!

> She tries to take a few steps, her strength fails her, and ERNESTO again tries to support her. She repulses him and draws away.

ERN. Why won't you let me?

TEO. [*Harshly*] Because you defile me.

ERN. You say—I defile you?

TEO. Certainly.

ERN. [*A pause*] Good heavens, what is she saying? She, too! Impossible! . . . Death would be better than this! . . . It's not true! I'm going mad! . . . Say it's not so, Teodora!

In Heaven's name, speak one word of forgiveness, or comfort, or pity, señora! I agree to leave you and never see you again, though it breaks my heart—it is killing me! But I do this on the condition that your affection and your esteem shall follow me in my solitude, together with your forgiveness . . . at least your pity! I must believe that you believe I am faithful and honorable, that I neither defile nor have defiled, that I neither wrong nor will wrong you! I care little for the world. I scorn its curses, and its anger fills me with profound contempt. Even though it hits me cruelly, wantonly; though it whispers about what I have been, it can never think as ill of me as I think of it. But you—the purest being imaginable —you, for whom I swear I would gladly give a thousand times not only my life on earth, but my place in heaven,—for you to think me capable of treachery! Oh, not that, Teodora, not that!

TEO. You don't understand. We must separate, Ernesto.

ERN. It is impossible.

TEO. At once. I implore you. [*Pointing to the door*] Julian is suffering.

ERN. I know it.

TEO. Then we mustn't forget it.

ERN. No, but I'm suffering, too.

TEO. You, Ernesto? Why?

ERN. Because you despise me.

TEO. Oh, I don't.

ERN. You said so.

TEO. I lied.

ERN. No, you meant it. So we are not suffering equally. In this eternal struggle, in this relentless warfare, he suffers as men suffer on earth, and I as they do in hell.

TEO. Good heavens, my brain is on fire!

ERN. My heart is breaking.

TEO. Stop, Ernesto. Have some pity.

ERN. That's all *I* ask.

TEO. Pity?

ERN. Yes, pity. What is it that you fear from me,—or think of me?

TEO. Forgive me, if I have hurt you.

ERN. Hurt! No. The truth. I want the truth! I ask it on bended knees, with tears in my eyes.

> *He kneels before* TEODORA *and takes her hand. At this point* SEVERO *appears in the doorway of* JULIAN's *room and stands there.*

SEV. [*Aside*] The wretches!

TEO. Don Severo!

> ERNESTO *leaves* TEODORA *and goes to the right.* SEVERO *comes forward between him and* TEODORA.

SEV. [*To* ERNESTO, *with concentrated fury, but in a low tone, so that* JULIAN *may not hear*] Since I can find no words to express my anger and my contempt, I shall have to content myself with saying, "You are a scoundrel. Go at once!"

ERN. Out of respect to Teodora and to this house, because of him who is suffering on that bed, I shall have to content myself with answering . . . by silence.

SEV. [*Ironically, thinking that he is going*] To be silent and obey is the part of prudence.

ERN. You misunderstood. I don't obey.

SEV. You are going to stay here?

ERN. Provided that Teodora does not confirm your command, I stay here. A few minutes ago I was about to leave, but God or the devil detained me. You came, you tried to throw me out, and at once, just as though your harsh words were some devil's spell, I felt roots shooting out from the soles of my feet and taking firm hold in the ground.

SEV. I'll try calling the servants to see whether they can tear them out by force.

ERN. Try.

He takes a step toward SEVERO *with a threatening air.*
TEODORA *rushes between them and restrains him.*

TEO. Ernesto. [*Then turning to her uncle, with spirit and dignity*] You forget, doubtless, that in my house, while my husband, its master, is living, we, and we alone, have the right and the authority to command. [*To* ERNESTO, *sweetly*] Not for his sake—but for mine—because I am in trouble.

ERNESTO *cannot conceal his joy that* TEODORA *is defending him.*

ERN. Teodora, do you wish it?

TEO. I ask this of you.

[ERNESTO *bows respectfully and turns to go.*

SEV. Your audacity amazes and horrifies me as much— no, far more than Ernesto's. [*He approaches* TEODORA *with a threatening look.* ERNESTO, *who has taken several steps, stops; then, making an effort to control himself, goes on*] Do you dare lift up your head, unhappy woman, and before me, too! Bow your head to the dust. [ERNESTO *makes the same movements as before, but more markedly*] Where did you, poor, trembling little coward, find those spirited words to defend him? Passion is eloquent! [ERNESTO, *now at the back, stops*] But you forget that before throwing him out, Severo knew enough to turn you out of this house, which you have stained with Julian's blood. Why have you come back?

He seizes her brutally by the arm and gradually gets nearer and nearer to her.

ERN. Oh, I can't! No! [*He rushes up to* SEVERO *and* TEODORA *and separates them*] Let go of her, you scoundrel!

SEV. Again!

ERN. Again!

SEV. You come back!

ERN. Since you dare harm Teodora, what can I do but

[*He has lost all control of himself*] come back, come back and punish your insolence, and call you a coward to your face?

SEV. Me!

ERN. Yes!

TEO. No!

ERN. He brought it on himself. I saw him lay hands on you in anger. On you—on you! Like this.

[*He seizes* SEVERO *violently by the arm.*

SEV. Insolent!

ERN. True. But I'm not going to let go. Did you ever have a mother? Yes. Did you love her very much? Did you respect her still more? Well, you are to respect Teodora as much, and you are to humble yourself before the terrible grief of this woman! Of this woman, purer and more honorable than your mother, you hound!

SEV. You dare say these things to me?

ERN. Yes, and I've not finished yet.

SEV. You shall pay for this with your life.

ERN. With my life. But now . . . [TEODORA *tries to separate them, but he puts her gently aside with one hand*] You probably believe in a God. You must . . . a creator . . . a future hope! Good! Well, just as you bend your sluggish knees before the altar of God in heaven, you must bend them now before Teodora. Now, at once! Down! Into the dust!

TEO. Oh, have pity!

ERN. To the ground!

[*He forces* SEVERO *to kneel before* TEODORA.

TEO. Stop! Ernesto!

SEV. The devil!

ERN. At her feet.

SEV. *You* dare!

ERN. I!

SEV. Before *her!*

ERN. Yes.

TEO. Stop! Silence!

> TEODORA, *terrified, points to* JULIAN'S *room.* ER-
> NESTO *lets go his prisoner.* SEVERO *rises and goes
> back toward the right.* TEODORA *goes to the back,
> toward* ERNESTO. *In this way he and she form a
> separate group.*

JUL. [*Without*] Let me go.

MER. No.

JUL. It is they. Come!

TEO. [*To* ERNESTO] Go!

SEV. [*To* ERNESTO] My revenge!

ERN. I admit it.

> *At this moment* JULIAN *appears, pale, haggard, half-
> dying, supported by* MERCEDES.

JUL. Together! Where are they going? Stop them!
They're running away from me.   Traitors!

> *He tries to throw himself upon them, but his strength
> fails him, and he totters.*

SEV. [*Rushing up to support him*] No!

JUL. Severo, they deceived me . . . they lied. Wretches!
[*As he is talking,* MERCEDES *and* SEVERO *lead him over to the
settle*] Over there! Look! Both of them—she and Ernesto!
Why are they together?

TEO. ⎱
ERN. ⎰ [*Drawing away from each other*] No!

JUL. Why don't they come here? Teodora!

TEO. [*Stretching out her arms, but not going any nearer*]
Dear Julian.

JUL. Come to me! [TEODORA *rushes into* JULIAN'S *arms
and he embraces her violently. A pause*] Do you see? Now,
do you see? [*To his brother*] I know they are deceiving me
and I clasp her in my arms and hold her there . . . and I
could kill her! . . . And she deserves it! . . . And I look at her.
. . . *I look at her,* and I cannot!

TEO. Julian!

JUL. And that man? [*Pointing to* ERNESTO]

ERN. Señor—

JUL. And I loved him! Be still, and come here! [ERNESTO *goes up to him. He holds* TEODORA] I am still her master!

TEO. I am yours! I am yours!

JUL. Don't pretend! Don't lie to me.

MER. [*Trying to calm him*] Please!

SEV. Julian!

JUL. [*To both*] Hush; be still! [*To* TEODORA] I've found you out. I know that you love him. [TEODORA *and* ERNESTO *try to protest, but he will not let them*] Why, Madrid knows it! All Madrid!

ERN. No, father.

TEO. No.

JUL. They deny it; they still deny it. Why, I have evidence. I feel it in my very being. This fever that is burning me up lightens my mind with its flame.

ERN. These stories are all the children of the fever in your blood, of your deliriums. Listen, señor!

JUL. You're going to lie to me!

ERN. [*Pointing to* TEODORA] She is innocent.

JUL. I don't believe you.

ERN. By the memory of my father, señor—

JUL. Don't profane his name and his memory.

ERN. By my mother's last kiss—

JUL. Her last kiss is no longer on your forehead.

ERN. Then by anything you wish, dear father, I will swear it, I will swear it.

JUL. No oaths, no lying words or protestations!

ERN. Then what will satisfy you?

JUL. Deeds!

ERN. What does he want, Teodora? What is he asking us to do?

TEO. I don't know. What shall we do? What shall we do, Ernesto?

JUL. [*Who is watching them with feverish eyes full of instinctive distrust*] Ah, you're planning deceits before my very eyes. Wretches! You're plotting together. I see you.

ERN. You see with your fever, not with your eyes.

JUL. Yes, with my fever. My fever's a flame that has consumed the veil that you two drew in front of my eyes, and at last I see. Why do you look at each other now? Why, traitors? Why do your eyes shine? Speak, Ernesto. It's not the shining of tears. Come closer, closer! [*He forces them to come near, make him bow his head, and at last kneel before him.* JULIAN *now is between* TEODORA, *who is beside him, and* ERNESTO, *who is at his feet. In this position he passes his hand over* ERNESTO'S *eyes*] Do you see? It's not tears; they're quite dry.

ERN. Forgive me, forgive me!

JUL. Why, if you ask forgiveness, you confess your sin!

ERN. No!

JUL. Yes!

ERN. It's not true.

JUL. Then let your eyes meet before me.

SEV. Julian!

MER. Señor!

JUL. [*To* TEODORA *and* ERNESTO] Perhaps you're afraid? Don't you love each other like brother and sister? Then prove it. Let your souls look out of your wide pupils, and let the rays of their chaste light mingle before me so that when I look very closely I may see whether those rays are *light* or *fire*. You, too, Teodora! Come, you must! Do it, both of you!

> He makes TEODORA *kneel before him, faces them near together, and makes them look at each other.*

TEO. [*Drawing away with a violent effort*] Ah, no!

ERN. [*Tries to free himself, but* JULIAN *holds him*] I cannot.

JUL. You love each other, you love each other! I saw it clearly! [*To* ERNESTO] You shall pay for this with your life!

ERN. Yes.

JUL. With your blood!

ERN. With every drop!

JUL. Be still.

TEO. [*Trying to calm him*] Julian!

JUL. Do *you* defend him?   Defend him?

TEO. It's not for his sake!

SEV. By heaven!

JUL. [*To* SEVERO] Silence! [*To* ERNESTO] Unnatural son!

ERN. Father!

JUL. Deceiver! traitor!

ERN. No: father!

JUL. Today I am going to put the brand of shame upon your cheek with my hand! . . . later with my sword!

> *With a supreme effort he rises and strikes* ERNESTO *in the face.* ERNESTO *gives a terrible cry and goes away to the left, covering his face.*

ERN. Ah!

SEV. [*Pointing to* ERNESTO] A just punishment!

TEO. My God!

> [*She hides her face in her hands and sinks into a chair.*

MER. [*To* ERNESTO, *as though excusing* JULIAN] It was delirium.

> *These four cries are in quick succession, then come a few moments of stupefaction.* JULIAN *stands looking at* ERNESTO. MERCEDES *and* SEVERO *support him.*

JUL. Delirium? No: punishment! Wretch, what did you expect?

MER. Let's go, let's go.

SEV. Come, Julian.

JUL. Yes. I'm coming.

> *He walks painfully to his room, supported by* SEVERO *and* MERCEDES, *but stops from time to time to look at* ERNESTO *and* TEODORA.

MER. Quick, Severo!

JUL. Look at them, the wretches . . . It was justice! Isn't that true? Isn't that true? I think so.

SEV. Julian, for my sake!

JUL. You alone! You alone! You loved me.

> [*Embracing him.*

SEV. I? Of course.

JUL. [*Stops in the doorway and looks at them again*] And she is weeping for him, and she doesn't follow me! She doesn't even look at me! She doesn't see . . . that I'm dying! Yes, dying!

SEV. Julian!

JUL. Wait, wait! Shame for shame; good-bye, Ernesto.

> JULIAN, SEVERO, *and* MERCEDES *go out, right.* ER-NESTO *sinks into the chair by the table.* TEODORA *remains standing. A pause.*

ERN. [*Aside*] What good is loyalty?

TEO. What good is innocence?

ERN. My conscience is troubled.

TEO. Have mercy, God, have mercy!

ERN. Poor child!

TEO. Poor Ernesto!

SEV. [*Without, in great anguish*] Brother!

MER. Help!

PEP. Quick!

TEO. Cries of grief!

ERN. Of death!

TEO. Let's go at once!

ERN. Where?

TEO. In there!

ERN. [*Checking her*] We can"

TEO. Why not? [*Anxiously*] I want him to live.

ERN. And I, but I can't— [*Pointing to* JULIAN'S *room*]

TEO. I can. [*Rushing to the door*]

> SEVERO *comes out a moment after* PEPITO, *and blocks* TEODORA'S *way.*

SEV. Where are you going?

TEO. [*Desperately*] I want to see him.

PEP. It's impossible.

SEV. Don't let her in. Is that woman in my house! Quick—put her out, without pity. Immediately.

ERN. What is he saying?

TEO. I am going mad!

SEV. Even if your mother shields her, you must obey my commands, son. If she begs,—if she implores,—if she weeps ... Let her weep. [*With concentrated anger*] Get her far away, or I shall kill her.

TEO. Are those Julian's orders?

PEP. Yes, Julian's!

ERN. Her husband's? Impossible!

TEO. I must see him!

SEV. Well, you shall see him, and then leave this house.

PEP. [*As though wishing to oppose him*] Father—!

SEV. Let me be!

TEO. It can't be true!

PEP. It's terrible.

TEO. A lie!

SEV. Come, Teodora ... come and see!

> *He seizes her by the arms, drags her to the door of* JULIAN'S *room and points inside.*

TEO. He! Julian! My dear Julian! Dead!

> [*She falls, fainting.*

ERN. Father!

> *He hides his face. A pause.* SEVERO *watches them in anger.*

SEV. [*To his son*] Put her out!

PEP. [*Hesitating*] Señor—?

SEV. I command it. Do you hesitate?

ERN. Have some pity.

SEV. Pity. Yes. As she had for *him.*

ERN. Oh, my blood boils!—I'll leave Spain.

SEV. Very well.

ERN. I'll die!

SEV. Life is short.

ERN. For the last time—

SEV. No.

ERN. She's innocent, I tell you. I swear she is.

PEP. [*Trying to intercede*] Father—

SEV. [*Pointing scornfully at* ERNESTO] He lies.

ERN. So you turn me out to sink or swim? Well, I won't struggle. I'll go with the current. What she will think of the world, and of the wrong you have done, I can't guess, for her lips are mute and her mind is asleep, but I am going to tell you what I think.

SEV. It's useless. [*Starting to go to* TEODORA] You can't keep me from—

PEP. [*Restraining him*] Father!

ERN. No! [*A pause*] Let no one come near this woman. She is mine. The world decreed it; I accept its judgment. I carry her away in my arms. Come, Teodora. [*He lifts her up*] You turn her out of here! We obey!

SEV. At last. Scoundrel!

PEP. Rascal!

ERN. Yes, I am all that! Now you are right. Now I admit it! Do you want passion? Well, here is passion, madness! Do you want love? Here is love immeasurable! Do you want more? Then I'll give more! I'm not afraid. You thought of the plot. I only pick up my cue! Now tell all about it, tell all about it. Waken the echoes with this

fine bit of news! But if any one asks you who was the infamous accomplice in this infamous affair, say to him, "You
yourself; though you didn't know it. You and the tongues
of other fools!" Come, Teodora, my mother's spirit is watching over you. Good-bye. She belongs to me now! And in
due time may heaven judge between you and me!

Curtain.

BENITO PÉREZ-GALDÓS

BENITO PÉREZ-GALDÓS, like Echegaray, is one of Spain's foremost writers. He is best known as a novelist, though his activities in the field of the drama during the past twenty-five years have placed him high in the minds of his country-men as a dramatist. He was born in the Canary Islands, at Las Palmas, in 1845. At an early age he went to Madrid, to study law, but finding that the work was unsuited to his temperament, he turned to journalism. He soon began writing fiction, which was to be his life-work, and produced a series of romances—"National Episodes"—which, together with a subsequent series, have made his name celebrated throughout the civilized world. He did not seriously turn to the drama until comparatively late in his career.

CHRONOLOGICAL LIST OF THE PLAYS OF BENITO PÉREZ-GALDÓS

Electra, translated under the same title, is published in The Drama, May, 1911; *El Abuelo* as *The Grandfather* by Elizabeth Wallace, in Poet-Lore, 1911.

References: The Drama, May, 1911; Atlantic Monthly, vol. cii, p. 358; Era, vol. x, p. 535; Critic, vol. xxxix, p. 213, and vol. xlv, p. 447; Barrett H. Clark, The Continental Drama of Today (Henry Holt & Co.); Revue des deux Mondes, 5eme période, 1906; Manuel Bueno, Teatro Español contemporáneo (Madrid, 1909); L. Alas, B. Pérez-Galdós (Madrid, 2nd ed., 1889); J. Martínez Ruíz (Azorin), Lecturas Españolas (1912).

THE DUCHESS OF SAN QUENTIN
(*La de San Quentin*)

A COMEDY IN THREE ACTS

By BENITO PÉREZ-GALDÓS

———————

TRANSLATED BY

PHILIP M. HAYDEN

Presented for the first time in the Teatro de la Comedia, Madrid, January 27, 1894

CHARACTERS

Rosario de Trastamara, *Duchess of San Quentin* (*Age 27*)

Rufina (*Age 15*)

Lorenza, *Buendía's housekeeper*

Rafaela, *Rosario's maid*

Don César de Buendía, *Rufina's father* (*Age 55*)

Victor (*Age 28*)

Don José Manuel de Buendía, *Don César's father* (*Age 88*)

Marquis de Falfán de los Godos (*Age 35*)

Canseco, *Notary* (*Age 50*)

Two Gentlemen

Three Ladies

The action takes place in a seaport of northern Spain, designated by the imaginary name of Ficóbriga.

Time, the present. Summer.

THE DUCHESS OF SAN QUENTIN

ACT I

Room in BUENDÍA's *house. At the rear, on the left, a large door—back-drop beyond—through which enter those who come from outside or from the garden, and a large window through which trees are seen. Two doors at the right, and one large one at the left, leading to the dining-room. Furnishings of black walnut, a desk with drawers, chests, all neat and clean. Religious pictures, and two or three of ships and steamers; on the back wall a large painting of the ship "Rufina." The setting should give the impression of a pleasant village home, indicating comfort, neatness, and simple habits. Table at the right; small table at left. Daylight. "Right" and "left" refer to the spectator.*

DON JOSÉ, *seated, in the arm-chair near the table. At his side,* RUFINA. *At the left, by the small table,* DON CÉSAR *and a* LADY. *At the right, by the table, two* LADIES, *seated, and two* GENTLEMEN, *standing. In the center of the stage,* CANSECO, *standing.* LORENZA *is passing in and out, serving sherry. On each table, bottles and glasses, and a plate of cakes.*

When the curtain rises, CANSECO *is delivering a speech. He has just finished a sentence which has drawn applause and cries of "Bravo" from all those on the stage. With glass in hand, he waits for silence, and continues.*

CANSECO. I conclude, ladies and gentlemen, by proposing the health of our venerable patriarch, the pride and glory of

this fair city of commerce and shipping; that distinguished
landed proprietor, manufacturer and ship-owner, Don José
Manuel de Buendía, who today does us the honor of com-
pleting his eighty-eighth year—I mean—who today com-
pletes . . . and has so kindly invited us . . . in short . . .

[*Confused.*

ALL. Good! Good! Go on!

CANSECO. Let us drink also to the health of his noble son,
the gallant Don César de Buendía. [*Laughter.*

DON CÉSAR. [*Mocking*] Gallant!

CANSECO. I mean, of the noble Don César, heir to the enor-
mous name and brilliant fortune, real and personal, of the
patriarch whose anniversary we celebrate today. And
finally, I drink also to his grandson . . . [*Murmurs of surprise.*
DON JOSÉ *and* DON CÉSAR *start. Aside*] Ah! . . . A slip of
the tongue. [*Puts his hand to his mouth.*

FIRST LADY. [*Aside*] That *was* a slip!

DON CÉSAR. [*Aside*] Bungler!

CANSECO. [*Trying to cover his mistake with coughs and gestures, and amending*] To his . . . I mean . . . to his granddaughter, [*Turning to* RUFINA] that lovely flower, the delight
of the whole city . . .

RUFINA. [*Laughing*] Oh, heavens! . . . the whole city!

CANSECO. Of the family, of . . . of . . . [*Hesitating*] In short,
long life to Don José, and likewise to Don César and little
Rufina, for the greater glory of this fair city, celebrated
throughout the world for its mines and fisheries, and, parenthetically, for its incomparable pastries; of this city, I say,
in which I have the honor to serve as notary, and in that
capacity I can bear witness to the sentiment of the people,
and I take the liberty of indicating it to Señor de Buendía in
the form of a warm embrace.

Embraces him. LORENZA *passes cakes to the guests.*
All eat and drink. Laughter and applause.

DON JOSÉ. Thanks, thanks, my dear Canseco.

THIRD LADY. [*The one beside* DON CÉSAR] What a wonderful old man!

FIRST LADY. His presence is a benediction.

SECOND LADY. And just as strong as ever, Don José?

DON JOSÉ. Like an old oak. No wind can overthrow me, no lightning blast me. Tell that to those who envy my age. My sight is keen, my legs still firm, and my mind as clear as day. In fact, there are only two of us in the world: myself and Gladstone.

FIRST GENTLEMAN. Wonderful!

CANSECO. What a lesson, gentlemen, what an example! At eighty-eight years of age, he directs his immense business himself, and brings to everything admirable order and system. A marvelous executive, far-sighted, careful of every detail, from the greatest to the smallest.

DON JOSÉ. [*Modestly*] Oh, you exaggerate.

RUFINA. Not a bit. My grandfather handles a big lawsuit, with lots of papers, just the same as he decides the feed that we are to give the hens.

SECOND GENTLEMAN. And so this house is full of prosperity.

DON JOSÉ. Call it order, authority. All who live here under the rule of this old duffer, from my dear son to the last one of my servants, obey blindly the direction of my will. No one acts or thinks without me. I do the thinking for everybody.

FIRST GENTLEMAN. Just hear that!

SECOND GENTLEMAN. There's a man for you!

CANSECO. Born of very humble parents. . . . Parenthetically, I know that he's not ashamed of it. . . .

DON JOSÉ. Certainly not.

CANSECO. And from his earliest years, he showed an aptitude for saving.

DON JOSÉ. To be sure.

CANSECO. And soon after his marriage he began to be a perfect ant for industry. [*Laughter.*

DON JOSÉ. Don't laugh. The idea is correct.

DON CÉSAR. But the form is a little . . .

CANSECO. In short, in a long and industrious life he has come to be the chief citizen of Ficóbriga. He is allied with some of the most noble and illustrious families of Castile.

FIRST LADY. Don José, are you related to the family of San Quentin?

DON JOSÉ. Yes, madam, by the marriage of my sister Demetria to a poor cadet of the house of Trastamara.

SECOND LADY. And the present Duchess Rosario?

DON JOSÉ. My niece, a few times removed.

CANSECO. You have it all: nobility on one side, and on the other, or better, on all four sides, boundless wealth. Yours are the best country and city properties in the district; yours the two iron mines . . . two mines, gentlemen, and I might better say three [*To* DON JOSÉ] because the cannery that you own with Rosie the Fishwife is a mine, and a most productive one.

DON JOSÉ. Not bad.

FIRST GENTLEMAN. Add to that the tack factory.

CANSECO. And the two steamers that take the ore to Belgium. And then the two sailing-ships. . . .

RUFINA. [*Quickly*] Three.

CANSECO. That's so. I was not counting the "Rufina," which doesn't go out.

RUFINA. She does go out. There isn't a better ship on the sea.

CANSECO. [*Oratorically*] One more glass, the last one, in honor of this wonderful triumph of industry, gentlemen, of administration, of the sacred principle of thrift. . . . Oh, glorious example of the age of iron, of the age of legal paper, of the age of public confidence, which like . . . which like the . . . [*Confused.*

FIRST GENTLEMAN. The pipe is plugged. [*All laugh.*

CANSECO. Of the golden age of our literature, I mean of our political economy, of electoral light. [*Loud laughter*] No, of electric light . . . and of vapor, that is to say, of steam . . . of the locomotive . . . Ouf! I have done. [*Applause.*

DON CÉSAR. [*Rising*] Who is that coming?

RUFINA. [*Looking through the window at the back*] There's a handsome horse at the big gate.

DON JOSÉ. A horse, you said? It must be the Marquis de Falfán de los Godos.

RUFINA. [*Looking out*] Himself.

> *Enter the* MARQUIS DE FALFÁN DE LOS GODOS, *in an English riding-costume, simple, but elegant.*

MARQUIS. Many happy . . .

DON JOSÉ. My dear Marquis! This is kind of you . . .

DON CÉSAR. [*Aside. Vexed*] What brings him here? The good-for-nothing . . .

MARQUIS. I was just riding down from Las Caldas to Ficóbriga, and as I passed through the village toward the bathing-beach, I noticed a crowd of visitors at the door of this honored house. I inquired; they told me that today is the patriarch's birthday, and I hasten to add my congratulations to those of the whole town

DON JOSÉ. [*Taking his hand*] Thanks.

MARQUIS. And so it is eighty?

DON JOSÉ. Eighty-eight. Don't rob me of the little ones.

MARQUIS. We shan't last so long. [*To* DON CÉSAR] You especially.

DON CÉSAR. Nor you either.

MARQUIS. My health is good.

DON CÉSAR. What can I do to be able to say the same? Ride horseback?

MARQUIS. No. Have less money [*In a low tone*] and fewer vices.

DON CÉSAR. [*Aside to* MARQUIS] Your lordship is pleased to jest.

MARQUIS. It's not a joke. It's a fact.

FIRST GENTLEMAN. Marquis, is there any excitement at Las Caldas?

MARQUIS. So-so.

DON JOSÉ. Aren't you coming down for the bathing this year?

MARQUIS. Oh, yes. My beloved ocean! Within a couple of weeks I shall be established.

SECOND GENTLEMAN. Did you come with Ivanhoe?

MARQUIS. No, sir. With Desdemona.

THIRD LADY. [*Surprised*] Who's she?

DON CÉSAR. It's a mare.

THIRD LADY. Oh.

DON JOSÉ. [*With interest*] Tell me, did you leave Las Caldas about ten?

MARQUIS. I know why you ask.

DON JOSÉ. Has the Duchess come?

MARQUIS. Rosario? Yes, sir. She told me she would come over at once, in the same carriage that brought her from the station.

DON JOSÉ. And is she well?

MARQUIS. As fine and handsome as ever. Misfortune seems to have no effect on her. . She charged me to tell you . . . I've forgotten already.

DON JOSÉ. She will tell me. Won't you take a glass of wine?

MARQUIS. Yes, with pleasure. [RUFINA *serves him.*

DON JOSÉ. And try the cakes, which have made Ficóbriga famous.

MARQUIS. They are delicious. I like them immensely.

RUFINA. Home-made.

MARQUIS. Ah!

CANSECO. [*Taking another cake*] And much richer than those you buy.

> *The ladies and gentlemen prepare to leave.* RUFINA *and* DON CÉSAR *escort them.*

DON JOSÉ. Going already?

FIRST LADY. Many happy returns, once more.

FIRST GENTLEMAN. I repeat . . .

SECOND LADY. My dear Don José . . . Marquis . . .

> [*The* MARQUIS *makes a low bow.*

DON JOSÉ. We will come out to see you off. [*To the* MARQUIS] You will excuse me, I am sure.

THIRD LADY. Don't trouble.

> *Exeunt all but* CANSECO *and the* MARQUIS. *The former takes another cake.*

MARQUIS. Excuse me, sir. Have I the honor of addressing the doctor of the town?

CANSECO. No, sir. Canseco, notary, at your service.

MARQUIS. Ah, yes, I remember. I had the pleasure of seeing you . . . [*Trying to recall*]

CANSECO. Yes, three years ago, when we drew up that note . . . for the loan which Don César made you.

MARQUIS. Yes, yes. You will excuse me if I venture to ask you a question. If my curiosity does not seem impertinent. . . .

CANSECO. Oh, no, Marquis.

MARQUIS. Do you know this family well?

CANSECO. Intimately. I respect the family very . . .

MARQUIS. And so do I. I have great respect for the old gentleman. . . . But as for his son . . .

CANSECO. Well, Don César is . . .

MARQUIS. Is what?

CANSECO. A very handsome man.

MARQUIS. The biggest rascal God ever made . . . an example that He must have put into the world to make us wonder at the infinite variety of His creative power, for otherwise . . . Come, confess, Señor Canseco, that our limited intelligence is incapable of grasping the reason for the existence of certain noxious and venomous creatures.

CANSECO. For example, mosquitoes, and . . .

MARQUIS. And so when I get up in the morning, or in the evening, in the short prayer that I address to the sovereign power that rules us, I always conclude by saying: "O Lord, I still don't see the reason for the existence of Don César de Buendía."

CANSECO. [*Aside. Slyly*] He owes him money.

MARQUIS. And . . . tell me, if I am not too inquisitive: This immense fortune acquired by the two Buendías—without discussing the why and the how of its acquisition—will this immense fortune pass entire to the granddaughter, the lovely Rufina?

CANSECO. Entire? No. Half, as I understand it.

MARQUIS. [*Understanding*] Ah!

CANSECO. And parenthetically, Marquis, isn't it a pity that that girl, in whom I see an excellent match for either of my sons, should have taken the determination to enter the church?

MARQUIS. Parenthetically, it seems to me madness. . . . You said half. Well, here is my question.

CANSECO. What?

MARQUIS. I am not indiscreet?

CANSECO. No, indeed.

MARQUIS [*Fills two glasses*] Is it true that . . . ? [*Hands a glass to* CANSECO] Parenthetically, my dear Canseco . . . Is it true that Don César has a natural son?

CANSECO. [*Glass in hand, like the* MARQUIS, *without drinking*] Yes.

MARQUIS. Is it true that this natural son, the child of an Italian woman named Sarah, has been here?

CANSECO. For the last four months.

MARQUIS. Has his father legitimized him?

CANSECO. Not yet.

MARQUIS. Then he intends to do so?

CANSECO. Yes, sir, for only today he told me to prepare the necessary papers.

MARQUIS. Good, good.   [*They drink.*

CANSECO. He's a handsome lad, but he has the devil in him. Brought up in foreign parts, he has a head full of radical, revolutionary, and socialistic ideas. By the grandfather's decree, they have put him to work to reform him, at hard labor, with no rest or let-up.

MARQUIS. Here?

CANSECO. He lives at the tack factory, and works there from morning to night, except when they put him on repair jobs here, or on the ships, or in the warehouses . . . for parenthetically, he is a great mechanic, he can do anything. Indeed, as for talent and ability, I assure you, Victor is a remarkable man.

MARQUIS. [*Calculating*] He must be . . . twenty-eight years old.

CANSECO. About that. They have put him in overalls, like a slave. And in fact, such wild ideas, such a violent temperament, deserve a harsh treatment for education's sake, Marquis. They hope to tame him, and parenthetically, I believe they will tame him.

MARQUIS. Good, good. A thousand thanks, my friend, for having satisfied my curiosity—idle curiosity, since I have no reason . . .

  Enter DON CÉSAR.

DON CÉSAR. [*Aside*] That fool still here!

MARQUIS. Ah, Don César! It was not only to congratulate Don José that I stopped here, but also to have a few words with you.

DON CÉSAR. I can guess . . .

CANSECO. [*Moves away to the right and fills another glass*] He wants another extension. That makes six.

MARQUIS. No doubt you think that I have come to ask for another extension. . . .

DON CÉSAR. Naturally. [*With feigned regret*] And the worst of it is, Marquis, that with the greatest regret, I shall be obliged to refuse it.

MARQUIS. There is no occasion for regret. I have come to inform the man who has been my nightmare for ten years that . . . [*Puts his hand in his pocket*] Here is a telegram from my attorney, that I received last night. Read it. [*Shows it to him*] Yesterday the two notes were cancelled.

DON CÉSAR. The big one, too? The one for ten thousand and . . . ?

MARQUIS. That, and the other, and the whole business.

CANSECO. [*Aside*] He has paid up! Let us celebrate the miracle with another glass, and a cake to go with it.

[*He eats and drinks.*

DON CÉSAR. This is miraculous! Did you win it in the lottery?

MARQUIS. I have had a legacy. You are glad to get your money, and I am bursting with joy to find myself free of the humiliating chain that a debt of long standing becomes, especially when the creditor is morally—insufferable.

DON CÉSAR. [*With false humility*] You don't mean that for me.

MARQUIS. [*Ironically, but with formal courtesy*] Oh, no . . . Thank heaven, I am free now to talk about the fabulous multiplication of the interest, which in the last four years has tripled the sum that I owed to your generosity. That is the regular thing, I suppose?

DON CÉSAR. [*Affecting heartiness*] My dear fellow, it was the rate agreed upon.

MARQUIS. Oh, yes, agreed upon. Enough. Out of deference to you, and knowing business and human nature as I do, I will not be so vulgar as to call you a usurer, a Jew, a monster of avarice, as others do, . . . unjustly, no doubt.

DON CÉSAR. [*Touched, but concealing his anger under a false courtesy*] Those who say that are the same ones who presume to call you a worthless scamp. So unjust!

MARQUIS. [*Patting his shoulder*] We despise slanderers, don't we? Ah, my dear Don César, what a relief it is to pay! [*Drawing a deep breath*] I am free, free! I have struck off at last the degrading shackles. When a man pays his debts, my friend, he recovers the control of his faculties. The trials, the deep shame, the thousand devices that insolvency involves change our character. A debtor is a different man. . . . I don't know whether you understand me.

DON CÉSAR. And so, on fulfilling your obligations, you become again . . .

MARQUIS. What I always should have been, what I am in reality.

DON CÉSAR. [*As if trying to close the conversation*] I am very glad. And so our account is closed.

MARQUIS. Closed?

DON CÉSAR. So far as I know.

MARQUIS. Think it over. We may have some old score to settle.

DON CÉSAR. Score? With you? There is nothing.

MARQUIS. It is not a matter of money.

DON CÉSAR. Of what, then? Ah! Some supposed offense. . . .

MARQUIS. Just so.

CANSECO. [*Aside*] This looks bad.

DON CÉSAR. Well, if I have offended you—unconsciously, no doubt—why didn't you demand an explanation at the time?

MARQUIS. Because the unhappy debtor, if I must repeat

it, cannot stand up to the arbiter of his life and of all his acts. A feeling of delicacy, second nature to well-bred men, intervenes, and the man is bound hand and foot, like a criminal. A loan of money works a tremendous revolution in the normal order of human feelings.

CANSECO. [*Aside*] The aristocrat is getting metaphysical!

DON CÉSAR. I don't understand a word, Marquis. Ah! About some woman, perhaps.

MARQUIS. I am addressing the greatest lady-killer and heart-breaker in the world.

DON CÉSAR. That was long ago. Bah! After all these years you sound that old note again! [*Laughs*] The good Marquis is digging up antiquities.

MARQUIS. I like to revive old memories.

DON CÉSAR. I don't. I am a practical man. The past is dead. And the present, my noble friend, is sad enough for me. [*Sitting down, sad and weak*] I am very ill.

MARQUIS. Really?

DON CÉSAR. [*Dejectedly*] Seriously ill, as good as done for.

MARQUIS. That would be a pity. [*Putting his hand on his shoulder*] Poor fellow! Avarice and lust will undermine the strongest constitution.

DON CÉSAR. But, after all, what offense is this? I don't remember . . .

MARQUIS. There is no haste. When you recover your health, we will review different periods of cur lives, and in some of them we shall find certain acts which had no excuse —and needed one.

DON CÉSAR. [*Remembering, and trying to palliate the fact*] Ah! Do you attach much importance to an innocent jest?

MARQUIS. [*Seriously, repressing his wrath*] Jests, eh? Well, now that I am free, don't be surprised if I also . . . And beware of mine!

DON CÉSAR. Or perhaps you refer to occurrences, or accidents, due to a lamentable mistake, to a misunderstanding ...

MARQUIS. [*With emphasis*] I, too, can make lamentable mistakes when I want to make trouble. ... Stabs in the back that I have learned from you.

CANSECO. [*Aside. Confused*] Why, what does this mean?

DON JOSÉ. [*Entering, weary*] They've gone. ... Thank heaven!

MARQUIS. I must be off, too. [*Shaking hands with* DON JOSÉ] Good-day, sir.

DON JOSÉ. My good friend ... César, go with him. If you meet Rosario on the way, tell her that I am waiting for her eagerly. Good-bye.

MARQUIS. I will do so. [*Bowing to* CANSECO] Señor Canseco.

RUFINA. [*Entering quickly*] Here is Don Buenaventura de Lantigua.

DON JOSÉ. More callers? [*To* DON CÉSAR] You receive him. Tell him I'm tired out. And then come back. I want to speak with you.

DON CÉSAR [*In disgust*] Confound the callers!

Exeunt the MARQUIS *and* DON CÉSAR *at the back.*
Enter LORENZA, *who gathers up the glasses, etc., aided*
by RUFINA.

CANSECO. I also will bid you good-day. [*Embraces* DON JOSÉ] Of course you're coming to the tax-payers' meeting at the town hall?

DON JOSÉ. [*Sitting down, tired*] I'll be there. Good-bye. [*Exit* CANSECO] How much sherry did they drink?

LORENZA. Eleven bottles.

DON JOSÉ. A half-dozen would have been enough.

LORENZA. And see what's left of the seven pounds of cakes we made today.

DON JOSÉ. In these times, it is pretty evident ... [*Remembering*] Ah! Before I forget it ... [*Takes out several keys and gives one to* LORENZA] Get out three bottles of claret for dinner today.

LORENZA. Very well. And shall I add another meat course?

DON JOSÉ. No.

LORENZA. Since you told me that you would perhaps have a guest . . .

DON JOSÉ. [*Surprised*] Whom?

RUFINA. Yes, grandfather: the Duchess . . .

DON JOSÉ. Oh, yes. But I don't know whether she will dine with us. Anyway, kill a hen.

RUFINA. The tufted one?

DON JOSÉ. No; keep the tufted one; she's the best. Kill the speckled one. Lorenza, how many eggs did they lay yesterday?

LORENZA. [*Preparing to go*] Nine.

DON JOSÉ. That's not much. Doesn't pay for the corn they eat.

LORENZA. The poor things! If they could figure like you, they'd fit their production to the food they eat. But God hasn't made the fowls so . . . mathematical.

[*Exit with the crockery.*

DON JOSÉ. And on the other hand He has made you impertinent. [*To* RUFINA] Your accounts for today.

RUFINA. [*Getting out paper and pencil*] Here they are. Meat, seven-and-a-half. Fish, five . . .   [*Writes.*

DON JOSÉ. Put it all down, and tonight enter it in the book. I want the accounts and expenses of the house kept up to the hour of my death. Order is heaven's first law, and regularity is my joy. Blessed be figures, which give peace and joy to a long life!

RUFINA. I must add bird-seed for the canaries, six. And bran for the hens. I bought them both at wholesale to get a better price.

DON JOSÉ. [*With enthusiasm*] You are an angel. The administering angel. No wonder God wants you for Himself. Are you going to church now?

RUFINA. [*Putting away her papers*] I can't go yet. There are more people coming.

DON JOSÉ. That's so.

RUFINA. The captain and crew of the "Rufina." Didn't you know? They are bringing you a pastry ship, with candy masts, and a cargo of sweetmeats.

DON JOSÉ. [*Pleased*] Ha, ha! That will be fine! How many presents today! The capons from the mayor, beauties!

RUFINA. Yes, and the smoked tongue from Don Cosme.

DON JOSÉ. And the ham from the priest.

LORENZA. [*Hastening in from the back*] Señor, the coastguard men are bringing a dozen cocoanuts; and the tenant of La Juncosa is here with a lot of lard and sausage, and no end of dainties.

RUFINA. [*With joy*] I'll go and see him.

DON JOSÉ. Give them a glass of wine.

      Exeunt RUFINA *and* LORENZA. *Enter* DON CÉSAR.

DON JOSÉ. [*Indicating the nearest seat*] I wanted to see you alone.

DON CÉSAR. [*Sitting down wearily*] Plague take the callers!

DON JOSÉ. We have things to talk over.

DON CÉSAR. Go ahead.

DON JOSÉ. You are fifty-five years old.

DON CÉSAR. [*Sighs*] Yes, sir. What of it?

DON JOSÉ. You're a mere boy.

DON CÉSAR. Compared with you. . . . But if we consider health, my father is the boy, and I the old man. If you only knew how badly I have felt for the last few days!

      [*Puts his elbows on his knees and his head in his hands.*

DON JOSÉ. Come, come, you imagine it. César, be a man. If you're going to get married, there's no time to waste.

DON CÉSAR. [*Without raising his head*] Perhaps you think a second marriage is gaining time!

DON JOSÉ. In this case it is. I tell you again that the interests of the firm require your marriage to Rosita Moreno. A worthy widow, if they do call her the Fishwife.

DON CÉSAR. And you insist on my walking into her net.

DON JOSÉ. Precisely. I have weighty reasons for desiring this marriage. It is your duty to raise a family, to insure the dynasty, so to speak.

DON CÉSAR. I have a daughter.

DON JOSÉ. [*Quickly*] But Rufina wants to be a nun.

DON CÉSAR. I have a son.

DON JOSÉ. A natural son, not yet legitimized.

DON CÉSAR. I am going to legitimize him. I have told Canseco . . .

DON JOSÉ. Yes, but . . . I have forbidden the adoption until we have assured ourselves that Victor deserves to belong to our family. In view of the bad reputation he brought from abroad, where he was educated, and from Madrid, where he had been living for some months, I decided, and you agreed to it, that we should observe him for a while under a reformatory system. Now if it turns out to be impossible . . .

DON CÉSAR. Victor has ability.

DON JOSÉ. If he had some sense along with his ability . . .

DON CÉSAR. I hope that the severity with which we treat him will straighten him out. You see that I am inexorable. I keep forever at him.

DON JOSÉ. That's all very well; but his radical ideas are so fixed in his mind that . . .

DON CÉSAR. The result of bad company and perverted books. I tell you, books are the curse of humanity.

DON JOSÉ. Don't exaggerate. There are good books.

DON CÉSAR. But in order to find out which are good and which are not, you have to read them all, and that's impos-

sible; and so the best thing to do is to forbid reading entirely.
. . . Anyway, I am trying to form Victor to our own image
and likeness, before admitting him legally into the family. . . .
And how that rascal can work. Everything is easy for him.
Such intelligence, quickness, skill!

DON JOSÉ. But those qualities alone mean little. The
workman who hasn't the gift of silence along with his ability
is good for nothing.

DON CÉSAR. For that reason I have forbidden him to
speak to the laborers except to say "Good-morning," "Yes,"
and "No." I am afraid he may sow some seed of insubordina-
tion in the shops. [DON JOSÉ *begins to nod*] To tell the truth,
he bewitches me, in spite of myself, hard and dry as I am.
And although his ideas about property, labor, politics, and re-
ligion seem to me absurd, he puts his nonsense in such a glit-
tering way that he captivates me, fools me. . . . Ah! if I could
only succeed, with this training of hard labor, in bringing
that genius back to the straight path. . . . [*Noticing that* DON
JOSÉ *has fallen asleep, with his head on his chest*] Why, father!
Are you going to sleep?

DON JOSÉ. [*Waking slowly, and thinking he is talking to
some one else*] Rosario de Trastamara, Duchess of San
Quentin. . . . Forgive me if I tell you that . . . [*Waking up*]
Ah! I thought . . . I have that woman's visit so much on
my mind that . . .

DON CÉSAR. Is that so? Is Rosario coming here?

DON JOSÉ. You heard the Marquis of Falfán. She can't
be long now. She said in her letter she was coming to ask
my advice.

DON CÉSAR. To ask advice! Translate that into the language of the day—to ask for money.

DON JOSÉ. Why, is she so badly off?

DON CÉSAR. Poor as a church mouse.

DON JOSÉ. Is it all gone?

DON CÉSAR. Soon after her spendthrift husband died the real estate passed into the hands of three or four creditors. Rosario had to sell the pictures, armor, and tapestries, the plate and china, and even the servants' liveries.

DON JOSÉ. What a pity!

DON CÉSAR. She disposed of her jewels in Paris, so I heard. Now she has nothing left but her wardrobe, a collection of fashionable clothes that are worth nothing.

DON JOSÉ. Merciful heaven! To think that so great a house should end like that! Tell me, did you see Rosario in Madrid lately?

DON CÉSAR. No, sir. Since the bitter quarrel that I had with her father, the proudest, most obstinate imbecile I ever saw in my life, I have nothing to do with any of the family, and the relationship is a dead letter for them and for me.

DON JOSÉ. Poor Rosario! I can't forget that I used to hold her on my knees and kiss her. . . . Surely, if her poverty is as great as you say, we shall have to help her out.

DON CÉSAR. [*Rising*] You can do as you like. I wouldn't give her a penny. She won't ask for it; no, but she will weep. You'll see how she weeps. In that noble family tears are the refined way of begging for alms.   [*Starts to go.*

DON JOSÉ. Wait. Listen to me.

DON CÉSAR. I must go to the town hall.

RUFINA. [*Running in gaily, through the dining-room*] Grandfather, papa, the captain, pilot and sailors from the "Rufina." Come! Come and see the sugar-ship.

DON JOSÉ. I am coming. Show them into the dining-room.

RUFINA. Shall we give them sherry?

DON JOSÉ. No; Jamaica rum, the kind that burns your throat. I am coming. Coming, César?

DON CÉSAR. No. [*Preoccupied*] This visit of the Duchess looks suspicious. To ask advice! What for? Can it be she

wants to marry again? Poor woman! Pride and poverty
are a bad pair. [*Seeing* VICTOR, *who enters upper right*] Ah!
Victor . . . [*Harshly*] What are you doing here?

VICTOR. [*Laborer's dress, blouse. He carries various tools*]
You told me to come at eleven for some work. . . . I don't
know what.

DON CÉSAR. Oh, yes, I remember now. First, did you in-
spect the "Rufina"?

VICTOR. Yes, sir. Yesterday.

DON CÉSAR. Can she make another voyage, just one?

VICTOR. Hardly. Some of her ribs are broken; nearly all
her deck timbers need to be replaced. The stern-post and
the stem are weak and the mainmast is cracked at the
deck.

DON CÉSAR. So that it will be dangerous. . . . But one voyage, just one, in calm season—she can do that, surely.

VICTOR. If she doesn't get back before the October equi-
nox, she might not come back at all.

DON CÉSAR. Well, all right. We'll send her with ore to
England. A return cargo of coal, and then we'll put the ax
to her.

VICTOR. As you please.

DON CÉSAR. Have you repaired the rolling-machine that
got out of order last week?

VICTOR. It is done, and works perfectly.

DON CÉSAR. Good. Now bring your rule, hammer, and
cold-chisel.

VICTOR. [*Showing them*] I have them here.

DON CÉSAR. [*Leading him to door at right*] I have told you
that I plan to put up another story over these rooms. Meas-
ure the three rooms carefully, and make me a plan of them.
Examine the thickness of the walls, locate the supporting
beams so that you can find them again. . . . And do it right
off. Get the plans done today.

VICTOR. Very well.

> *Exit upper right.* DON JOSÉ *and* RUFINA, *returning from the dining-room, see him go out.*

RUFINA. Oh, papa, on a day like this isn't there any rest for poor Victor?

DON JOSÉ. He will rest later, my dear.

DON CÉSAR. What he is doing today is not work for him.

DON JOSÉ. Idleness is his worst enemy.

RUFINA. What tyranny! Everybody is against him. [*Firmly*] Well, let me tell you that I am here to defend him.

DON CÉSAR. You? It seems to me . . .

> LORENZA *hurries in at the back.*

LORENZA. Señor, here she is.

DON CÉSAR. The Duchess?

LORENZA. The carriage has just stopped at the gate. She has a maid with her, and there's a cart behind loaded with trunks.

DON CÉSAR. I'll make my escape. Good-bye.

> [*Exit through dining-room.*

DON JOSÉ. I will receive her here. [*Exit* LORENZA] In case she stays to dinner, they had better make some preparation in the kitchen. Order a tin of preserves—the good coffee, white sugar.

RUFINA. Yes, yes.

DON JOSÉ. And put some flowers on the table.

RUFINA. Don't worry. Shall I stay?

DON JOSÉ. No. Rosario will want to see me alone. You will see her later. You can go to church.

RUFINA. Very well, I will.

> *Exit through dining-room. Enter* ROSARIO *at back, dressed in an elegant traveling costume.*

ROSARIO. Señor de Buendía . . .

DON JOSÉ. Rosario, my child!

ROSARIO. [*Examining him*] A little older, yes,—but so well preserved. What a handsome old fellow you are!

DON JOSÉ. And what a handsome young person you are!

[*They sit.*

ROSARIO. This reminds me of my dear grandfather. Do you remember?

DON JOSÉ. [*Sadly*] Ah!

ROSARIO. And my father.

DON JOSÉ. Poor Mariano! If he had done as I said, you would not be in this sad situation today. But with him as well as your mother, the good advice of this old preacher went in one ear and out the other. While I handled the extensive interests of the house of San Quentin in this district, I worked like a dog to put some order in the budget of the family. Ah! it was like putting up gates in an open field. I had to abandon the task. Our relations were broken off, and finally I neglected to write to you—you probably don't remember—when the Juncosa property went under the hammer.

ROSARIO. Yes, it makes me sad today to pass by the Juncosa. To think that that lovely grove was mine, and the hill, and the meadow. There in that old house, that looks like a feudal castle, with its ivy, its battlemented walls, its lonely mystery and romance, I passed the happiest days of my childhood. And now, the Juncosa, and San Quentin, and the ancestral palace . . .

DON JOSÉ. [*Embarrassed*] Are mine. Yes. I bought them from the bidder. Other good farms of San Quentin have come into my possession in the most legitimate fashion. Gossip, my child, which respects nothing, has tried to insult me by whispering that I made loans to your family on usurious terms.

ROSARIO. Oh, no. If I mentioned the fact of our property being in your hands, it was not to complain. I state a fact, a coincidence . . .

DON JOSÉ. A very natural coincidence, which happens every day. Riches, like an eel, slip away from the weak, delicate, effeminate grasp of the aristocrat, to be seized by the strong, calloused hands of the laborer. Accept this lesson, and learn it by heart, Rosario de Trastamara, daughter of princes and kings, and my niece once removed . . .

ROSARIO. And proud of it.

DON JOSÉ. And I will add, to drive the lesson home to you, that my father was a poor pastry-cook of this town. Not that he was without superior qualities. The tradition is that he invented, [*proudly*] that he invented the rich cakes that have made Ficóbriga famous.

ROSARIO. Oh!

DON JOSÉ. Sixty years ago, when your grandfather, the Duke of San Quentin, was astounding the simple countryside with his prodigal luxury, José Manuel de Buendía married Teresa Corchuelo, the daughter of a worthy confectioner. Well, on the day of my wedding I did not possess four pesetas. I got married, and they put me in charge of the cakes, which began to find a market outside, and I made money, and I was able to increase it, and I became a man, and look at me today.

ROSARIO. An example for everybody!

DON JOSÉ. Ah! if I had only taken you under my care! [*Shaking his fist playfully*] Now tell me how things are going with you. All about it.

ROSARIO. Ah! Don José, I have so many troubles that I don't know where to begin. Soon after I lost my husband, who was, as you know . . .

DON JOSÉ. A calamity. God rest his soul! Go on.

ROSARIO. I found myself involved in disagreeable lawsuits and discussions with my aunts, the Gravelinas, and with my cousin, Pepe de Trastamara. That, and the complete ruin of the family, made life impossible for me in Madrid.

I took refuge in Paris, and there, new trials, humiliations, daily discussions, a life of misery.

DON JOSÉ. Yes, yes, I know. You must have suffered a great deal, poor child, with your proud spirit.

ROSARIO. Proud?

DON JOSÉ. That's what they tell me.

ROSARIO. Oh, my troubles have humbled my pride more than you think. If you only knew! I feel in me a vague dissatisfaction, a regret at having been born into the upper circles. And at the same time I have here [Gesture] some strange ideas. I find in myself a yearning for a practical life in a modest home.

DON JOSÉ. It's a bit late, a bit late now.

ROSARIO. I long for solitude, quiet, simplicity, to live with truth, with my own feelings, thinking my own thoughts.

DON JOSÉ. Oh! You want to withdraw from the world. Does the life of the convent call you?

ROSARIO. It may be my only salvation. I want to consult you about it.

DON JOSÉ. We will think it over, and discuss it. Don't worry. Listen. You have come to ask my advice, and without refusing you that, I will give you something better. I will give you shelter in this humble home.

ROSARIO. [Joyously] Oh, thank you, thank you!

DON JOSÉ. While you are deciding whether to enter a convent or not, and which one it's to be, you will be quiet here.

ROSARIO. Perhaps I shall be in the way.

DON JOSÉ. Not a bit. I assure you I shall not change my simple habits. If there is enough for four, there's enough for five. The old-fashioned table, you know—only soup, meat, and dessert. The house is big, with a fine view, light, and air, and cheerful all through.

ROSARIO. Don't tempt me, Señor de Buendía. How happy, how restful, how enchanting it is! I love these old family homes, this perfect neatness, this black-walnut polished by time and by industrious hands. [*Rises and looks out of the window*] And there's the garden. I saw it as I came in. What fine apple-trees, and so laden with fruit! And the chicken-yard! And that terrace, where they are ironing, under the arbor. And there's the oven . . . And a dove-cote—I can hear the cooing. This is a paradise!

[*Returns to* DON JOSÉ.

DON JOSÉ. Besides the repose that I offer your weary mind, the life here will be like a course in domestic science for you. My granddaughter will teach you many things that will be new to you.

ROSARIO. [*Clapping her hands*] Yes, yes! I have heard so much about that dear child.

DON JOSÉ. She is an angel, a real ministering angel, capable of filling a chair of house-management.

ROSARIO. Where is she? I want to meet her.

DON JOSÉ. You will see her presently.

ROSARIO. And only you two in the family.

DON JOSÉ. My son is here also.

ROSARIO. Don César! [*With a start, rising.*

DON JOSÉ. Yes. What's the matter?

ROSARIO. I thought your son was still in Madrid.

DON JOSÉ. He returned last month.

ROSARIO. [*Much disturbed*] No, no. I can't accept your hospitality. I cannot remain under the same roof with that man.

DON JOSÉ. What foolishness! Why are you afraid of César?

ROSARIO. It is not fear. It is rather dislike.

DON JOSÉ. Ah! I understand. The friction with your father some years ago.

ROSARIO. [*Very nervous*] Friction? It was more than that. I saw my father on his death-bed, at the hour of the sacrament, shed tears of rage at not finding it in his heart to forgive Don César.

DON JOSÉ. Your father was extreme in everything. My dear child, forget, and forgive. Bah! I assure you that my son will not bother you. Come, César is not a bad man at heart. But my paternal affection does not blind me, and I see in him a grave fault.

ROSARIO. What?

DON JOSÉ. His weakness for the fair sex. It has been in him a disease, a blind passion. He fell in love with every woman he saw. From that defect came all his errors, all the grievous sorrow he caused his poor wife and me.

ROSARIO. What a deplorable character!

DON JOSÉ. But we must be just. There was one good thing about his madness, and that was, that he never gave them money, or very little.

ROSARIO. He wanted to be loved for himself alone. And by the way, my cousin Falfán spoke to me of . . . It appears that Don César has a son.

DON JOSÉ. And he is a very grave problem for us.

ROSARIO. Tell me, isn't this young man the son of an Italian woman named Sarah, who died several years ago?

DON JOSÉ. Exactly. A fine present to make to his father!

ROSARIO. And you expect me to be kind to Don César, when you yourself . . .

DON JOSÉ. But your injuries are purely imaginary, and besides, it is all over now. You will offend me if you refuse for so slight a cause the hospitality I offer you.

ROSARIO. I don't want to offend you.

DON JOSÉ. [*Taking her hands*] You'll stay?

ROSARIO. For your sake, and your granddaughter's.

DON JOSÉ. Good. I will try to make life pleasant for you in this humble, but peaceful kingdom of mine.

ROSARIO. [*Moved*] Thanks, thanks. I suspect, my dear

old friend, that I shall find it so pleasant that in the end you will have to turn me out.

DON JOSÉ. [*Jokingly*] Good! We'll turn you out when you are in the way.

    Enter LORENZA *and* RAFAELA *and two men who bring*
        in four trunks.

DON JOSÉ. Put those down here. [*To* ROSARIO] Take out the simple things that you will use here, and leave the rest packed away.

ROSARIO. That's what we'll do.

DON JOSÉ. [*Indicating the door at the right, front*] You will occupy these three rooms, which were my wife's. From the windows you can see the sea, and the bathing-beach.

ROSARIO. Let's go and look.

        [*Exit, right, followed by* DON JOSÉ.

LORENZA. [*To* RAFAELA] Say, are all those full of clothes?

RAFAELA. Surely. All the summer things, and some of the spring and fall dresses. Twenty-seven in all.

LORENZA. Oh, how rich your mistress must be!

ROSARIO. [*Coming back with* DON JOSÉ] Charming! Rafaela, open all these; I want to change at once. Take out the dotted percale.

DON JOSÉ. Well, I'll leave you alone now. I am in the way. I must go to the town hall for a while. [*To* LORENZA] My hat. [LORENZA *gives him his hat*] Try to be ready, and to get into the habit of punctuality. [*To* LORENZA] Don't forget . . . you know . . . [*Speaks to* LORENZA *rapidly, and in a low tone.*

RAFAELA. [*Who has opened one of the trunks and is taking out some dresses, which she puts on the chairs*] Now I remember, the blue, dotted dress isn't in here.

ROSARIO. [*Indicating another trunk*] In here, stupid!

DON JOSÉ. This is your house. Lorenza, and all the servants, at your disposal.

    [*Kisses* ROSARIO's *hand, and exit, rear, with* LORENZA.

ROSARIO. Good. [*Jocosely*] Then we don't need you any longer. [*Takes off her hat and puts it on the table*] Get me out a couple of waists, too.

RAFAELA. [*Struggling unsuccessfully with the lock*] Madam, I can't get it open.

ROSARIO. Then leave it. Take the things out of this one, [*The one that is open*] and put them away in that black-walnut wardrobe. [*Pointing through door, right.*

RAFAELA. [*Impatient*] Plague take the lock!

ROSARIO. There must be some one around here who will help you. [*Loud pounding on the wall, at the right*] What's that?

RAFAELA. It sounds as if they were tearing the house down.

ROSARIO. Come, hurry up. Here, I'll take these out. Go and get me some water. [*Turning over a tray of dresses which* RAFAELA, *on going out, left on a chair*] Here is the checked one. I don't like it.

> *Pulls it out, and, turning to the right to put it on a chair, sees* VICTOR, *who comes in through the door, upper right, with hammer, chisel, and rule.* ROSARIO *is startled and gives a little scream.* VICTOR *stands motionless, in surprise, looking at her.*

ROSARIO. Oh! It's a workman. Excuse me, I was startled. If you would be kind enough to open that trunk . . .

VICTOR. [*Aside*] Yes, . . . it is she.

> [*Continues looking at her, in ecstasy.*

ROSARIO. Don't you hear what I say? Was that you pounding on the wall in my rooms?

VICTOR. [*Aside. Unable to conceal his joy*] She lives here!

ROSARIO. [*Observing him with an expression of doubt and wonder*] Why. . . .

VICTOR. I beg your pardon, Duchess. What did you say?

ROSARIO. [*Aside. Confused*] How strange! I know that man.

VICTOR. [*Noticing the attention with which* ROSARIO *is looking at him*] You will have some difficulty in recognizing me in this dress.

ROSARIO. Recognizing you! Why . . . Have I seen you before?

VICTOR. Yes, madam. [*Surprise and increasing confusion of* ROSARIO. *A pause*] But what was it you asked of me?

Enter RAFAELA *with two pitchers of water.*

RAFAELA. This trunk is the one I can't open.

Exit, right. VICTOR *examines the lock.* ROSARIO *continues to look at him.*

ROSARIO. [*Aside*] Either I am mad, or I really . . . do know that man. But who is it? Where have I seen him? That costume . . .

VICTOR. [*Who, after several trials, has opened the trunk*] There it is.

ROSARIO. Now you may go.

VICTOR. [*After a pause, hesitating whether to venture or not*] Without satisfying your curiosity? For you are cudgeling your brains, Duchess, at this moment, to recall where and when you have seen me.

ROSARIO. That is true. [*Aside*] He is a bit forward.

VICTOR. If madam will allow me, I will refresh her memory in two words.

ROSARIO. Are you Don César's son?

VICTOR. Yes, madam.

ROSARIO. Oh! And how is this? Condemned to hard labor for your hot-headedness?

VICTOR. Yes, madam.

ROSARIO. Yes, I can't restrain my curiosity. Tell me how and when . . .

VICTOR. First, if my boldness has displeased you, I beg you to pardon me.

ROSARIO. [*Haughtily*] You are forgiven. Come, answer me.

VICTOR. Where and when I had the honor of being in your presence?

ROSARIO. Yes.

VICTOR. And the greater honor of speaking with you?

ROSARIO. [*Quickly*] Speaking with me? Oh, no.

VICTOR. Oh, yes. Hear me a moment. I have not always been dressed as a workman. My father, a stern man, has imposed this costume—as a discipline. I was brought up in France.

ROSARIO. [*Interrupting*] And in Biarritz, perhaps . . . you saw me.

VICTOR. No, madam. Five years ago my father sent me to Liège to study mechanical engineering. After the theoretical course, I went to Seraing and worked in the big factory by the name of Cockerill. On Saturdays three or four of us young fellows of different nationalities would get together and go to spend Sunday at Antwerp, Malines, or Bruges. One day we went to Ostend. It was the height of the bathing season. Putting together the little money we had, we played a few turns of roulette in the Casino, and fortune favored us.

ROSARIO. [*Laughing*] You won?

VICTOR. Enough to feel rich for a few hours. There were three of us: an Alsatian, a Swiss, and your humble servant. Determined to play a gorgeous prank, we established ourselves luxuriously in the Hotel del Círculo de Baños, announcing ourselves as Russian princes.

ROSARIO. Oh, you rascals! Yes, yes, now I remember. . . . One afternoon in August. Yes, I remember the young Russian prince.

VICTOR. It was I. I invited you to take a walk in the grounds during an intermission. We went to the dairy, we talked awhile, and in the evening at the ball, I ventured . . . I had the incredible audacity to make a declaration of love to you.

ROSARIO. [*Laughing*] Yes, yes, and it was a most violent and passionate one. Now I remember. . . . But tell me. . . . It seemed to me that you spoke German with your comrades.

VICTOR. I speak German as well as I do Spanish.

ROSARIO. With me you spoke French . . . like a Parisian.

VICTOR. Yes, madam.

ROSARIO. You learn languages easily?

VICTOR. I have that gift, lacking others. I speak English also. Unfortunately, at that time not one of us knew a word of Russian. For that reason, and because our money was soon gone, we had to abandon our deception and escape by the first train Monday morning.

ROSARIO. And we never met again.

VICTOR. Oh, yes, we did.

ROSARIO. [*With great curiosity*] But when?

VICTOR. There is a great deal more to tell.

ROSARIO. Really?

RAFAELA. [*Enters, right. Indicates another trunk*] This one too. I don't know what's the matter with it. [*To* VICTOR, *imperiously*] Here! Open this one, too. [*Aside*] What a handsome fellow! [*Picks up some dresses to take away*] You might help me carry these trays.

ROSARIO. Let him alone. [*Aside, while* VICTOR *opens the other trunk*] This is like a novel. How extraordinary! The Russian prince of Ostend opening my trunks in Ficóbriga!

[RAFAELA *goes out again with clothes.*

VICTOR. [*With one knee on the ground, opening the lock*] Shall I go on?

ROSARIO. Yes, yes. I like to get away from the beaten track. But take care! Don't tell me anything but the truth.

VICTOR. If you knew me, madam, you would know that I adore truth, and that I sacrifice everything to it. [*Opens the trunk*] There it is.

ROSARIO. You adore truth, and pretended to be a Russian, and a prince!

VICTOR. A student's prank. And what a day it was! You were then newly married, and most beautiful.

ROSARIO. That was long ago.

VICTOR. Now you are much handsomer.

ROSARIO. [*Aside*] He goes too far. [*To* VICTOR] That will do. You probably have something to do elsewhere.

VICTOR. [*Disconsolate*] You dismiss me, . . . without hearing what . . . Do you think that you lower yourself in listening to me?

ROSARIO. Oh, no. Speak, say what you like. What a rascal you must have been, for them to treat you like this!

VICTOR. I recognize that my father is right. I have been at fault.

ROSARIO. Rebellious to study, perhaps.

VICTOR. Yes. I did not study,—or rather, I did study, and a great deal, but alone. I read what I liked, and learned what interested me. I always disliked instruction in regular schools, I refused to work for marks and degrees. What I know, I have no diploma to show for, and I have no stamp of official education. In Belgium I learned more by practice than theory. I am something of an engineer, something of an architect—without the title, it is true. But I can make a locomotive, and if necessary I can build a cathedral, and if I set about it, I can make needles, glass, pottery.

ROSARIO. So many talents, and to come to this sad state of simple laborer!

VICTOR. You shall see. In Belgium I was carried away by the idea of socialism. I was captivated by a German, an agitator, who preached the transformation of society, and I took part in a big strike. I made speeches, aroused the masses. A wild career, which ended in prison.

ROSARIO. You deserved it.

VICTOR. They kept me six months in the prison at Antwerp. My father wrote to me reproaching me, and refusing any help.

ROSARIO. And quite right. The idea of defending such absurdities! But you did not believe in all that: you engaged in it as a pastime, for fun.

VICTOR. No, madam. I believed in it . . . and I still believe in it. When I got out, I went to England. But I could not give myself up to the study of my beloved theories, because in London I met a Spaniard who insisted on reconciling me with my father, and succeeded. My father came for me, and brought me to Spain, and set me down in Madrid.

ROSARIO. And were you a workingman there?

VICTOR. No, I was a gentleman. My father took every precaution to keep me away from socialistic propaganda. I went with a crowd of young men of the best society, some of them very rich. In the evening I would put on evening dress, and thanks to the easy democracy that reigns there, I was able to go everywhere.

ROSARIO. Ah! [*Comprehending*] And once perhaps you saw me. Well, I don't recall . . .

VICTOR. I do. Besides, I saw you continually at theaters, on the avenue, at church . . .

ROSARIO. You went to church, too?

VICTOR. I went everywhere where I might see the person who fascinated me, whom I was crazy about, who . . .

Enter RAFAELA.

RAFAELA. [*Aside*] That young workman still here! What can he be telling my mistress?

ROSARIO. And did you also preach in Madrid the destruction of society, and all that nonsense?

VICTOR. I made oral and theoretical propaganda, but without success.

RAFAELA. [*Aside. Carrying off more clothes*] He is handsome. I'll hook him, as sure as two and two are four. [*Exit.*

ROSARIO. No! you didn't dare!

VICTOR. I tell you in all sincerity, and in all modesty, that I dare do anything. There is nothing in the world, nothing, that I am afraid of.

ROSARIO. [*With admiration*] Truly?

VICTOR. And difficulties and dangers increase my courage.

ROSARIO. Bravo! It's for your courage that they keep you in this servitude. Heaven knows what atrocities you committed in Madrid.

VICTOR. No: my life in Madrid was quite innocent. I did nothing but follow the woman who was my delight and my torment, since she fascinated me without looking at me.

ROSARIO. She didn't look at you? Heartless creature!

VICTOR. She did not know—she does not know—my wild passion.

ROSARIO. Such unrequited love is madness, self-deception.

VICTOR. [*With heat*] It is a love whose reality is beyond question, since in it I've lived and shall live; a love of spotless purity, since I never hoped for it to be returned, nor do I now. A love that flames as high in the absence as in the presence of the lovely being who . . .

ROSARIO. [*Laughing*] Enough, enough. What a deluge of poetry! I must get under cover. [*She moves away*] Frankly, I don't believe in love at first sight; even in plays and novels it seems to me of questionable taste. To fall suddenly in love with a lady of rank, follow her carriage, pursue her shadow in the street, assailing her with unnoticed glances in parks and theaters, adore her in pure, ethereal ecstasy. Tell that to some one with less experience of the world!

VICTOR. I tell it to you, because it is the truth, and because you asked for it. I live with that delusion and I shall die with it. It is the best of life to me. I cannot endure life without the continual presence of my idol here, [*Gesture*] and here I carry her, and here I adore her, peerless being, Nature's masterpiece, image of divinity. . . .

ROSARIO. Ha, ha, ha! But, man, tell me who this goddess is. I want to know who she is. Perhaps I know her?

VICTOR. Pardon my presumption, which is the reward of my insignificance. One who is nothing, has nothing, and perhaps never will be anything, can permit himself the luxury of sincerity, of frankness.

ROSARIO. Oh, but I like sincerity. It is a great relief for one who has lived so long in a world of pretense and lies.

VICTOR. [*Warmly*] Bless you for those words!

ROSARIO. [*Impatient*] The name! What is her name?

VICTOR. Why do you wish to know?

ROSARIO. Come! Who is she?

VICTOR. No, no.

ROSARIO. Well, if you won't tell, I will, and make you blush. The lady whom you idolize so foolishly— [*Pause*] is I.

VICTOR. Oh!

ROSARIO. I guessed it at once. Do you think I have never read novels?

VICTOR. Madam, notice that I make no plea. I have no hope, and never shall have.

ROSARIO. Naturally.

VICTOR. If what you have discovered seems to you unpardonable, crush me with your indifference.

ROSARIO. [*Still jestingly*] Oh, as for crushing you. . . . Nobody minds being an idol—more or less false.

VICTOR. And I have told you that it is not inconsistent with the greatest respect. I swear to you not to speak of it again.

ROSARIO. Yes, these things don't bear repeating. So much poetry is cloying. You think yourself a socialist, and you are only a poet; a poet who wants to destroy the world and set me up as a statue upon the ruins. What nonsense!

VICTOR. Don't notice me. Don't even look at me.

ROSARIO. What, forbid me to see you! If you come near me . . . I shall not close my eyes when you pass.

VICTOR. Then if my existence means anything to you, make me your slave.

ROSARIO. All right. Let's begin now. [*Enter* RAFAELA, *right*] Be kind enough to assist my maid.

[*Pointing to the trays of clothing which are on the chairs.*

RAFAELA. [*Giving them to him*] Here. It is late. The gentlemen have returned already.

VICTOR. My father and grandfather.

[*Exit, right, carrying the trays.*

ROSARIO. [*Aside. Admiringly*] Such assurance! I never saw his equal.

Enter, at back, DON JOSÉ *and* RUFINA. *Behind them, with some constraint,* DON CÉSAR.

DON JOSÉ. [*Presenting* RUFINA] My granddaughter.

ROSARIO. What a pretty girl! [*They embrace affectionately.*

DON CÉSAR. [*Remaining at the back, right, looking at* ROSARIO *with admiration. Advances and makes a low bow, which* ROSARIO *acknowledges coldly. Aside*] Beautiful. A splendid woman. [RAFAELA *and* VICTOR *re-enter, right, after more clothes. To* VICTOR, *with displeasure*] What are you doing here? Go back to the factory at once. Leave the work I gave you. . . . And you may take the afternoon off. But keep away from here.

VICTOR [*Going out by the door at right, upstage*] Very well, sir. I will go away . . . a long way.

DON JOSÉ. [*To* ROSARIO] Well, shall we eat? It is time.

ROSARIO. [*In haste*] Just five minutes. I will be ready directly. [*Runs to her room.*

DON JOSÉ. Five minutes, girl. [*Calling through door, left*] Lorenza, the soup!

Curtain.

ACT II

Terrace at BUENDÍA'S *house. At back, a line of apple and other fruit trees, and trellis, with opening in center, through which enter those who come from the garden. Background, a rustic landscape. Doors at each side, front. That on the left, covered with vines, leads to the kitchen and service-rooms; beside it an opening in the wall leads to the place where the oven is supposed to be located. The door on the right leads to the living apartments. Left, front, a large table which serves for ironing and for kneading. Two chairs and a wooden bench.* ROSARIO, RUFINA, LORENZA *are discovered, all three wearing large aprons.* ROSARIO *is ironing a blouse,* LORENZA *directing and instructing her.* RUFINA *is piling on a bench the linen already ironed.*

LORENZA. Bear down harder, ma'am.

ROSARIO. [*Doing so*] Still harder?

LORENZA. Not so much.   Ah! the gentlemen's shirt-bosoms are the real test.

ROSARIO. How awkward I am!

LORENZA. Oh! You are doing well. Many a girl . . .

RUFINA. Don't tire yourself out.   Lorenza will finish.

ROSARIO. [*Tired, laying down the iron*] Yes, I can't do any more.   I've earned my salt today.

LORENZA. [*Ironing vigorously*] I'll have it done in a jiffy.

RUFINA. We'll be putting it away.

ROSARIO. [*Piling pillow-cases and sheets on a wicker tray*] Let me do it.

RUFINA. No, let me.   You are getting tired.

130

ROSARIO. Oh, no, I'm not. What fun to fill the wardrobes with this clean, white, fragrant linen! And to put it all in order, the different sizes and kinds together. [*Picking up the tray*] Up with it! [RUFINA *helps her to put it on her head*] There we are!

RUFINA. [*Pointing, right*] In the big wardrobe there.

[*Exit* ROSARIO, *right.*

LORENZA. She doesn't look it, but she has strength . . . and so willing!

RUFINA. Indeed she is.

ROSARIO. [*Re-entering, briskly, right*] Now the sheets.

RUFINA. Now it's my turn.

[*Takes up a pile of linen. Exit, right.*

ROSARIO. What shall I do? Lorenza, give me the iron again. Since I came here I have lost the habit of sitting with my hands folded, and now idleness is torture for me.

LORENZA. I am just finishing.

RUFINA. [*Entering, right. Firmly*] There now, Duchess of San Quentin, the ironing is done. What do we make today?

LORENZA. Butter.

ROSARIO. No, today it's cakes. Don José said so.

RUFINA. And I have already told Victor to start the oven.

LORENZA *gathers up the last of the linen and carries it in. Then she clears away the ironing implements.*

ROSARIO. Today I am going to tend the oven myself, and you shall see. [*Gestures of putting cake in the oven.*

RUFINA. No, you don't know how. You have had no practice, and you'll burn them. Leave the oven to me.

ROSARIO. All right, all right.

With childish uneasiness, making the motions of kneading at the table.

LORENZA. Are you going to mix them here?

ROSARIO. Right here, where it is cool.

RUFINA. And Victor will bring them to me.

ROSARIO.   But will they let him come here?

RUFINA.   He's here already. [*Pointing to the garden*] Papa has told him to fix the asparagus and replant the old strawberry bed.

ROSARIO.   What?   Does he understand gardening too?

RUFINA.   That boy can do anything. [*Goes to the back and calls, beckoning*] Oh, Victor!

ROSARIO.   Mr. Socialist, Social Leveler, come here!

Enter VICTOR *at the back.*

VICTOR.   What is the will of the fair Proletarians?

RUFINA.   Get ready.   We need your reformatory and revolutionary co-operation.

ROSARIO.   We are the masses.   We ask for bread and work; and as they don't give us bread, we make it, but not for the rich to eat.

VICTOR.   [*Laughing*] Are you going to make bread?

ROSARIO.   Cakes, man, for the sovereign people.

[*Pointing to herself.*

RUFINA.   And you are to bring out here the mixing-board, the pans, and all the things.

ROSARIO.   And then you will condescend to carry the cakes to the oven.

VICTOR.   It is already hot, glowing like a loving heart. You will have to wait until it cools a little.

ROSARIO.   The cold light of reason and sanity.

RUFINA.   Go back to the garden.   Papa mustn't say that we keep you from your work.

VICTOR.   [*Aside, gazing at* ROSARIO] Divine creature!   Poor me. [*Aloud*] Will you call me presently?   Promise to call me.

ROSARIO.   Yes, yes.

VICTOR.   Au revoir, then.   [*Exit, back.*

RUFINA.   How handsome and good-natured he is!

ROSARIO.   Indeed he is.   A big heart, and gentle as a child.

LORENZA. [*Who has been in and out several times, carrying off the ironing things*] Don't forget the hens. It's time to feed them.

ROSARIO. Yes, let's go and feed them.

As they start for the back, they are detained by DON JOSÉ *and the* MARQUIS, *who enter. Exit* LORENZA, *left.*

DON JOSÉ. Here she is.

MARQUIS. [*Laughing at* ROSARIO'S *appearance*] Ha! ha! ha! Rosario, is that you? What a metamorphosis!

ROSARIO. [*Indicating* DON JOSÉ] Here is the worker of the miracle.

DON JOSÉ. What do you think? She gets up at five in the morning.

MARQUIS. Just the time she used to go to bed in Madrid.

ROSARIO. And how are you?

MARQUIS. Yesterday I moved down to the shore, and my first visit in all Ficóbriga is to the daughter of kings, now a laundress.

DON JOSÉ. She goes from one task to another all day. She is busy, healthy, and happy.

MARQUIS. She must be. Will you take me for your assistant?

RUFINA. Don't forget that this is real work.

DON JOSÉ. Don't forget that you have a lot of fun too, laughing and playing pranks.

ROSARIO. Yesterday we were up on the mountain. What a splendid view, what clear sky, and what fragrance! I never felt so fully the charm of nature and solitude.

MARQUIS. They told me at the baths that you were nearly killed one day, going up the mountain.

ROSARIO. I?

RUFINA. It was nothing.

DON JOSÉ. It was Victor's stupidity. I have scolded him for it. He persisted in leading the donkey through a pass.

RUFINA. It wasn't Victor's fault. You blame poor Victor for everything.

ROSARIO. It was my fault. I myself told him to take me over those rocks. We nearly fell off, rider, and donkey, and guide. But thanks to the courage of the brave fellow, nothing happened.

DON JOSÉ. And it won't happen again. He will be careful now.

ROSARIO. Well, Currito Falfán, cousin mine, illustrious scion of the younger branch of the Otumbas, will you help us make some cakes?

MARQUIS. [*Laughing*] Really? Can you . . . ?

DON JOSÉ. She kneads them like a professional.

MARQUIS. I will help . . . to eat them. And I also accept Don José's invitation. He claims there is no cider like his.

DON JOSÉ. [*With emphasis*] Home-made. You shall see what cider is.

ROSARIO. And now, to the chicken-yard.

MARQUIS. Wait, Rosario. I want to speak to you. Am I less important than the fowls of the air?

RUFINA. You stay here. I'll go. [*Exit, back.*

DON CÉSAR *enters briskly at back.*

DON CÉSAR. Hasn't Canseco come? Hello, Marquis. [*Aside, suspicious and displeased*] That spendthrift here again!

DON JOSÉ. The notary will be here soon.

MARQUIS. Tell me, Don César, is it true that you intend to buy the Marquis of Fonfría's coach horses, and the mare, which are to be auctioned off today?

DON CÉSAR. [*Proudly*] Yes, sir. What of it?

DON JOSÉ. Have you gone crazy? What do you want of horses like them?

DON CÉSAR. I, I . . . The Marquis, who is an expert in horseflesh, will advise me.

MARQUIS. With pleasure.

DON JOSÉ. [*Aghast*] Have you fallen into delusions of grandeur? César, come to your senses.

MARQUIS. The two coach horses, Eclair and Nestor, are of my brother's stock, mixed breed. The mare Sarah was mine. She came from the Duke of Northumberland's stables . . . a thoroughbred, fine as coral, and swift as the wind.

> ROSARIO *cleans the table, and finishes putting away some things that are left.*

DON CÉSAR. Will you give me, if it is not too much trouble, the exact pedigree of all three animals?

MARQUIS. I have it all in my book, descent, age. . . . You need not hesitate to purchase; it is a bargain.

DON JOSÉ. [*Uneasy*] This isn't a joke? Such recklessness!

ROSARIO. [*Approaching the group*] Don César intends to have his carriage like the rest of the nobility, so that Rosita the Fishwife may ride in state.

DON CÉSAR. You'll see who rides in it.

MARQUIS. He's going to get married? You don't mean it!

DON JOSÉ. [*In ill humor*] If the choice is not good, it is better not to think about it.

ROSARIO. Get married? Why, he says he's going to die soon.

MARQUIS. That's the way to persuade them.

DON CÉSAR. I'm good for a while longer. [*To* ROSARIO, *abruptly, in an affectionate tone*] Rosario, don't work so hard, you'll spoil your hands.

ROSARIO. What's that to you?

DON CÉSAR. To me . . . ? It may be a good deal to me. And you shouldn't be out in the sun so much if you care about the delicacy of your skin.

DON JOSÉ. She is prettier so.

MARQUIS. The pastoral type, the simple country lass!

DON JOSÉ. [*Scolding*] A nice time to get these high-toned notions!

ROSARIO. Just when I am turning to the populace.

DON CÉSAR. My dear Rosario, don't quarrel with me. You know how much I think of you. . . .

DON JOSÉ. [*Disturbed*] There, there, enough of your jokes.

DON CÉSAR. It's not a joke. [*To* ROSARIO] Did you take what I said as a joke?

MARQUIS. What's all this? [*Joking*] Don José, this is grave.

DON JOSÉ. I declare, my son has lost his wits.

DON CÉSAR. And moreover . . .

DON JOSÉ. [*Moving away angrily*] I will not listen to any more foolishness. I ought to treat you like a child. Marquis, are we going to try that cider or not?

MARQUIS. Whenever you like.

DON JOSÉ. I am going to the store-house for a moment. I'll meet you in the dining-room. [*In the doorway, aside, looking at* DON CÉSAR] Oh! what a son! We shall see, we shall see who comes out ahead. [*Exit, back.*

LORENZA. [*At right*] Señor de Canseco.

DON CÉSAR. Show him into my room. [*To* ROSARIO] I have some serious business to attend to. We will talk later. [*To the* MARQUIS] Excuse me. You won't forget to send me . . .

MARQUIS. The pedigrees? Yes, yes, don't worry.

DON CÉSAR. I'll see you later. [*Exit, right.*

ROSARIO. [*Seeing* DON CÉSAR *depart*] What a boor!

MARQUIS. I would swear that he has fallen in love with you.

ROSARIO. Unfortunately for me, he has.

MARQUIS. And has he declared himself?

ROSARIO. He asks me every day, in a different form. Yesterday a long, stupid, ungrammatical letter proposing marriage.

MARQUIS. And you . . . !

ROSARIO. Hush, for heaven's sake! I swear that I would

sooner marry a mason, a day-laborer, a jail-bird, than that man.

MARQUIS. Well said. Anything rather than this family of parvenu pastry-cooks. The one that invented the cakes must have been an excellent man. But the stock has deteriorated, and Don César is a perfect scoundrel. You hate him, but not so much as I do.

ROSARIO. No, I hate him more than you do. I claim the right. The sting of that reptile has been more fatal to my family than to yours.

MARQUIS. Ah! you don't know. I won't mention to you the humiliation in which I have lived for ten years, suffering his treachery, without the power to defend myself. Besides, the man, with a refinement of hypocrisy, feigned a servile attachment to me, and after playing some trick on me, would outdo himself in compliments and protestations of friendship. And always slily criticising my acts and spying upon me . . . ! He wouldn't let me alone, followed my every move. . . . He was my shadow, my nightmare. Have I never told you what he did? You shall see. He came into possession of seven letters of mine to Stephanie . . .

ROSARIO. And sent them to your wife. Yes, I knew that.

MARQUIS. He had a certain sum to send to Dolores in bank-notes. He put the letters in the same envelope.

ROSARIO. Infamous! And you didn't kill him!

MARQUIS. I went after him like a wild beast. Ah! you should have seen and heard him, trembling, cringing, trying to cover his cowardice by hypocrisy. He swore that he had made a mistake . . . that he thought he was sending the letters to me. In fact, he was sending me at the same time in another envelope a memorandum of interest due.

ROSARIO. You ought to have strangled him.

MARQUIS. Yes, I ought to have. But that night I had to

have two thousand dollars. A debt of honor . . . a case of shooting myself if I did not get them.

ROSARIO. I understand.

MARQUIS. And I had to humiliate myself. My dear Rosario, nothing degrades a man so much as certain kinds of debt. Don't get into debt. If in order to keep free from such entanglements you have to go down in the social scale, do it without hesitation. Marry a gatekeeper or the watchman on your street.

ROSARIO. You are right. I, too, have been a slave and martyr. Thank heaven, I am free, though poor.

MARQUIS. And now, cousin, I have resolved not to die without administering to my tormentor a blow like those he gave to me; I take pleasure in informing you that I have it all prepared and waiting for him.

ROSARIO. A blow?

MARQUIS. A mistake—of the choicest—like his own.

ROSARIO. Tell me. What is it?

MARQUIS. A big thing.

ROSARIO. [*With great interest*] Tell it to me. Is it a secret?

MARQUIS. Not for you.

ROSARIO. Then what are you going to do?

MARQUIS. [*Fearful of being overheard*] Destroy the illusion of his life. You know that there is around here a son . . .

ROSARIO. Yes, I know him. He is here.

MARQUIS. And moreover, an agitator, partisan of socialism, of atheism, of the devil himself. But with all that he is doubtless a better man than César.

ROSARIO. Indeed he is. He is not disagreeable. He doesn't seem like the son of such a father.

MARQUIS. Well, he isn't . . . he isn't. Is it clear now?

ROSARIO. [*Stupefied*] What are you saying?   [*Pause.*

MARQUIS. Just as I am telling you. I can prove it. That

is to say, what I can prove is that the parentage of the young
social reformer is an enigma, an unknown quantity.

ROSARIO. [*With great curiosity*] Explain yourself. Is it
possible that . . .

MARQUIS. Did you ever know a certain Sarah Balbi?

ROSARIO. An Italian, governess in the Gravelinas family?
I have heard my mother speak of that woman. Ah! now I
begin to see. And César loved her, and thought her faithful . . .

MARQUIS. Human nature is a strange thing.

ROSARIO. A man who knows counterfeit money so well
that in a hundred thousand good coins he can pick the bad
one, by merely turning them over on the table—and not
know what Sarah was!

MARQUIS. And take her for pure gold! Such blindness is a
punishment from heaven.

ROSARIO. But you . . . how do you know?

MARQUIS. You remember that poor Barinaga died a few
months ago, at my house.

ROSARIO. A colonel in the army, very distinguished, with
a white beard.

MARQUIS. He got mixed up in politics, and ended his days
in poverty. I took him in to save him from the poorhouse.

ROSARIO. Yes, yes, and the poor fellow also had an affair
with the Italian woman?

MARQUIS. Yes.

ROSARIO. At the same time as Don César.

MARQUIS. Two days before he died, the poor colonel told
me his story. Now you see. He loved her madly; he kept
seven letters from her—seven! Notice the number—seven
letters, which he gave to me.

ROSARIO. And you have them now?

MARQUIS. And they will be the bomb of dynamite which
I intend to place in the hands of that gentleman who makes

mistakes. Ah! I forgot to say that Barinaga suffered the torments of jealousy.

ROSARIO. So that Sarah deceived him also . . .

MARQUIS. He believed so, or feared so. That woman was a mystery, a mystery full of charm: I know that. Let us draw a veil . . .

ROSARIO. Yes, draw the veil.

MARQUIS. In the seven letters, which I call the seven manifestoes, it becomes evident that she was exploiting Don César's blind confidence . . .

ROSARIO. With the argument of her maternity.

MARQUIS. Which she used as a lever to force the money box that was so hard to open.

ROSARIO. A horrible story! And that poor youth! But how is he to blame? Rob him of his name, deprive him of his fortune! No, no, cousin, don't do that. Let him . . .

MARQUIS. It is a serious matter. Don't think that I . . . I too hesitate sometimes . . .

ROSARIO. [*Suddenly changing her mind*] Oh! what possibilities! Yes, you must . . .

MARQUIS. You think then . . .

ROSARIO. [*Retracting, horrified at herself*] No, no.

MARQUIS. Then it seems to you that . . .

ROSARIO. [*After hesitating*] Yes, yes. I feel a bitter, revengeful impulse. Don César deserves a hard blow, and I'll not be the one to spare him. My hatred for him I have inherited from my father.

MARQUIS. I know.

ROSARIO. And from my mother also. That man presumed to make love to her, and angry and spiteful at seeing himself repulsed with horror, he slandered her infamously.

MARQUIS. Don't I know it? He said that she . . .

ROSARIO. [*Indignant, closing his mouth*] Hush!

MARQUIS. Then it's settled. I am to—make a mistake?

ROSARIO. [*Firmly*] Yes.

MARQUIS. He has asked me for the history of the mare, whose name is also Sarah. A coincidence from on high! And so I—make a clerical error, and instead of putting in the envelope . . .

ROSARIO. I understand. [*Agitated and disturbed*] Oh! I don't know what to think. I don't understand my own feelings! If you knew, cousin, in how many ways this matter interests and concerns me!

MARQUIS. Yes, I think that as a matter of duty we ought . . .

ROSARIO. [*Making up her mind*] Will you do as I tell you?

MARQUIS. What is it?

ROSARIO. Give me the seven letters.

MARQUIS. And you will . . . ?

ROSARIO. Leave it to me.

MARQUIS. I will send you the packet by some one I can trust.

ROSARIO. I will take upon my conscience the care and the responsibility for the mistake. [*Hearing voices, right*] Hush. I think the old gentleman is calling you.

MARQUIS. [*Hastily*] Oh, yes, the cider. Then it's agreed that I will send it to you.

ROSARIO. Yes.

DON JOSÉ *enters from the back, behind him*, LORENZA.

DON JOSÉ. Marquis, I am waiting for you.

MARQUIS. I was just coming.

DON JOSÉ. [*Searching the terrace with a look*] Hasn't that crazy son of mine come back? [*To* LORENZA] Where's César?

LORENZA. In his room. Señor Canseco has gone. He said he would return.

DON JOSÉ. Hum! [*Aside*] The adoption.

MARQUIS. But you don't know the worst of it.

ROSARIO. That I am the cause of his madness, my dear Don José.

DON JOSÉ. Don't you suppose I could see that? For days the volcano has been smoking under my very nose.

ROSARIO. I, alas, have not given him the slightest reason.

DON JOSÉ. I should hope not. My dear child, I beg you to do everything in your power to put the foolish idea out of his head. It is not a suitable thing for him, nor . . .

ROSARIO. Certainly not for me.

DON JOSÉ. I want to marry him to a plain, unpretentious woman.

ROSARIO. A very natural match. And thus you make sure of the fish business.

DON JOSÉ. That is nothing to joke about. [*Suspiciously, aside*] I wonder if she encourages him? We must be on our guard.

RUFINA *enters from the back with a basket of eggs.*

RUFINA. Eight today.

DON JOSÉ. [*Examining the eggs with pleasure, and showing them to the* MARQUIS] See what beauties they are.

MARQUIS. Yes, indeed.

DON JOSÉ. You can tell your friends that my hens are the best layers in the world.

MARQUIS. I shall proclaim it far and wide, and woe to him who doubts it!

LORENZA. [*To* RUFINA] Give me the key to get the sugar.

DON JOSÉ. [*Surprised*] Sugar?

ROSARIO. Surely. For the cakes.

DON JOSÉ. Oh!

RUFINA. We are going to make five pounds, grandpa.

DON JOSÉ. Then one pound of sugar. Get the sugar and cinnamon. [*Feeling in his pockets*] Have you the keys? [RUFINA *gives the keys to* LORENZA] A pound and a half of butter, you know. First you separate the whites from the yolks; beat the yolks with the sugar, and when it is well beaten, you . . .

LORENZA. [*Interrupting*] I know that, sir.

DON JOSÉ. I say you are to mix it for them to save them trouble. You may go. [*Exit* LORENZA] Now then, Marquis, shall we try the cider?

MARQUIS. *Allons!* And then I'm going down to the shore. So good-bye. [*To* ROSARIO] You have your work laid out for you. [*Meaningly*] Knead it well.

DON JOSÉ. Come along.

[*The* MARQUIS *gives him his arm. Exeunt at back.*

VICTOR. [*Entering, left, with cake-board, rolling-pin, and several pans*] Where shall I put these?

ROSARIO. Here. Has Lorenza beaten the eggs?

VICTOR. She is at it now. The yolks and the sugar, representing the union of the aristocracy of blood with that of wealth.

ROSARIO. [*Joking*] Hush, envious proletarian!

VICTOR. What is the matter with the simile?

ROSARIO. It is not bad. Then I take the aristocracy, and [*Gesture of kneading*] mix it, amalgamate it with the populace, common flour, which holds everything together. . . How's that? And make a rich pastry.

RUFINA. But this populace, alias flour, where is it?

ROSARIO. And the butter—the middle class, so to speak?

VICTOR. I'll go and get the mass.

ROSARIO. But don't bring us the masses.

RUFINA. And don't preach the social revolution to us.

ROSARIO. [*Pushing him*] Quick, quick.

VICTOR. Full speed.   [*Exit, left.*

RUFINA. [*Arranging the cake-board and wiping it*] How good he is!

ROSARIO. Are you fond of him?

RUFINA. Indeed I am. It is so good to have a brother. Isn't it?

ROSARIO. [*Looks at her, fixedly. Sighs sadly. Pause*] Yes.
> *Enter* LORENZA *with a basin and towel, which she puts on the end of the table. Then* VICTOR *with the dough on a board.*

LORENZA. It is all mixed now.

ROSARIO. Plenty of butter in it?

LORENZA. Yes, ma'am.
> *She puts the dough on the cake-board and begins to pound it.*

ROSARIO. [*Impatiently*] Let me; let me.
> [*Pushes* LORENZA *away, and pounds the dough.*

LORENZA. Before you roll it out . . . so, so.
> [*Indicates the motion of working it with the fingers.*

RUFINᴀ And turn it and press it well so that it will be firm.

ROSARIO. [*Burying her hands in the dough*] I know, stupid. You go to the oven. Is it good and hot?

LORENZA. You ought to see it.

RUFINA. Come.

ROSARIO. I'll have the first batch ready in a jiffy.
> [*Exeunt* RUFINA *and* LORENZA, *left, upstage.*

ROSARIO. [*Interrupting her work*] Thank heaven we're alone!

VICTOR. Fleeting moments of happiness for me, stolen from the sadness and solitude of this prison.

ROSARIO. [*Working again*] I am going to scold you, young man. Last night when you met me as if by chance on my way back from a walk on the beach with Rufina and the priest's nieces, you said hard things to me. I dreamed of the masses in revolt, of the guillotine and of pillage.

VICTOR. That's not for you.

ROSARIO. Because I'm poor and have nothing to pillage.

VICTOR. That is not the reason.

ROSARIO. Then, when they start destroying idols, you will make an exception in my favor. For this socialist flouts all his ideas by falling madly in love with an aristocrat.

VICTOR. Madly, yes.

ROSARIO. Traitor! deserter! apostate! make a joke of principles.

VICTOR. I laugh at them.

ROSARIO. You abandon one absurdity to aspire to another.

VICTOR. [*Quickly*] No, I aspire to nothing. I know that you cannot love me.

ROSARIO. Then if I can't love you, control yourself. Take your heart and do with it [*Kneading the dough*] as I am doing with this unfeeling mass.

VICTOR. And then take it to the furnace of the imagination.

ROSARIO. [*Quickly*] Your imagination is your ruin.

VICTOR. On the contrary, it is my salvation. Blessed imagination! My only consolation is to mount it and speed away through infinite space to the region of the ideal, of thought, free and unconfined. Giving rein to my fancy, I construct my life to suit my desires. I am not what others try to make me, but what I wish to be. Laws are nothing to me, because there I make them to suit myself. I plant myself on the fairest planet: I am a king, a demigod, a god! I love and am loved in return.

ROSARIO. Enough. That reminds me of my childhood when I played supposing games with my little friends.

VICTOR. What is that?

ROSARIO. Didn't you play supposing games as a child? It is great fun. I was crazy about it. It was like this: we would see which could invent the biggest stories, and the one who brought forth an absurdity that no one could surpass, won.

The actress will determine, according to the meaning of the speeches, when she will interrupt and resume the work.

VICTOR. What fun!

ROSARIO. Let's play at supposing. Let's see which of us can contrive the most preposterous thing.

VICTOR. The most impossible.

ROSARIO. Exactly. The other night I thought I was an ant, and that I kept travelling around the world, always in the same path, until I wore a path so deep that I split the earth in two. Imagine how many centuries I should need to . . .

VICTOR. [*Laughing*] Yes, that's clever. Well, I supposed something more nonsensical than that:—that you and I were living on a planet where the trees could speak . . .

ROSARIO. And the animals grew leaves.

VICTOR. And we were like a couple of walking shrubs, and our eyes laughing flowers, and our mouths flowers that kissed each other. . . . In that far-off world, you were not an aristocrat.

ROSARIO. Probably I was a pumpkin, perhaps a nice little nettle. Bah! Your nonsense is good for nothing, Victor. I can suppose an impossibility far greater.

VICTOR. What?

ROSARIO. An absurdity almost inconceivable. [*Pause. They look into each other's eyes for a moment*] That I, not in that planet where the grass speaks, but here on this earth, should come to love you, to sympathize with your ideas first, and then with yourself.

VICTOR. Duchess, do you want to drive me mad?

ROSARIO. Why don't you invent some nonsense like that?

VICTOR. You! Love me? Duchess . . .

ROSARIO. Why do you keep saying, Duchess, Duchess? If you are so frosty these cakes will be covered with icing. Call me Rosario.

VICTOR. Just Rosario like that?

ROSARIO. Don't you know that the Duchess of San Quentin is also a revolutionist and an anarchist? Yes, sir, I think that everything is going very badly in this world; that with all our laws and pretences we have come to inextricable confusion, and now no one understands it. And we shall have to mix it up again like this, [*Kneading vigorously*] and shape it and make it over, and pound it, and roll it out, [*Suiting the action to the word*] to arrive at something different.

VICTOR. Admirable! I go farther than that.

ROSARIO. Yes, you will go now and see if the oven is ready.

VICTOR. I know it is.

ROSARIO. Go and see, I tell you.

VICTOR [*Smiling*] Tyrant! [*Moving away.*

ROSARIO. I am not the tyrant; it is the baking, the public interest. [*Exit* VICTOR, *left, upstage.*

ROSARIO. [*Stops kneading, and takes the rolling-pin*] Ah, me! [*Sighs deeply*] I hardly dare admit it to myself. But it is true, and I confess it, and reproach myself. . . . The ideas of this man seduce me, charm me. . . . No, it is not his ideas; it is the man himself. [*She has rolled out the dough, and cuts it with the knife. She stops work, and takes up a piece of the dough, working it mechanically, abstractedly*] What! Rosario, shame on your weakness! In love with a poor nameless . . . Ah! if I could make a new world, new society, new people, as I make of this pastry the forms I please! [*Looking at a figure which she has moulded rapidly*] No, no. We must accept the human gingerbread man as he is, as the cooks of old formed him. [*Destroying the figure and trying the dough*] It is not hard enough. [*Rolls it up and uses the rolling-pin again*] Poor Victor! A hard fate is his.

[*Stands in thought, both hands on the rolling-pin.*

RAFAELA. [*Enters, back, with a package*] From the Marquis. He charged me to place it in your own hands.

ROSARIO. Ah, the letters. . . . Sarah . . . [*Unable to take it*] Put it in the pocket of my apron.

RAFAELA. [*Putting the package in the pocket*] Do you wish me to help you?

ROSARIO. [*Rolling again*] No. Leave me alone. [*Exit* RAFAELA] It frightens me to contemplate the abyss that is opening between Victor and Don César. [*Takes the knife and cuts the dough. Remains motionless in thought*] Shall I dare? No. Impossible.

VICTOR *enters, left, upstage.*

VICTOR. Ready in two minutes.

ROSARIO. [*Absent-minded*] Who?

VICTOR. The oven.

ROSARIO. [*Begins to make the cakes, twisting strips of dough*] Come, Rosario, hurry up.

VICTOR. When I came in, you seemed to be talking to yourself.

ROSARIO. Yes, and I was saying that it is foolish to sacrifice everything to truth, and that the great art in life consists in adapting ourselves blindly to this mass of fiction and pretence that surrounds us.

VICTOR. I don't believe that. For me it is war to the death against all falsehood of whatever kind.

ROSARIO. Do you love truth?

VICTOR. Above everything else.

ROSARIO. And do you maintain that the truth should always prevail?

VICTOR. Always.

ROSARIO. Even when it causes great unhappiness?

VICTOR. The truth can do no harm.

ROSARIO. You say that very confidently. You are very puritanical.

VICTOR. You are very curious.

ROSARIO. One more question. I like to know all your tastes and desires. Do you care about money, wealth?

VICTOR. [*Disconcerted*] That question . . . in that form. . . . Why, it all depends.

ROSARIO. You are an enemy of capital. So that it will be

very disagreeable to you to see that rascally capital coming your way. You will take a stick and . . .

VICTOR. As for that . . .

ROSARIO. Come, that hatred of capital is theoretical, especially when the capital is one's own. [VICTOR *starts to speak. She goes on*] Wait and let me make the question more concrete. You have in prospect wealth, a position, a name. If you should lose all that, should you regret it?

VICTOR. Wealth and poverty will be all one to me if you love me.

ROSARIO. I love you! You're coming back to our game of impossibilities.

VICTOR. Let us come back to it, and tell me that it is not an impossibility—that it is possible.

ROSARIO. [*Looking into his eyes*] Ah! Victor, between you and me there is a horrible phantom.

VICTOR. [*Surprised*] A phantom?

ROSARIO. Yes, and in order to destroy it,—note well what I say,—I should have to commit a crime.

VICTOR. [*Stupefied*] A crime!

ROSARIO. Yes, sir, a little crime—a village crime. [*Laughing*] What a face!

VICTOR. Really, I don't understand.

ROSARIO. Don't you see? I am wicked, very wicked.

VICTOR. You are an angel.

ROSARIO. An angel that can kill; the angel of assassination, as they said of Charlotte Corday.

VICTOR. [*With increasing astonishment*] You, capable of killing!

ROSARIO. Yes.

VICTOR. Whom?

ROSARIO. You.

VICTOR. [*Taking it as a joke*] Me? Very well, from your

hand I will accept death, if only it brings me love at the same time.

ROSARIO. And you won't be angry with me . . . if I kill you?

VICTOR. Never. If you doubt it, put me to the test. What must I do?

ROSARIO. [*Handing him a pan of cakes*] For the present, take Rufina the first panful. [*Alarmed at seeing* DON CÉSAR *entering, right*] Ah! Don César. Careful!

DON CÉSAR. [*Brusquely, surprised at seeing* VICTOR] What brings you here?

ROSARIO. Don't scold him. I told him to come.

DON CÉSAR. This is an occupation, my dear lady, suitable for children and women. Your maid . . .

ROSARIO. I have given her something else to do.

DON CÉSAR. Then Pepita . . . And you, take that away, and then I want the drainage plan for the lower field this afternoon.

VICTOR. Very well. [*As he goes out, aside*] Unbearable tyranny! [*Exit, back.*

DON CÉSAR. You and Rufina have upset the whole house with your little tasks and your . . .

ROSARIO. Don José doesn't mind what we're doing. But if you don't like it . . .

DON CÉSAR. No, no. You are the mistress here. Allow me to sit down. I am very weak.

[*Brings up a chair and seats himself by the table.*

ROSARIO. As you reproved me . . .

DON CÉSAR. Reprove, no. Go on, go on, since you have the poor taste to descend to occupations so far beneath you.

ROSARIO. [*Preparing cakes rapidly*] Ha, ha! You are still harping on that old idea of class distinctions? Remember that I am poor, Don César. [*Sighing*] And I must be learning to earn my living.

DON CÉSAR. And you will still have your joke. Duchess of San Quentin, taking everything into account . . .

ROSARIO. I never was any good at accounts.

DON CÉSAR. I mean, when you think it over—for of course you will marry . . .

ROSARIO. Oh, no.

DON CÉSAR. If you take a second husband in the aristocracy, you may easily fall again into the hands of some one like poor Gustave. I am not an attractive man, at first blush, as they say, but when you know me. . . . Oh, Rosario, I will love you with my heart and soul; I will give you a fine position.

ROSARIO. I am sick of fine positions.

DON CÉSAR. Mere fancy.

ROSARIO. It's true. Ah, Don César! After a life of grasping and usury, you have taken a fancy to become a Duke. If my father could raise his head and see you asking me to be your wife . . .

DON CÉSAR. He would be glad.

ROSARIO. And if my poor mother could come to life again . . .

DON CÉSAR. She would be glad, too. Come, Rosario, my dear, let us forget old disagreements . . . which never had any basis of truth. Tell me, in heaven's name, what shall I do to overcome this aversion?

ROSARIO. You'd have to be born again.

DON CÉSAR. I will be your slave, and fit myself to your wishes and caprices. I will be as yielding as that dough that you take in your fingers and mould as you like.

ROSARIO. You would be hard to twist.

DON CÉSAR. That would be on account of the coating of sugar.

ROSARIO. Sugar—money. Ah! Don César, a mountain of sugar-cane wouldn't be enough to sweeten you!

Don César. We would add soft butter, sentiment, affection, domestic peace.

Rosario. No, the mixture would still taste bitter.

Don César. [*Rising and thumping his chair on the ground*] The devil take your pastry! You drive me mad. You play with me like a kitten with a spool, and you confuse my soul and make me a snarl, a tangle, and I don't know what to think. [*Firmly*] Come, let's make an end of this.

Rosario. That's what I want, to end it.

Don César. Did you read my letter?

Rosario. Surely.

Don César. Why don't you answer?

Rosario. Be calm.

Don César. How can I? I like to have things definite. Yes, or no. I'm not like you. As an aristocrat, you like to exercise your fickle disposition, and it disgusts me.

Rosario. Thank you.

Don César. No. I have a better opinion of you than I've any reason to have. I believe firmly that you will answer me, that perhaps you have already written the answer.

Rosario. That may be.

Don César. [*Aside*] She is flirting with me, pretending to despise what she really wants. I know women!

Rosario. What are you saying?

Don César. [*With a show of sincerity*] That you are playing with me. And with all this teasing, you are preparing for me a pleasant surprise.

> *He approaches the table, and leans over it with his hands upon it, looking at* Rosario, *softening his voice.*

Rosario. A pleasant surprise? Are you sure of it?

Don César. Yes. And you are going to give me a yes flatly and frankly that will make me happy. [*Noticing the package which* Rosario *has in the pocket of her apron*] Ah! What have you there? A letter?

ROSARIO. Maybe.

DON CÉSAR. [*Moving away from the table*] Aha! That is the reply I am asking for. I am a prophet, Rosario. I am, unfortunately, an old hand at the wiles of feminine diplomacy.

ROSARIO. I can see that.

DON CÉSAR. I penetrate their intentions, I catch their thoughts on the wing.

ROSARIO. Oh, indeed! Then guess the reply that I have here.

DON CÉSAR. Well, I'll wager you accept, but with a lot of delicate circumlocution . . . the eternal feminine. A woman after all—I mean a lady.

ROSARIO. It's all the same.

DON CÉSAR. [*Showing great impatience*] Will you permit me to approach? [*Without waiting for permission, he comes up to* ROSARIO *and looks at the packet, which is sticking half out of the pocket*] It's a thick one. I see my name—the Marquis's writing.

ROSARIO. It is a paper that my cousin has sent for you.

DON CÉSAR. [*Disappointed*] About the horses? Why don't you give it to me?

ROSARIO. I can't use my nands.

DON CÉSAR. Then let me take it.

> *Starts to take the packet.* ROSARIO, *with a sudden start, prevents him by putting her hand over her pocket.*

ROSARIO. No.   [*Pause.* DON CÉSAR *is surprised.*

DON CÉSAR. Why . . . ?

ROSARIO. [*Aside*] I dare not . . . No. Let fate take its course, let falsehood triumph.

DON CÉSAR. [*Very serious*] If that package is only what I think it is, why don't you give it to me?

ROSARIO. [*At a loss*] The fact is that . . . [*She has an inspiration*] You were right, Don César. This is my reply. I put it with the papers that the Marquis gave me, and tied it all together with this red ribbon.

DON CÉSAR. [*Impatient*] Then give it to me, for God's sake!

ROSARIO. No, no.

DON CÉSAR. [*Bitter and sarcastic*] Is what you said to me so horrible?

ROSARIO. Naturally. I specify my grievances, as you asked in your letter.

DON CÉSAR. [*Showing himself gross and insulting*] And you bring up the case of your father. Well, your father, the noble Duke of San Quentin, had a lot to thank me for, madam. I saved him from going to prison. And I am not one of those who say, "Aha! He deserved to go." Not I . . .

ROSARIO. [*Unnerved, stammering with anger*] And why do they say that you are as treacherous as you are base?

DON CÉSAR. And you will also talk about your mother . . .

ROSARIO. Don't take her name upon your vile lips!

DON CÉSAR. Her name! Innocent creature! What do you know about it?

ROSARIO. [*Furious*] You dare repeat . . . ! Oh, if I were a man I'd strangle the infamous . . . [*She stops, overcome with anger. Looks at him with scorn*] Don César, let us have no more words. You deserve no consideration, nor even pity. [*Giving him the packet*] Take this.

DON CÉSAR. At last! [*Takes it.*

ROSARIO. I beg you to leave me.

DON CÉSAR. Good. I will retire. [*Starts to the door, right, and stops, hesitating, as if dissatisfied with himself. Aside*] The devil! I have been a fool. Blinded by anger. [*Trying to reopen the conversation*] Rosario . . .

ROSARIO. Enough.

DON CÉSAR. [*Humbly*] But you. . . . Did you take seriously what I said? [*Hypocritically*] Without meaning to, one word led to another, and I ran on without thinking. . . . I was impertinent. [ROSARIO *moves away, turning her back*] What? Won't you hear me? [*Takes a few steps toward her*] You know, my nerves are all upset, from not sleeping, and not eating. I get mixed up. . . . Anybody is likely to make a mistake . . . especially a sick man.

ROSARIO. [*Aside*] His cringing apologies are more offensive than his insults.

DON CÉSAR. Won't you let me explain?

ROSARIO. [*Sharply*] No.

DON CÉSAR. You are angry with me?

ROSARIO. [*With disdain, not unmixed with compassion*] Oh! No.

DON CÉSAR. [*Going toward the door*] I will read your reply, and then we will have a talk. You will do me justice.

ROSARIO. Justice! That's exactly the idea.

DON CÉSAR. [*From the door, looking at her with eyes of passion. Aside*] You little savage! I'll catch you yet, though it be in a trap.

> *Exit.* VICTOR *has entered, left, upstage, a few moments before* DON CÉSAR'S *departure, and has waited for him to leave.*

VICTOR. He has gone. It seemed to me that you were speaking with some excitement. What is happening?

ROSARIO. [*Agitated and embarrassed*] Nothing . . . no.

VICTOR. [*Taking up the pans*] Shall I take these?

ROSARIO. [*Takes them from him*] No, not now. Heavens! what have I done? [*Hastily washes her hands in the basin*] Victor, forgive me! No, you will never forgive me. Impossible.

VICTOR. [*Alarmed*] For what? What are you doing?

ROSARIO. You see: washing my hands—like Pilate. Or rather, no; I am guilty. . . . There is blood on them.

VICTOR. [*Not understanding*] Rosario!

ROSARIO. Ah! my dear Victor! . . . Truth above everything. . . . You believe that, don't you?

VICTOR. Yes.

ROSARIO. Always, and under all circumstances?

VICTOR. Always, always.

ROSARIO. [*Dropping the towel, runs to* VICTOR *and puts both hands on his breast, questioning him with an affectionate look*] Victor!

VICTOR. What?

ROSARIO. Will you always love me? Always?

VICTOR. [*Overcome, not knowing what to say*] Rosario!

ROSARIO. Oh, I must be crazy to talk to you like that! So immodest!

VICTOR. It is the truth rising and coming out.

ROSARIO. Yes, that's it. Now I repeat: Will you always, always, love me, in spite of . . .

VICTOR. [*Quickly*] In spite of what?

ROSARIO. Of this . . . Because your love is what I care for most in the world, and I am condemned [*With emotion*] to have your hate.

VICTOR. I? What nonsense! Why . . . you're weeping.

ROSARIO. [*Drying her tears*] No, no.

VICTOR. [*Passionately*] Ask of me the greatest sacrifices, the hardest service; put me to the test. My love will not be complete unless I can suffer for it.

ROSARIO. [*Sadly*] Don't ask for sacrifices. They will come.

VICTOR. But explain to me . . .

ROSARIO. I can say nothing. I am going now.

VICTOR. [*Trying to detain her*] No.

ROSARIO. Let me go! I am going—to the oven. [*Forcing a laugh*] You see, I have to take this, [*Indicating the two pans of cakes*] and I want to see how the baking has come out.

[*Exit rapidly, left, upstage.*

VICTOR. [*Agitated*] Love, yes, love! It is revealed in her

eyes, in the trembling of her voice. Can I be mistaken? [*Doubtful*] I wonder. [*Thoughtful*] What is this intangible mystery that floats about me? Rosario . . . this house . . . my family . . .

DON JOSÉ. [*Enters, back*] I smell something burning. Those crazy girls have let the baking. . . . Ah! Victor.

VICTOR. [*Vehemently*] Grandfather, I want to be different. I am different. I declare myself changed, transformed . . .

DON JOSÉ. Good. But you must prove it.

VICTOR. Do you doubt it? Command my acts, my thoughts. I renounce all the ideas that offended you; I surrender. I will identify myself with the family which is about to receive me into its midst . . .

DON JOSÉ. In fact, your father intended today . . . Here is Canseco with the papers.

CANSECO *enters, back.*

CANSECO. My dear patriarch . . . Don Victor.

DON JOSÉ. [*Looking at the document that* CANSECO *takes from his pocket*] Is that the act?

CANSECO. Yes, sir. [*Gives it to him.*

DON JOSÉ. [*Calling, right*] César, my son.

DON CÉSAR. [*Enters, right, with an expression of confusion and anger, which he restrains with difficulty.* VICTOR *and* CANSECO *look at him in surprise*] What is it, father?

DON JOSÉ. [*To* CÉSAR, *giving him the document*] Look this over. [CÉSAR *snatches it and crumples it convulsively*] What are you doing?

DON CÉSAR. My duty.

[*Tears the paper and throws the pieces to the ground.*

DON JOSÉ. [*Aghast*] Why, my son, what's this?

DON CÉSAR. To destroy, annihilate. . . . Oh, fool that I am! I can easily tear up this paper . . . but the shame, the deception with which I have lived, how can I destroy and remove that? Who will destroy the years, the acts of treachery, the infamous deceit, my stupid blindness? [*Overcome, looking at* VICTOR, *who remains at the left of the stage, waiting, troubled and silent, and without understanding what is happening*] Ah! There he is! That living sham, my deception through all these years! His person which was pleasing to me but yesterday, now shames and offends me!

VICTOR. [*Aside*] God! what is he saying?

DON JOSÉ. My son, you are raving.

DON CÉSAR. [*Wildly, with staring eyes*] Oh! if I only were raving, dreaming! But no, no. I have not even the consolation of doubt.

DON JOSÉ. What?

DON CÉSAR. [*Aside, to* DON JOSÉ, *in a low and mournful tone*] It is certain, father, the living truth. It is her hand, her delicate writing, fair and false; it is herself, coming back from the grave to reveal to me her vile imposture.

VICTOR. [*Understanding by* DON CÉSAR'S *manner that something serious is happening, but not knowing what it is*] What mystery is this? [*To* CANSECO, *who approaches*] Have they told him something about me? Slander perhaps . . .

CANSECO. [*Confused*] I don't know.

VICTOR. [*Taking two or three steps toward* DON CÉSAR] Sir . . .

DON CÉSAR. [*Terrified*] Don't come near me.

DON JOSÉ. Victor, have you caused sorrow to your father?

> RUFINA *and* ROSARIO *enter, left, upstage.* ROSARIO *remains near the wall, and does not advance until* VICTOR *is left alone.*

RUFINA. [*Running up to* VICTOR] Victor, what are you doing? We have been waiting for you.

DON CÉSAR. Rufina, come away from that man.

RUFINA. [*Startled*] Why, papa?

CANSECO. Don César doesn't want anybody to go near him.

RUFINA. [*To her father*] Papa, what has Victor done?

DON CÉSAR. [*Aside to* RUFINA *and* DON JOSÉ] Nothing. He is innocent.

RUFINA. I don't understand.

DON JOSÉ. I do. But explain to us.

DON CÉSAR. [*Dejectedly*] I can't. The truth burns my lips. It is impossible for me to tell my disgrace. [*Falls fainting in a chair*] I feel very ill. . . . I am dying. [*All surround him except* VICTOR] My strength leaves me in this crisis of honor, of conscience. I can only suffer, and curse my fate, and revile heaven and earth. [*Nervously sitting up in the chair, supported by* DON JOSÉ *and* RUFINA] I feel fire, gall, shame, coursing through my veins.

VICTOR. [*Overwhelmed*] What is this horrible enigma? But great heavens, of what am I accused? [*With rage, clenching his fists*] What have I done?

DON CÉSAR. Done? Nothing, nothing. No, I can say nothing. My courage fails me. . . . I can't, I can't.

VICTOR. Good God!

RUFINA. [*Embracing her father*] Are you ill?

DON JOSÉ. Let us take him in.

CANSECO. And call the doctor.

DON JOSÉ. Yes, yes.

DON CÉSAR. [*Led by* DON JOSÉ, RUFINA, *and* CANSECO] My daughter. . . . My only true . . .

[*Kisses and puts his arm around her.*

DON JOSÉ. Come. [*Exeunt, right.*

VICTOR. [*Angrily, running to the right*] No, no! You must tell me . . .

ROSARIO. [*Advances and detains him*] Wait. I will tell you.

VICTOR. You, Rosario? You possess the key to this horrible mystery?

ROSARIO. Yes.

VICTOR. And you know . . . In heaven's name, explain to me. . . . My father . . .

ROSARIO. Don't call him that.

VICTOR. Why?

ROSARIO. Because he isn't.

VICTOR. [*Horrified*] He isn't! I am not . . .

ROSARIO. [*Rapidly*] Don't ask me anything more. You are not to blame. [*Seriously*] The guilty ones are no more. God has punished them . . .

VICTOR. [*Covering his face*] Oh! [*Drops into a chair.*

ROSARIO. Life is a fickle thing, and surprises us with sudden revolutions and changes. Do not the rich and powerful, and even kings fall? Then if the great fall, why should we wonder if ordinary mortals fall too and disappear, and vanish into nothing?

VICTOR. [*Not listening*] The proofs, the proofs of this . . . whatever it is.

ROSARIO. They are undeniable.

VICTOR. [*Greatly agitated*] Who told my father—Don César? You? Why? For what purpose?

ROSARIO. For the sake of truth. I thought that one who loves truth above everything would not reproach me for that.

VICTOR. [*Confused*] Yes, but . . .

ROSARIO. The truth, always the truth! Does your moral standard permit you to accept a name and a position that do not belong to you?

VICTOR. Oh, I would never do that.

ROSARIO. And do you regret the loss of the wealth you thought was yours?

VICTOR. I should be a hypocrite to pretend that this blow does not wound me deeply. Just when I wanted a name and a fortune to be able to aspire . . .

ROSARIO. To what?

VICTOR. [*Bitter and disconsolate*] Can you ask me? You are cruel to impress upon me the distance, now infinite, that separates us.

ROSARIO. [*Tenderly*] Victor, console yourself. How many times, in talking with me, you have protested against social distinctions, cursed property, and even names. Names—vain idols, according to you, to which so often the purest instincts of the heart are sacrificed! Well, now your ideal is realized; now you have no property, not even a name. Now you are nobody.

VICTOR. [*Recovering himself*] Nobody? Oh! not quite, not so low as that. [*Rising abruptly*] Away with weakness that is unworthy of me! It is over now, the shock of the fall. I still live. . . . I am myself. [*With courage*] I will accept with a tranquil heart the most difficult and desperate situations. I fear nothing. The abyss into which I have dropped does not dismay me, and its shadowy depths will not cause a shudder. I thought I possessed the riches of the earth—all of them, all: those that make life peaceful and happy, that stir the mind, that rejoice the heart. A dream, an illusion! It is my fate —a cruel fate. [*Boldly*] Well, with all its cruelty and pain, I accept it, I face it, I welcome it, and I will go on living. Forward, then. What am I? Nobody? Good! I am a man, and that is enough.

ROSARIO. A man, yes, of powerful intelligence and firm will.

VICTOR. My will! That is all I have left.

ROSARIO. Not quite. [*Meaningly*]

VICTOR. I have a sad and hopeless love, more hopeless now than ever. [*Vehemently, and with curiosity*] But tell me, Rosario, in God's name, what motive had you in revealing to my father—to Don César—this . . . this . . . thing?

ROSARIO. A great interest . . . immense.

VICTOR. What?

ROSARIO. [*Embarrassed*] That I wanted to say to you . . .

VICTOR. [*Anxiously*] What?

ROSARIO. Something that I could not say to the son of that

man, whom I hate. Between the false father and the supposed son I have opened an impassable abyss. [*Tenderly*] And now that you are alone in the world, now that you no longer have over you the despicable shadow of Don César de Buendía, I can say to you . . .

VICTOR. What?

ROSARIO. [*With a burst of love and enthusiasm*] Son of Adam, outcast of fortune, wanderer in the wide world—my poor darling . . . [*Pause. She rests her eyes on* VICTOR. *He, opening his arms, goes toward her*] I love you.

VICTOR. My angel!

ROSARIO. My love!   [*They embrace. Quick curtain.*

End of Act Two.

ACT III

(The Scene is the same as in Act One)

LORENZA *discovered putting the room in order;* RUFINA *enters at back, wearing a hat and walking-suit.*

RUFINA. How animated and gay the whole town is! The plaza is full of people, and the whole square of San Roque, and Lantigua Avenue all the way to the church.

LORENZA. Yes, yes. Rarely has the pilgrimage of Our Lady of the Sea been so big as this year. Ah! the fifteenth of August, the great festival of this town, is hardly recognizable nowadays! Today it is all excitement, and eating and drinking, and lots of people from inland and from overseas . . . but devotion, real devotion—don't look for that, because it isn't there. Well, did you girls go as far as the sanctuary?

RUFINA. It was hard to make our way through the crowd, such pushing, and swaying . . . But finally we got there, and offered to the Holy Virgin the three wreaths, ours and yours. [*Anxiously looking toward the right*] But Rosario . . .

LORENZA. Didn't she come home with you?

RUFINA. No, I thought she had come on ahead.

LORENZA. I haven't seen her come in.

RUFINA. In San Roque's square the Lantigua girls kept me talking a few minutes—such chatterers—and when I succeeded in getting away, Rosario wasn't with me. I looked for her all through the streets and shops of the fair, and couldn't find her. The Duchess of San Quentin had disappeared. I thought she had come home, and that I should find her here.

163

LORENZA. [*Alarmed*] Do you suppose she is lost in the crowd, and can't find her way home?

RUFINA. What? Rosario? She can find her way anywhere. She is not lost.

LORENZA. But what has happened to the Duchess, anyway? She doesn't get up early any more; she doesn't work; she spends the morning gathering wild flowers, and the nights looking at the moon, and counting the stars to see if they are all there.

RUFINA. Just her whims.

LORENZA. A strange whim to be as gloomy as a funeral, when she ought to be as happy as a lark.

RUFINA. Oh, you think . . .

LORENZA. Yes. They haven't told us about it, but everybody in town is talking about it.

RUFINA. Why, what do they say?

LORENZA. That you will soon have a handsome stepmother.

RUFINA. Come, come. Don't talk nonsense. What do you know about it?

LORENZA. More than you do.

RUFINA. You don't understand what has happened here, and you can't understand.

LORENZA. [*To herself*] My word, the girl is stupid! [*Mysteriously*] Since the day of the revolution in this house . . .

RUFINA. Hush. Don't remind me of it.

LORENZA. Since the day they repudiated Mr. Victor, leaving him in the class of the sovereign people, strange things have been happening in the house of Buendía. The poor boy! When we were just becoming fond of him, it turned out that . . .

RUFINA. [*Sadly*] That he is not my brother. For me he always will be. I regarded him as my brother from the time he came to the house, and I shall consider him so as long as I live. When I become a nun,—and the religious life attracts me more strongly every day,—I shall pray for him night and morning, asking the Lord to give him some happiness—of the little that exists on this earth.

LORENZA. He deserves it, the dear boy. I shall never forget that afternoon when I saw him go out of the house, never to return. And don't imagine that he was downcast and dejected. I said then, he seems too haughty for the common herd.

RUFINA. [*With interest*] You haven't seen him since?

LORENZA. No.

RUFINA. Tell me the truth.

LORENZA. I assure you I haven't.

RUFINA. And you haven't heard from him?

LORENZA. No. I ask all the workmen I know, and nobody can tell me anything.

RUFINA. I can't understand it.

LORENZA. He must have gone away.

RUFINA. No, no. He is here. Canseco must know where, because grandfather and papa have sent him—that I know, I overheard it—have sent the notary to propose to him . . .

LORENZA. They have? What . . . ?

RUFINA. You shall see. I begged grandfather not to abandon poor Victor and he—you'll never guess what my dear old granddaddy said—Well, he'll give him the "Rufina," which is now ready to sail, loaded with ore, and with provisions for two months. Last night he told the captain to clear for Boston or Philadelphia, with cargo for sale on arrival. They will give Victor the ship, with the papers all in order, on condition that he leaves at once. The ship and everything in it is his, and when he reaches the United States he can sell it, and buy land in the west, and make a big, big ranch.

LORENZA. Ah! what a man! How he runs everything, and gives everybody his due. He is a regular Providence. And Victor, does he accept?

RUFINA. We shall know soon, because the captain wants to sail on tomorrow's tide.

LORENZA. [*Seized by an idea*] Oh, do you suppose Victor is already on board?

RUFINA. [*Quickly*] Oh, that hadn't occurred to me. We must find out at once.

LORENZA. Yes, John will know—my nephew, he is the quartermaster. [*Goes to back.*

RUFINA. Listen. Rosario's delay worries me.

LORENZA. I will send Rafaela to look for her. [*Looking out at back*] Ah! Here she is. [*Enter* ROSARIO, *back*. LORENZA *stops on seeing her, as if about to enter into conversation*] Have you had a pleasant walk, ma'am?

RUFINA. Go and do what I told you, and leave us. [*Exit* LORENZA] Thank heaven! Where have you been?

ROSARIO. [*Downcast*] Oh, I wasn't lost. I was . . . [*Anxiously*] Tell me, have you heard anything?

RUFINA. Nothing, dear.

ROSARIO. And Lorenza, who knows everything and hears everything, hasn't she found out . . . ?

RUFINA. Not yet.

ROSARIO. [*Very much agitated*] I am so uneasy! Since that day, which I shall never forget, we haven't seen him nor heard from him. Why is he hiding? Is he trying to avoid me?

RUFINA. Oh, no.

ROSARIO. It would be an inexplicable change. His last words, when he said good-bye to me and left the house, indicated tender affection and Christian fortitude. I don't know which touched me more, his love for me or the proud courage with which he faced misfortune. But since then . . . now . . . this disappearance, this flight, if he is really gone. . . . I don't know what to think. If you only knew the things that I imagine!

RUFINA. What?

ROSARIO. That when he was alone, his courage dropped away, and he fell into that dejection that stifles one's energies, and leads to despair, and bitterness, and anger.

RUFINA. Oh, don't believe that.

ROSARIO. It may well be that the love he felt for me has been stifled by the memory of the harm I did him.

RUFINA. Come, come. That is impossible. I can sooner believe that his feelings have been affected by the reports that are current in the town.

ROSARIO. That I am going to marry your father? Ridiculous gossip!

RUFINA. That is what my friends were talking about this afternoon, and every one I met on the way home. Now of course, if Victor believes it too . . .

ROSARIO. He can't, he won't believe it. Oh, dear, I don't know what to do. If I were only sure he received the letter I wrote to him yesterday!

RUFINA. I gave it to the teamster at the factory, and I am sure he is searching the town and the country round to find him.

ROSARIO. Oh, I hope so! Why do you think I left you this afternoon at San Roque, when you were talking with your friends? I thought I saw him in the crowd.

RUFINA. Victor?

ROSARIO. I would have sworn it was he. I ran after that face that appeared for a moment in the shifting mob. It was not he. With a sudden impulse, I began to run through the whole fair, with the idea, the presentiment, that I should find him. In that turbulent throng, through the excited hubbub, I made my way rapidly—people coming and going, dancing here, eating there. All, old and young, men and women, were full of the joy of living, that simple gaiety which is unknown to us who have been born and have lived in a world of artificiality, of dry and empty formalities, like puppets hung on wires. And I was seeking, seeking, seeking, with anxious eyes, searching the sea of faces, that mass of humanity abounding in joy and flesh and blood and life. I saw weather-beaten sailors, with the look of the sea in their eyes; workmen's faces, marked with the dust of the mines; I saw farmers, teamsters, all kinds of people, but among all those faces I did not find the one I sought. And I was so blindly confident that the Virgin would grant me what I asked! You see, it was such a little thing I wanted. I have been very unhappy. I have lived in the desert of fashionable life; I prayed that she should let me see again the only man who ever reached my heart—and stayed there.

RUFINA. Oh, she might grant you that! You took the wrong path. Instead of going down to the fair, you should have gone down to the harbor.

ROSARIO. I did. I went down to the shore, and went over it from the ore-works to the fishermen's beach. I saw three, four, a dozen boats arriving from the other shore, their masts gay with flags, leaves, and masses of flowering shrubs; they were filled with pilgrims, all bearing branches of laurel and garlands of flowers to offer to the Virgin. He was not there, either. And those people arriving so gaily as if they thought they had discovered a new world as soon as they set foot on shore, passed close to my great grief without noticing it. My grief is so small, so diminutive, so invisible to others— and so great to me!

RUFINA. Be calm. We shall surely know today. For pity's sake, have patience.

ROSARIO. That is just what I can't do. Recommend to me all the virtues, but not patience.

RUFINA. Take care. Here are father and grandfather.

Enter DON JOSÉ, *leaning on* DON CÉSAR'S *arm.*

DON JOSÉ. Ah! there you are. Have you been to the fair?

ROSARIO. Yes, sir, and we took flowers to the Virgin.

RUFINA. And we prayed to her to give you both good health.

DON CÉSAR. To me, too? Did you pray for me?

ROSARIO. Yes, for you, too.

DON CÉSAR. Thanks. But so far the Virgin has not paid any attention to you, for I am no better today than yesterday.

ROSARIO. Our Lady of the Sea is not very generous this year. She doesn't grant anything we ask.

DON JOSÉ. Are you going tonight to the dance at the Casino?

ROSARIO. I'm not.

RUFINA. If we wanted to go, would you let us, grandfather?

DON JOSÉ. My dear children, I am not the one who commands here now. Do you know what I have decided to do?

RUFINA and ROSARIO. What?

DON JOSÉ. Well, considering that my dear son disapproves of the authority that I have exercised in this house for more than half a century, considering that he is determined to follow new paths which are not to my liking, I—abdicate.

[*He sits down.*

ROSARIO. Do you really mean it?

DON JOSÉ. [*Seriously*] Yes, and there is something more important, which I ought to say to you today, and which he will tell you. You can settle it yourselves. [DON CÉSAR *talks with* ROSARIO, *aside;* DON JOSÉ *with* RUFINA] He insists upon ruining himself, and he will.

ROSARIO. But, Don César, do you still persist?

DON CÉSAR. To be sure. Persistence is my only virtue. Yes, I still persist.

ROSARIO. In spite of our disagreeable quarrel the other day?

DON CÉSAR. In spite of all quarrels, past, present, and future.

ROSARIO. I thought you would still be angry with me.

DON CÉSAR. Why? Oh, for having revealed to me . . . On the contrary, I ought to be grateful. For what purpose or reason I know not, you saved me from a great mistake. You wounded me, but you told me the truth, and say what you like, one should always be thankful for the truth. You see I speak frankly. Imitate my frankness, and tell me . . .

ROSARIO. [*Displeased*] If you please, we will leave this for another occasion. I must write to my family—I have been very neglectful.

DON CÉSAR. Cruel. You are always fleeing from me.

ROSARIO. Au revoir. [*To* RUFINA] Are you coming?

[*Exeunt, right.*

DON JOSÉ. From what I can see, her disdain does not cure you of your mad infatuation.

DON CÉSAR. You are right: blind infatuation, madness. I cannot help it. It is my temperament, my character to seek to overcome obstacles, especially when I know that they are more affected than sincere. She is simply wild to enrich her dried-up aristocracy with the prosperous, if lowly house of Buendía. Only, with the greatest shrewdness she dickers over her consent, to get a better bargain.

DON JOSÉ. [*Rising angrily*] I tell you . . .

DON CÉSAR. [*Calmly*] Father, have you abdicated or not?

DON JOSÉ. [*Sitting down*] Ah! I forgot. Do what you like. I have nothing to say. I have withdrawn from the world, and from my humble cell, watching my own funeral. I shall see how you govern alone.

DON CÉSAR. I shall rule as best I can.

DON JOSÉ. I shall not interfere again except to see the fulfillment of one of the last acts of my reign. Tell me, will Canseco be here soon?

DON CÉSAR. I expect him any moment.

DON JOSÉ. And he will tell us whether that poor boy accepts or not.

DON CÉSAR. Do you doubt it? What more can he expect? I don't know. We are giving him, for love, a magnificent ship.

DON JOSÉ. Yes, rotten in every timber, like us. Well, we shall see if that diligent notary . . .

DON CÉSAR. [*Approaching the back as if to give some orders*] Talk of the devil . . . here he is.

Enter CANSECO.

DON CÉSAR. What news?

CANSECO. [*Pompously*] A great, a stupendous event.

DON CÉSAR. Out with it.

CANSECO. Parenthetically, [*Shaking* DON CÉSAR'S *hand, effusively*] accept my warmest congratulations, my dear Don César.

DON CÉSAR. What for?

CANSECO. They are talking of nothing else all over town. It will be a happy day for all the inhabitants of Ficóbriga when we come to greet the new Duke of San Quentin.

DON CÉSAR. Oh, there is nothing to that yet. Maybe . . . But come, my friend, what about . . . ?

DON JOSÉ. Have you seen him?

CANSECO. Yes, sir.

DON CÉSAR. Where has he been?

CANSECO. Prepare for a great surprise. [*Pause*] Are you prepared?

DON CÉSAR. Yes, but tell us . . .

DON JOSÉ. Where is he?

CANSECO. At Saint Mary's.

DON JOSÉ. In the sanctuary?

CANSECO. In the rectory, at the home of the priest.

DON CÉSAR. Father Florencio?

CANSECO. Yes, it appears they are great friends.

RUFINA. [*Peeping in at the right, hears the last words*] Ah!

[*She goes back to* ROSARIO'S *room.*

DON JOSÉ. Did you speak with him?

CANSECO. Yes, sir, more than half an hour.

DON CÉSAR. Of course, he accepts our aid, and will embark immediately.

CANSECO. Well, he has not agreed specifically.

DON CÉSAR. He hasn't?

DON JOSÉ. Well . . .

CANSECO. Let me proceed in due form. He told me that on the day following his departure from this house, he went to Socartes, summoned by a Belgian engineer, a friend of his, and former comrade at Liège.

DON CÉSAR. Ah, yes. Trainard, who is the Belgian consul here.

CANSECO. Accompanied by his friend and his friend's wife, he returned here this morning.

DON CÉSAR. And what else?

CANSECO. Why, nothing. . . . He requests that you give him an interview, and I have come in his name to ask for it.

DON JOSÉ. An interview, here?

DON CÉSAR. No, no; he must not set foot here. That would be the last straw. . . . Tell him, no, no.

CANSECO. The petitioner instructed me to say that he has a communication of the greatest importance to make to you.

DON CÉSAR. Bah, bah! Tell him to let us alone.

CANSECO. I presume—of course, I do not speak of my own knowledge—that it has something to do with the sad revelation made by the Duchess. And, parenthetically, since I have mentioned the lady's name . . .

DON CÉSAR. What?

CANSECO. [*Confidentially*] Well, when in the course of our conversation the name of the Duchess was mentioned, I observed on Victor's face an expression, an emotion. . . . Well,

... I understood it instantly. My natural perspicacity leads me to observe and read such things. ... Clearly, as the noble relative of the house of Buendía was the one who rectified that serious family mistake, it is perfectly logical that the petitioner, innocent victim of the declaration of the deponent, should have conceived a violent hatred for her. It is proper that you should be warned.

DON CÉSAR. What? Would he dare ... ?

DON JOSÉ. I don't believe it.

CANSECO. Have him arrested and taken to Segura. Let us with wise prevention forestall any diabolical plot that his desire for vengeance may have conceived.

DON CÉSAR. Oh, it is impossible.

CANSECO. I do not affirm. ... I suspect. The natural pessimism of an officer of justice who has seen much villainy. And, parenthetically, what do you reply to his request?

DON JOSÉ. It is for you to say.

DON CÉSAR. I told you no, absolutely.

ROSARIO and RUFINA *enter, right.*

ROSARIO. [*From the door*] Is it a secret, what you are saying?

DON CÉSAR. No, come in.

CANSECO. [*Advancing to greet her*] Dear lady ... [*Officiously and mysteriously*] Have no fear.

ROSARIO. Fear!

CANSECO. You are quite safe. There is no danger. We are all here to watch over your precious life. The only precaution you can take is not to leave the house until ...

DON CÉSAR. But if the petitioner, as you say, is to leave Ficóbriga soon anyway. Why it would be absurd ...

ROSARIO. Ah! I know whom you are speaking of.

DON CÉSAR. And now he comes with the ridiculous request that we grant him an interview.

CANSECO. An audience, here.

DON JOSÉ. He wants us to give him something more.

RUFINA. Let him come, grandfather.

DON JOSÉ. I have nothing to say. He will decide.

DON CÉSAR. Receive him here! In my house!

RUFINA. Papa, receive him. What difference does it make to you? [*To* CANSECO] Where is he?

CANSECO. He is close by. He came with me as far as the door, and is now in the square awaiting the decision.

ROSARIO. [*Aside to* RUFINA] Quick, go and call him. [*Exit* RUFINA, *back*] As a matter of conscience, Don César, remembering the important part I played in the lamentable affair, I am obliged to intercede for the unfortunate victim. Gentlemen, you are noble and generous; you owe it to yourselves to hear him at least, and find out what he asks.

DON CÉSAR. [*Excusing himself*] Rosario, I am very sorry to . . .

RUFINA. [*Enters quickly, back*] Here he is.

ROSARIO. Let him come in.

DON CESAR. You demand it?

ROSARIO. And you consent.

DON CÉSAR. Well, so be it.

> *All sit down.* DON JOSÉ *at the right, having on his right,* RUFINA, *on his left,* ROSARIO; *opposite* DON CÉSAR, *with* CANSECO *at his side. The center of the stage is empty.* VICTOR *appears in the door at the back; his dress is that of a gentleman, but unostentatious. He stops for a moment in the door, awaiting an invitation to enter.*

DON JOSÉ. Come in. [VICTOR *does not move*]

RUFINA. Grandfather says to come in.

> [VICTOR *advances and bows gravely to the two groups.*

ROSARIO. [*Aside*] How my heart beats! I must control myself.

CANSECO. You see, these gentlemen have yielded to my persuasion, and consented to receive you in this house.

VICTOR. I am very grateful for their kindness. I shall return it by making this visit as short as possible, for I realize that my presence cannot be agreeable to all the members of this household.

RUFINA. [*In a low tone, to* VICTOR] Sit down.

VICTOR. Thank you, no.

DON CÉSAR. [*Alarmed*] What did he say?

VICTOR. Your daughter invited me to be seated, and I replied that it does not tire me to stand.

DON CÉSAR. Very well. Now if you desire to be brief, so do I. I will save your time by saying in advance that if the assistance which you desire, in addition to the ship, is reasonable . . .

VICTOR. Oh! I am not asking for assistance. I do not need it. Poor and nameless, alone in the world, I shall be able to find some spring in the midst of the desert that surrounds me. Gentlemen, you can give me no assistance, nor can I accept any. An error brought us together. The truth, or an appearance of truth, has separated us forever. Don César, I break off all relations with you, leaving you only my gratitude, since to you I owe my education, the little that I know, the little that I am.

DON JOSÉ. [*To* ROSARIO] Not bad.

ROSARIO. No indeed.

DON CÉSAR. Then . . .

CANSECO. [*Aside to* DON CÉSAR] He is not asking for help. Shall I tell him to be seated?

DON CÉSAR. No. [*To* VICTOR] Then what do you want? I don't understand. Have done, for your presence is torture to me. The sight of you, unfortunately, plunges me into a mad frenzy. You are innocent of the harm that you have done me, and still I cannot love you; you represent my disappointment, and still I cannot hate you. To relieve me of this horrible recollection, it is necessary that you go away, [*Rises*] a long, long way, to the ends of the earth.

CANSECO. [*Forcing him to sit down*] Calm yourself, my friend. Don't excite yourself unnecessarily. I will continue for you. [*To* VICTOR] The important thing, sir, is that you should leave Ficóbriga, and Spain,—and Europe. To that end, the generous gentlemen in whose name I speak, offer you a magnificent ship.

DON JOSÉ. Ah! Here is where I come in. This belongs to my reign. Victor, tell me simply whether you are willing to embark for the United States on the ship which I give you.

CANSECO. That's it.

VICTOR. I am deeply grateful for the offer of the venerable patriarch, and for the interest which he takes in me. But I do not accept it; I cannot accept.   [*All are astonished.*

ROSARIO. [*Aside, with emotion*] What noble pride! I love you for it.

DON JOSÉ. Do you mean that? What reason . . . ?

RUFINA. [*Aside*] Good! He will stay here.

ROSARIO. That is quite natural. Victor does not wish to withdraw from useful commerce a ship so handsome, so strong and safe.

VICTOR. The principal reason is that I will die rather than accept from this family, which I respect, the value of a pin.

CANSECO. Come, come.

DON CÉSAR. [*Aside*] What's that?

DON JOSÉ. Then what do you want of us? What have you come for?

VICTOR. To ask a question of Don César.

DON CÉSAR. Of me!

ROSARIO. [*Aside*] Now we have it!

VICTOR. I desire that Don César affirm or deny what the

notary here present has told me—a report, moreover, which is current throughout the town.

CANSECO. [*Aside*] I see.

DON CÉSAR. What?

DON JOSÉ. What?

VICTOR. [*To* DON CÉSAR] I desire to know whether it is true that you have proposed marriage to the Duchess of San Quentin.

DON CÉSAR. [*Alarmed and angry*] You . . . You . . . What's that to you?

DON JOSÉ. How dare you?

DON CÉSAR. Why, you . . .

VICTOR. I, I. I ask you if your proposal is a fact, because, I tell you now, I declare it to all of you, I oppose it.

DON CÉSAR *and* DON JOSÉ. You!

VICTOR. Yes, I, with all the will and determination I possess, I protest. The reason is very simple. I love Rosario.

>*Astonishment.* DON JOSÉ *and* DON CÉSAR *jump to their feet.*

DON JOSÉ. Good Lord!

RUFINA. [*Aside*] Heavens!

DON CÉSAR. Disgraceful! Be silent, you wretch! [*Looking at* ROSARIO *and* VICTOR, *wildly*] Rosario! Victor! Horrible, horrible! And you are silent, you do not protest!

DON JOSÉ. [*To* ROSARIO, *sitting down again*] But you . . .

DON CÉSAR. Begone from here. Rosario, crush him with your scorn.

DON JOSÉ. Come, girl, speak.

RUFINA. [*Going around to* ROSARIO'S *side*] Answer, Rosario.

>[ROSARIO *remains seated, motionless and silent.*

DON CÉSAR. But you . . . at least . . . Are you not indignant that this unfortunate . . . ? [*Seized by a horrible suspicion*] Perhaps . . . God, what an idea! [*Overcome by the thought*]

Say that this suspicion which has come into my head is absurd. . . . Speak quickly!

RUFINA. Speak.

VICTOR. [*Imploring*] Speak, in heaven's name.

DON JOSÉ. Come, what have you to say?

ROSARIO. [*Rises. All are expectant. Pause. In a solemn tone she speaks as follows*] I am of noble race, born in the highest rank. As a child, they taught me to recite the names of great men, princes, kings, whose heroic virtues adorned the history of my family. Well, my noble birth, the tradition of my race, the spiritual bond which unites my present humble state to the grandeur of my ancestors, makes it incumbent upon me to proceed in all the circumstances of life in accordance with the eternal dictates of honor, of justice, of conscience. I deprived this man of all the riches of the earth. He believes that my hand is the only compensation for his ill-fortune, and I give it to him, and with it my heart and soul.

[*Goes to* VICTOR's *side.*

DON CÉSAR. [*Beside himself*] Him, love him! Impossible!

VICTOR. [*Proudly*] She loves me, me alone.

DON JOSÉ. [*Praying*] In the name of the Father . . .

DON CÉSAR. [*Overcome, drops into his chair*] I must be crazy. The world is coming to an end, the universe is breaking into a thousand pieces. The descendant of kings . . . the nameless son of Sarah! An impossible alliance! Lucifer himself must have had a hand in it. Oh, no! Tell me it is a dream, a lie!

CANSECO. Be calm, my dear Don César, compose yourself.

VICTOR. Forgive me, it is not my fault.

DON CÉSAR. You have invaded my house, you have robbed me, carried off my hope, my happiness. I thank God for showing me that you are not my son!

[CANSECO *tries to calm* DON CÉSAR.

DON JOSÉ. [*Severely, taking* ROSARIO *by the hand*] Disturber of my home, even if my son's madness deserves this disillusionment, yours deserves the madhouse.

ROSARIO. Yes, my dear patriarch. Victor and I are two maniacs who are about to enter upon the incredible adventure of seeking life and happiness in ourselves.

DON CÉSAR. [*To* CANSECO, *anxiously*] What are they saying?

CANSECO. [*To* DON CÉSAR] She admits that she is crazy.

DON CÉSAR. [*Aloud*] And she throws her ducal coronet in the mud.

ROSARIO. My ducal coronet! The gold of which it was composed crumbled to powder, to a fine, almost impalpable flour. I mixed it with the milk of truth and from that refined and delicate mass I have made the bread of life.

DON JOSÉ. And now, Victor, since you are not going to America . . .

VICTOR. I am going.

DON JOSÉ *and* RUFINA. And you?

ROSARIO. I shall go too. To complete his existence, he needs a family, a well-ordered and tranquil home, the affection and companionship of a woman—and I shall be that woman, here, or in the uttermost corner of the earth.

VICTOR. [*Embracing her*] Which will be a heaven for me.

DON JOSÉ. Praised be the infinite Mercy!

VICTOR. Yes; ask heaven's favor for those poor emigrants.

DON CÉSAR. [*To* CANSECO] What are they saying? What are they talking about?

CANSECO. Nothing. It seems they are going together to the other world. [DON CÉSAR *listens to what follows.*

VICTOR. Through the influence of a Belgian engineer, a friend of mine, I am going to an industrial district in the state of Pennsylvania, as an emigrant. They require that I take my family, and here it is. We embark on the Royal Mail steamer, which stops at this port.

RUFINA. She arrives tonight.

VICTOR. And leaves tomorrow.

DON CÉSAR. [*Wildly*] She goes away with him. . . . She loves him! Hell raised on high, to the zenith, and heaven plunged into the depths of the abyss!

DON JOSÉ. You can't go away like that.

RUFINA. You have no time to get married.

DON JOSÉ. Wait, and . . .

ROSARIO. After what has happened, I cannot remain here an instant.

RUFINA. Where will you go?

VICTOR. The Belgian consul and his good wife will receive us, and will be the witnesses of our wedding.

ROSARIO. That solves it.

VICTOR. [*With emotion, drawing* ROSARIO *to him*] Come, my life, my dream, my inspiration.

CANSECO. [*Approaching the group in the center*] It is better that you should withdraw.

ROSARIO. [*To* DON JOSÉ] Good-bye.

DON JOSÉ. [*Sadly*] Farewell, my daughter. [ROSARIO *and* RUFINA, *in the center of the stage, kiss each other affectionately, and remain for a moment in close embrace. Then* RUFINA *bids farewell to* VICTOR, *who embraces her. During this mute scene,* DON JOSÉ, *taking* CANSECO'S *hand, says to him*] Ah! what desolation in my home! My son half mad; my granddaughter to become a nun when I pass on. . . . So ends this family.

CANSECO. And all your care and labor comes to naught.

DON JOSÉ. [*To* RUFINA, *who, after the farewells, returns to his side, weeping*] You are crying?

RUFINA. Yes, I love them both.

DON JOSÉ. My son . . . César . . .

DON CÉSAR. [*Rising, angrily*] Let this horrible nightmare come to an end. [*To* ROSARIO *and* VICTOR] Begone from here!

[*As if seeking consolation at his father's side*] Father, it is all over for me. I have no illusion, no hope but death.

DON JOSÉ. Come here. [*He throws one arm around* RU-FINA *and the other around* DON CÉSAR, *forming a group*] Let us stand close together, that our loneliness may be less sad.

RUFINA. They are going away forever.

VICTOR. Over the sea, to a new world.

ROSARIO. Let us turn our backs on the ruins of this one.
They go to the door at the back, turn, arm in arm, toward the stage and wave their free hands joyously.

ROSARIO *and* VICTOR. [*Together in firm, clear voice*] Good-bye!

DON CÉSAR. They have gone. It is the death of a world.

DON JOSÉ. No, my children, it is the birth of a world.

Curtain.

ANGEL GUIMERÁ

ANGEL GUIMERÁ was born in Catalonia, but went as a young man to Barcelona, where he has since remained. He soon became identified with the nationalist and separatist movements of Catalonia, and has always, at first through the medium of a periodical, then, more or less directly, through the medium of his plays, preached nationality and separation. After Guimerá's astonishing success with "María Rosa," his plays were translated—by Echegaray—into Spanish and played in Madrid, many of them by the famous Guerrero and Mendoza company. Of late years, however, for political reasons, Guimerá has not been popular outside his native province, where he is held in reverence by his followers. So great is his belief in nationalism that he never writes nor speaks in Spanish.

CHRONOLOGICAL LIST OF THE PLAYS OF ANGEL GUIMERÁ

Gala Placidia 1879
Judith de Welp 1883
Lo Fill del Rey 1886
Mar y Cel 1888
Rey y Monjo 1890
La Boja 1890
L'Anima Morta 1892
En Pólvora 1893
Jesús de Nazareth 1894
María Rosa 1894
Las Monjas de Sant Ayman 1895
La Feste del Blat 1896
Terra Baixa (Tierra Baja)[1] 1896
Mosseu Janot 1898
La Farsa 1899
La Eilla del Mar 1900
Arrán de Terra (Schivolando culla Terra)[2] 1901
La Pecadora 1902
Aygua que corre 1902
Lo Camí del Sol 1904
Andrónica 1905
Sol Solet 1905
La Miralta 1905

[1] *Terra Baixa* was translated as *Marta of the Lowlands* by Wallace Gillpatrick, with an introduction by John Garrett Underhill (Drama League Series, Doubleday, Page & Co., New York, 1914).

[2] Originally produced in Italian.

References: Introduction to *Marta of the Lowlands;* Manuel Bueno, *Teatro Español contemporáneo* (Biblioteca Renacimiento, Madrid, 1909); Joseph Yxart, *Prólech á las Poesías de Angel Guimerá,* 2d ed., Barcelona, 1905; *La Escena Catalana,* Barcelona, 1906 et seq.

DANIELA
(*La Pecadora*)

A DRAMA IN THREE ACTS
BY ANGEL GUIMERÁ

TRANSLATED FROM THE CATALAN BY
JOHN GARRETT UNDERHILL

PERSONS REPRESENTED

DANIELA

ANTONIA

MONSA

TOMASETA

PONA

HUGUETTE

JEANNE

ANNA

RAMON

DON JOAQUIM

M. ALBERT

RICHARD

MAX

ANDREW

VALENTINE

MICHAEL

Four girls, playmates of ANNA; *also Village People, Men, Women and Children*

The time is the present. The scene is laid in the mountains of northern Spain.

ACT I

Entrance hall of a farm-house on the outskirts of a small mountain village. A door to the right and another to the left. At the rear on the right a door opens upon the highway; at the rear on the left a second door opens upon a broad step or landing. A staircase ascends from this to the second story, and beneath it are placed a table and chairs. Through the outer door a number of whitewashed houses may be seen. Midday.

When the curtain rises, the stage is empty. The sound of a cradle, rocking, comes from the right and a woman's voice is heard singing:

> Mother of God, a little child
> Is laid upon thy breast,
> Best of the blessings of the world
> And of life's joys the best.
> Rest, little baby, rest!
> Rest! Rest!

After a moment, RAMON enters by the main door, followed by VALENTINE and MICHAEL. The song continues a little longer.

RAMON. I knew it would be so. Of course nothing has been done. [*To* VALENTINE] I told you to be ready before twelve o'clock.

VALENTINE. Humph! We will be soon enough; we began cleaning the pens and getting the corrals ready for the sheep before daylight.

189

RAMON. Before daylight? You did nothing until then? Is this the way to set an example to the men? What have you been doing all this time?

VALENTINE. Oh, going on with the spading and setting out the tomatoes; they were all broken down with the rain.

RAMON. Didn't I tell you to clean the pens out first? Suppose the sheep had come last night?

VALENTINE. They didn't come.

RAMON. But suppose they had.

VALENTINE. They didn't, just the same.

RAMON. But they will come.

VALENTINE. Yes, and the pens will then be clean.

RAMON. They will be clean! The pens will then be clean! About it, man, about it! Here, Michael, boy! Run along, run along! To work! To work!

MICHAEL. [*Without moving*] To work—hungry?

[*He looks wistfully toward the door on the left.*

RAMON. [*To* VALENTINE] Has any one been in since I went away?

VALENTINE. No one—that is, no one except the doctor. Nobody's sick, though.

RAMON. [*To* MICHAEL] What! Are you still here?

MICHAEL. I—I—haven't had my dinner yet.

RAMON. I haven't had mine either. Run along! When there is work to do, about it!

MICHAEL. Without my dinner?

RAMON. Pst! As if I didn't hear you!

Exit MICHAEL, *running out at the back.* ANNA *enters from the right.*

ANNA. Papa! [*Running up to him*] Papa!

RAMON. [*To* VALENTINE] Have they sent for the wine by Sumell?

ANNA. Papa! Papa!

[RAMON *runs his hand carelessly through her hair.*

VALENTINE. Oh, the wine?   Yes, they sent for the wine.

RAMON. Then why didn't you tell me about it?   Ola, man! When I ask you who's been here, you stand there like a blockhead, tilting back on your heels, without so much as opening your mouth.

ANNA. [*Running to the door on the right*] Mamma! Mamma!

VALENTINE. Of course they sent for the wine.

ANNA. [*Calling*] Here's papa!

RAMON. Who stood by and saw it was measured out?

ANTONIA *enters.   She goes straight up to* RAMON. ANNA *follows, jumping up and down.*

ANNA. Papa! Papa!

VALENTINE. Why, I did; I never moved from the spot.

ANTONIA. [*To* RAMON] How have you been getting on?

RAMON. Well, Antonia. [*To* VALENTINE] And who kept the count?   How many skins did it make?

ANTONIA. [*Dusting off* RAMON *with her hand*] You are all covered with dust.

VALENTINE. Anna kept the count.

RAMON. Anna? [*To* ANTONIA] So we've been trusting to a child, have we?   That is the way things are done in this house.

ANTONIA. I kept an eye on her, Ramón.

ANNA. I made a little dot for every skin.

ANTONIA. The poor dear!

RAMON. Antonia, I've just bought two droves of sheep. They'll be up from the village this afternoon.

ANTONIA. I hope they won't turn out like those that you bought last year.

RAMON. No fear of that.   It would take somebody to cheat me now, I can tell you.   I have eyes in my head.   A man doesn't have to learn a hundred times.   That old miser, Pardinas, came down from the village—he knows a sheep from a goat when he sees one—and he was looking over the flock.

As soon as he turned his back for a moment, up I stepped, and before he knew it I had struck a bargain for the lot. It didn't take me long, I can tell you.

ANTONIA. It won't take you long to want to get rid of them, either.

RAMON. [*Preoccupied*] Where is the boy?

ANTONIA. In the cradle.   He cried all night.

RAMON. Let me see the wine count.

ANTONIA. Valentine.   Where is the wine count?

> VALENTINE *makes a gesture, indicating that he does not know.*

ANNA. Didn't you bring me anything, father?

RAMON. Where is the count?   It is never safe for a man to go away from home. Everything is at sixes and sevens. *Santísima!* The count?   I won't put up with it any longer. And then they wonder that a man has a temper!

> ANTONIA *and* VALENTINE *run about looking for the count, opening the drawers of the table, looking in the closets, and in every place conceivable.*
>
> ANNA *retires to a corner and begins to play with an old ragged doll.*

ANTONIA. Mercy!   But we'll find it.   He's in a fine temper.

RAMON. That's it.   In a temper!   I am in a temper!   Can't you keep your heads?

VALENTINE. We'll find it, man.

RAMON. That fellow will drive me mad. [*To* ANTONIA] And you, too, running about the house like the rest of them, as if you had nothing at all to think about—as if you were all millionaires!

ANTONIA. Millionaires?

RAMON. [*Pounding on the table*] The count, I say!   Why don't you find the count?

ANTONIA. Do you know where the count is, child?

ANNA. What count? [RAMON *continues to pound on the table.*

ANTONIA. The count of the wine by Sumell.

ANNA. I put it in my pocket, mamma.

[*She draws the paper from her pocket, all crumpled up.*

ANTONIA. Praise be to God!

RAMON. Give it to me.

[*Taking it from* ANTONIA, *he begins to read.*

VALENTINE. [*To* RAMON] Now I remember. I gave it to her myself.

RAMON. [*Abstractedly*] You did? So. Go out and mind the sheep.   [*Exit* VALENTINE *at the rear.*

ANTONIA. [*To* ANNA] Was there ever such a pother?

ANNA. [*To* ANTONIA] He never brought one thing for me.

MONSA *enters.*

MONSA. Good - morning, Antonia. [*Seeing* RAMON] So Ramon's home again?

ANTONIA. [*Excusing herself*] Just a minute, Monsa. [*To* RAMON] I have something to tell you.

RAMON. [*With the count*] Let me run through this first. Here are twenty loads—correct; not a penny more, not a penny less. Ca! Who would ever have expected it would have turned out so, trusting to a child?

ANTONIA. I told you I was by.

ANNA. I did just as I was told, mamma.

[RAMON *continues to run through the paper.*

ANTONIA. Of course you did.

MONSA. That child has sense. I'd take her to help me with the school, Antonia, if she were only a little bit older.

RAMON. To help with the school, would you? You would be a likely one to teach her. What do you know, anyway? Because we send the children to you, you think you must be wise. Huh! She'd turn out a simpleton like yourself.

ANTONIA. That's a nice way to talk to Monsa. When the baby was sick, she came here and gave up everything to help us.

MONSA. I don't mind what he says.

ANTONIA. You oughtn't to be so rough, either, with the child. She loves her father.

RAMON. Have I nothing to do but listen to you talk? What a mess! I have been gone four days, and when I come home everything is wrong. [*He goes toward the door at the rear, pacing up and down, examining the account*] What a mess!

MONSA. Don't mind him, Antonia.

[*The two women converse apart.*

RAMON. [*Aside, still pacing up and down*] What? They haven't checked the count? Here, there are four skins short. Was there ever such a mess?

ANTONIA. [*Leading* MONSA *aside*] He's not well today.

MONSA. [*To* ANTONIA] What difference does it make?

RAMON. [*In a low voice*] Pst! Anna, Anna.

[*The child runs up to him.*

ANNA. Father!

RAMON. [*Aside, still pacing up and down*] What a mess! Women, women! [*He kisses* ANNA] They are no use at all. I'm off to the corrals.

He disappears. ANTONIA *retires for a moment to the room at the right.* MONSA *stands looking after her.*

ANTONIA. I wanted to see whether the baby was asleep.

MONSA. He's such a good child.

[ANNA *begins to play again with the doll.*

ANTONIA. It will be no miracle if he takes after his father.

MONSA. He is very fond of us all.

ANTONIA. Of course; but he's wrapped up in his work.

TOMASETA *enters.*

TOMASETA. I just ran in to hear the news about Daniela.

ANTONIA. Yes. I suppose everybody will be coming now.

MONSA. Poor Daniela!

ANTONIA. How did you hear about it?

TOMASETA. Valentine told Andrew, the shoemaker, while he was working on his shoes.

ANTONIA. Andrew the shoemaker is a cobbler of gossip.

TOMASETA. What do you mean?

ANTONIA. [*To* MONSA] Some foolishness of Valentine's.

PONA *enters.*

PONA. I am so busy today that I really haven't any time.

TOMASETA. So am I. We are whitewashing our house.

PONA. I had to hear, though, about Daniela.

ANTONIA. Well, it seems she's alive. There can be no doubt about that—though for a long time we never heard a word of her.

PONA. Valentine says that you've just had word.

ANDREW *enters, carrying an unfinished shoe.*

ANDREW. What does Ramón say about Daniela?

ANTONIA. I haven't had a chance to speak to him yet. You see we really don't know anything at all about her.

MONSA. [*Simply*] They were so fond of each other— Ramón and Daniela.

TOMASETA. [*Leaving the door*] I was looking for Ramón so as to be able to get out in time. He says that women are a nuisance in this house.

ANTONIA. Sit down a minute and I'll try to tell you everything I know. Yesterday afternoon I was standing out by the gate, when all of a sudden in comes the Doctor, and begins straight off to tell me about some letter which he had just received from a French doctor who wanted to know if this place was healthy; because he had a patient, a woman who had come from here, and who was sick, and who wanted to come home again to see if she could regain her health.

ANDREW. Was that all?

ANTONIA. I don't think there was anything more.

ANDREW. Hm! But how do you know who this sick woman is?

PONA. It may be—pst!—it may be they want to put up some game on us.

TOMASETA. Put up some game on us? They'd never put up a game on such a little place.

ANTONIA. No, for Daniela's name was mentioned in the letter.

ANDREW. Oh! Then that's a different matter.

TOMASETA. I supposed she was dead and buried long ago.

PONA. The hussey!

TOMASETA. That's what my husband says. I'd better go home to my whitewashing.

ANTONIA. You must have all known her. I didn't live in the village in those days. Of course she was a friend of yours.

TOMASETA. [Coldly] Hardly that.

PONA. [With disdain] We know her. She was a good deal older than we were.

MONSA. No, Pona; you were older.

TOMASETA. You ought to know, Monsa. You were a good deal older than she was—and than the rest of us, too, for that matter.

MONSA. Suit yourselves; it doesn't bother me.

ANTONIA. Ramón says she was twelve years old when she went away.

ANDREW. My wife says twelve or thirteen.

TOMASETA. She must be thirty-two by this time. Good-bye, girls.

PONA. Oh, more! More.

MONSA. She's exactly twenty-eight.

PONA. And I'm sure she looks it, after the life she has led.

ANDREW. Maybe it won't show, eh? In France, you know, they say the girls fix themselves up so that they look like new—yes, and a good deal fresher.

ANTONIA. Anna, run out and mind the boy. I thought I heard him cry.

[ANNA *stops playing with the doll and runs out.*

TOMASETA. [*To* ANTONIA] If she really does come back, don't know what we're going to do about it.

ANTONIA. That would be for Ramón to say.

TOMASETA. She's his first cousin; they used to play together.

PONA. I'd never want to look her in the face again.

ANTONIA. Nonsense! You don't think she'll ever come?

ANDREW. Perhaps she's starving to death.

TOMASETA. Who'd want to take her into their house?

PONA. Sick, and without a penny! There are places for such people without eating an honest woman out of house and home.

ANDREW. She might repay you with a "God bless you" at least.

ANTONIA. When it comes to that, it will be time enough to speak to Ramón about it.

TOMASETA. What do you think, Monsa?

MONSA. I? If Daniela should come back and no one else would have her, I'd take her in myself.

ANDREW. You? With your work?

MONSA. Yes.

PONA. I dare say you would take her in. But what would you give her to eat? How would you pay for the medicines?

MONSA. I'd show you. Everybody would help me. The mothers of the children at the school . . .

TOMASETA. [*Hotly*] They'd help you, would they? For that woman?

PONA. The men might. [*Laughing*]

ANTONIA. Don't talk like that, Pona.

ANDREW. When you took that woman into your house,

I'll tell you what would happen—the mothers would take their children away.

MONSA. But maybe she's penitent.   Maybe she's dying.

ANTONIA. Maybe she's reformed.

[ANDREW *laughs out loud.*

TOMASETA. Penitent?   Now I *am* going!

PONA. If she is penitent, it's because nobody wants her any more.

MONSA. I wouldn't let her starve, just the same.

[*They all laugh at her.*

ANTONIA. What are you laughing at?

MONSA. No, I say no!   No, I wouldn't give her up.   I'd sooner starve myself, I'd sooner die; that's the way I feel.

TOMASETA. You could tell she was never married; she talks like a fool.

PONA. Or worse.   Ay, Señor!

[ANDREW *laughs.*

MONSA. I know it.   I'm only a poor woman, an unfortunate.   I'm not like the rest of you.   But I would take her in —I'd not give her up.   [*She begins to cry.*

ANTONIA. Don't you mind what they say, Monsa.

MONSA. No, I don't mind; but I am so tired.   I have done my best.   I have done the best I could.

TOMASETA. She always takes things like this.

ANDREW. Well, Antonia was teasing, too.

PONA. To hear her you'd think we didn't have any consideration at all.

DON JOAQUIM *and* M. ALBERT *enter.*

DON JOAQUIM. Thanks be to God, here we are at last!

ANTONIA. The Doctor!

DON JOAQUIM. Good-afternoon, everybody. . . . What's the matter with Monsa?   What's the trouble, child?

MONSA. Nothing, Doctor.

DON JOAQUIM. Nothing? [*To the others*] What are you

making this woman cry for? Shame, shame on you! Isn't she worth all the rest of you put together? [*To* ANDREW, *who is about to speak*] Yes, and your prattling wife, too, in the bargain!

ANDREW. Better include me in the bargain, Doctor.

DON JOAQUIM. You idle fellow! . . . Come, come now, what's the matter? What have they been doing to you, Monsa?

MONSA. Nothing, Doctor; nothing. [*Rising*] I must be going back to school. There are too many children to be left in the care of a child.

> As she approaches the door, ANDREW *and the others pro-
> test that they did not wish to hurt her.* MONSA *shows
> that she is not offended, and passes out, drying her
> eyes. Meanwhile the dialogue proceeds.*

DON JOAQUIM. [*To* MONSA] Adios, adios! [*Then to* AN-TONIA] Is Ramón back yet?

ANTONIA. Just back, Doctor.

DON JOAQUIM. Then I would like to see him immediately.

ANTONIA. [*Calling*] Anna! [*To* DON JOAQUIM] Have you had your lunch? I hope there's nobody sick, Doctor.

> ANNA *enters from the right.*

ANNA. Mamma!

ANTONIA. Run and tell your father to come straight here. The Doctor is waiting with a strange gentleman.

DON JOAQUIM. And tell him to hurry. I am very busy this afternoon.

> ANTONIA *places chairs for the gentlemen.* ANDREW
> *and the others continue talking at the rear.*

TOMASETA. [*To* ANDREW] I'll do it, Andrew. I'll do it. [*To* DON JOAQUIM] Señor Doctor!

DON JOAQUIM. [*Thinking she is ill*] Well? What's the matter? What ails you? Come, come! Let me see.

TOMASETA. No, Señor, no!

PONA. No, Doctor, no; she isn't sick. But we all knew Daniela so well; we're dying to hear something about her.

DON JOAQUIM. Hm! I see. Well, I know nothing at all about her—nothing whatever. [*They retire.*

M. ALBERT. [*To the others*] Ah! So you knew Mademoiselle? [*With a slightly French accent*]

ANDREW. He's talking to us.

PONA. Yes, sir; we knew her.

TOMASETA. Did you know her, sir?

M. ALBERT. I did indeed!

> *The women go up to him to question him.* RAMON *is heard without, talking excitedly.*

PONA. Here's Ramón.

ANDREW. Hush! We want to hear about Daniela.

> [*He stops at the entrance of* RAMON.
> *Enter* RAMON.

RAMON. God be with you, Don Joaquím.

DON JOAQUIM. Ola, man! How are you? [*Aside to* ANTONIA] Send them away; send them all away. I want to speak with you alone.

> ANTONIA *dismisses* ANDREW *and the women, closing the door behind them.*

RAMON. Doctor, I'm expecting a drove of sheep that I've just bought in the village. I wish you could see the state that the pens are in. [*Turning to the others, he finds they have gone*] Where is everybody?

DON JOAQUIM. If you will let me have your attention for a moment, Ramón, I shall explain as briefly as I can what has brought us this afternoon. [*To* M. ALBERT] That is agreeable to you, is it not?

M. ALBERT. Perfectly, Señor Doctor.

DON JOAQUIM. Then I shall proceed. This gentleman has come from Paris with a message for you from a cousin, from . . .

RAMON. From a cousin? From—from Daniela?

M. ALBERT. Precisely. The Señor Doctor received a letter some days ago from a colleague in that city, and, as I believe, he has not yet condescended to answer it . . .

DON JOAQUIM. No; but that was for a good reason. It seemed to me that the question propounded by the Doctor was not likely to meet with a favorable answer.

RAMON. The question propounded by the Doctor? But I know nothing of any question.

ANTONIA. I tried to tell you, Ramón, when you first came in.

DON JOAQUIM. Kindly allow me to explain. The other day I received a letter from a physician in Paris, who is a great celebrity, informing me that your cousin had been lying for some time at the point of death, and that, as she was not improving in that city as rapidly as could be wished, it might be that she would make up her mind to return here to re-establish her health in this place. [*Addressing himself to* M. ALBERT] I believe that is correct?

M. ALBERT. Quite correct; except that you might add that whenever Mademoiselle makes up her mind to do a thing, it is her habit to do it immediately.

RAMON. [*To* DON JOAQUIM] Well?

DON JOAQUIM. I was asked further in the letter concerning the sanitary and climatic conditions of the place. I had intended replying to the distinguished physician . . .

M. ALBERT. Pardon. But you did not reply?

DON JOAQUIM. No.

M. ALBERT. Then it will be quite useless to do so now.

DON JOAQUIM. I should have to study the conditions first.

RAMON. [*To* DON JOAQUIM] Why didn't you speak to me about this letter before? Then you could have answered it at once.

DON JOAQUIM. But, man, you were away.

ANTONIA. [*Speaking for* DON JOAQUIM] He's going to tell you about it now.

DON JOAQUIM. It was a matter requiring some investigation —in fact, most thorough research.

RAMON. Then I will reply to the gentleman myself.

DON JOAQUIM. One moment, Ramón. First let me give you some notion of what my answer is going to be. I mean to explain to the physician that although I do not live in this village, fortunately I am able to assist him in what he desires to know because I am accustomed to visit it professionally from the neighboring town, which is, of course, my headquarters, a station on the railway, having telegraphic communication, and so on, and so on. [*The others begin to grow impatient*] Secondly, regarding the sanitary conditions of the place, considering them carefully from every point of view, I intend to write that I find them to be excellent, and that, take it all in all, I think the invalid may come whenever it may best suit her convenience to do so.

[M. ALBERT *laughs at the* DOCTOR.

RAMON. No, Don Joaquím, permit me. Not at all. Whether the village is healthy or not does not in the least concern me. But as to this woman's coming again into my house, I refuse absolutely to hear of it. [*To* M. ALBERT] You have my answer. It is the end of the matter. Say for me to—Daniela—that she shall never again set foot in my house. If she were in the last extremity, I would bar the door. Do I make myself clear?

M. ALBERT. I think I understand.

DON JOAQUIM. [*To* RAMON] But, it seems to me, friend, . . . [*Wishing to argue the point. They pause*] Well, after all, it's none of my business. Family matters are family matters, and that's all there is about it.

RAMON. Pardon, Don Joaquím, but this is not a family matter. It is a long time since Daniela was one of our family.

[*With growing emotion*] Why, whole years passed when we supposed that she was dead; then, at the last, along comes some chap and tells us he has seen her dancing somewhere in a hall, in a café, in I don't know what town in France . . .

M. ALBERT. In a café? That must have been a long time ago. [*Implying that she has risen in the world*]

RAMON. Yes, before I met my wife. And we have been married twelve years.

M. ALBERT. I can believe it. But now she never leaves Paris, unless to make some tour through Germany or Belgium . . . [RAMON *shrugs his shoulders.*

DON JOAQUIM. Well, well! Can it be possible? Adios, Antonia, adios!

ANTONIA. Adios, Señor Doctor.

M. ALBERT. [*To* RAMON] You see her condition is quite contrary to what you had supposed. [*They prepare to go.*

RAMON. [*Much offended, but restraining himself*] Then let those cure her who have made her ill. We have been happy here without her; she has been happy there without us.

DON JOAQUIM. [*To* M. ALBERT] Come, come! Let us go. [*Going straight to the door*] Why argue with such a fellow?

RAMON. If any one had said that but you, Doctor, I'd say to him . . .

DON JOAQUIM. Ha?

RAMON. That in coming here he was making extremely free with other people's business.

ANTONIA. Ramón!

DON JOAQUIM. How dare you? What right have you to talk to me like this? What do you know of life? You have no more than peeped at the world through the eye of a needle, you foolish fellow! Let me tell you, there are all sorts of creatures in the world—creatures that swim, creatures that fly, creatures that walk. We call the man a fool who cannot tell the fowl from the fish or the fish from the birds. But

there are greater differences between men, far greater!
Oh, I could teach you a few things! This fellow believes that
we are all like sheep that flock together, one just as the other,
living, feeding, dying the same, following the leader like
those he buys and sells and herds here upon the mountain.
We are all cast in one mould. The only question with him
is the care and pasturage of sheep. What's the use of talking
to such a fellow? Bah! Bring an unfortunate here? A useless burden! He's wrapped up in his business. No wonder
that he has prospered all these years. It's business, eh?
Good business? God bless such good business, man, and by
heaven, much may it profit you! Good-day, good-day!

[M. Albert *laughs at* Ramon.

Ramon. Stay, Don Joaquím! Stay! I don't want you
to go away like this. If I had spoken out—ah! But I had
no right. We've stood together through a lot of trouble,
Doctor; but this man, who does not know me—I don't
want him to go away and think I am a boor. And since he
knows that woman, I mean to tell him now, before he leaves
the house, with whom he has to deal.

Antonia. Be calm, Ramón.

Don Joaquim. No, let him speak. I prefer it so.

Ramon. Then listen. [*He shrugs his shoulders*] This woman,
who has made you believe that we are all unnatural folk,
who, alone in misery and distress, has led you to suppose that
we have abandoned her . . .

M. Albert [*Ironically*] But, sir, if she has led me to suppose nothing? If we do not in the least concern ourselves
about the matter?

Ramon. It's an absolute lie, the whole story. We have
not abandoned her. As a child she was left without father or
mother when she was seven years old. Her mother, a good
woman, was unfortunate in love, and set her heart on a
worthless fellow, one of those glib, smooth-tongued wretches,

half French, half Spanish, who hail from nobody knows where.
Well, one day they were married.   Years later, she died
from a blow that he gave her, and the man, for he was a
smuggler, was found dead one morning in a gully on the
French border, half across the line from Spain, slain in a
drunken brawl.   As for the girl, she was brought home to
us and she became to me—a sister.   I was just past six and,
as I told you, she became to me a sister.   [*Becoming more
excited*] But she was a very strange child, always making a
great outcry, passionate and wild, impetuously stamping
and weeping about, so that one day my father went to lay
hands on her to control her; and, because I defended her
and held him off, he became angry with me, till, choking
with rage, he could no longer bear to see her in the house.
She, seeing how his passion had possessed him, for she was
very near thirteen then and seemed much older, one day,
when a party of mountebanks or jugglers were passing through
the village, disappeared, and when it came to be vesper
time we could not find her.   Nowhere Daniela!   I ran through
the streets distracted—everywhere about.   At first I thought
I should go mad, for I feared she had fallen from some cliff
or that the rapid current of the river had carried her away.
I wanted to kill myself, believing that she was dead.   We
had lived so much together I did not really know her; I was
too young to understand.   Like a fool, for days I wandered
through the villages and towns, until, at last, one night I
learned that she had been seen crossing the frontier in a
tartana with those same mountebanks, laughing, chattering
there on the seat beside them, carousing in their arms, and
shamelessly making merry.   And this, this woman—this is
she, that Daniela you know, for whom I would have given
up my life, and who has never once since so much as troubled
herself to think of me, no, not once, nor of her home.   And
now that she finds herself sick and poor, without resources,

cast-off, rejected, despised, she has the shamelessness to propose to return home again to me and present herself again in my house. Ah! How does it appear to you now, gentlemen? Is it another story? Let her die and be buried in the deepest hole in the ground as befits such a thing, rather than that after what has happened, she should again enter my house. [*Much excited*] I have my wife, I have my children, we are happy because we believe in God and have done wrong to no man, no, not in all our lives, but good—nothing but good—and that you all can bear witness, and Monsa.

ANTONIA. Yes, Ramón, good, nothing but good. They see how it is.

DON JOAQUIM. Holy Mother! And all this happened fifteen years ago!

ANTONIA. [*To* RAMON] Say no more about it.

M. ALBERT. I still think that we labor under a misapprehension. From what I hear, the gentleman takes it that Mademoiselle is poor; that she may become a burden upon him; but it is quite the contrary. Mademoiselle is rich . . .

RAMON. Rich? So much the worse! What is that to me?

M. ALBERT [*Cynically*] Frankly I do not understand.

RAMON. How did she make this fortune?

M. ALBERT. As one makes fortunes. Pst! As best one can.

DON JOAQUIM. [*To* M. ALBERT] My dear sir, we really must be going.

RAMON. [*To* M. ALBERT] You attempt to defend her? Now that you know the worst—unless it be the life she has led afterward.

M. ALBERT. But if these things were true, she surely would have told me. Who do you think I am?

[*Turning on* RAMON.

DON JOAQUIM. [*Wishing to lead him away*] Señor!

RAMON. Yes, take him away, Don Joaquím. Take him away. Enough!

M. Albert. [*To* Don Joaquim] I see now in what light they regard me. [*Always cynically*]

Don Joaquim [*To* M. Albert, *going*] And we had as well understand each other. I receive a letter from a physician in Paris. Very well! Then you ask me to make arrangements for an invalid who is presently to arrive, and to accompany you to this house. Very well! I have done so, and I have fulfilled my obligation in the matter.

M. Albert. You have, and for my part I wash my hands of it.

Don Joaquim. And you do very well to do so.

> *Meanwhile* Ramon *is speaking with* Antonia, *who endeavors to quiet him.*

M. Albert. As a servant of Mademoiselle's I undertook this charge solely in order to oblige her. I have concluded my mission, and I am done.

Ramon. We are all done.

Don Joaquim [*To* M. Albert] And, my dear sir, we have also concluded our business. [M. Albert *bows to the* Doctor.

M. Albert. I have, however, one piece of information for you. [*To* Ramon] Mademoiselle will presently be here.

Ramon. You will advise her that she cannot come.

M. Albert. I? When Mademoiselle thinks a thing it is as good as done. By the last advice, she had already left Paris direct for Barcelona. In fact, she may be here now. —Let them digest that if they can. [*Aside*]

Ramon. Good-afternoon, Doctor.

Don Joaquim. Good afternoon, Ramón.

M. Albert. [*To* Ramon] Good-afternoon.

Ramon. [*As they near the back*] God give you better employment, gentlemen.

M. Albert [*Laughing*] Thanks, thanks.

> M. Albert *offers his hand;* Ramon *makes a movement to accept it, but then draws back.*

RAMON. His hand! What next?

> [*Exit, laughing nervously.*

M. ALBERT. [*To* DON JOAQUIM] I suppose you have no objection to my returning to the village in your tartana?

DON JOAQUIM. [*Going*] It will not trouble me.

> [M. ALBERT *and* DON JOAQUIM *go out.*

ANTONIA. Ay, Señor!

> [*Exit to the room on the right.*
> *Enter* MONSA *and* ANNA *by the outer door.* MONSA
> *is leading* ANNA *by the hand. They come forward
> slowly, and are audible before they appear.* MONSA
> *is repeating some lines of the Song of St. James of
> Galicia.*

MONSA. [*Entering*] "It was like a miracle sent from heaven."

ANNA. Like a miracle sent from heaven.

MONSA. "One of God's miracles."

ANNA. One of God's miracles. Tell me the rest of it, some other day, won't you?

MONSA. Listen, child. "They untied the young man."

ANNA. They untied the young man.

MONSA. Yes.

ANNA. Then they tied him?

MONSA. No, child. They untied him. And the little girl ...

ANNA. Did they untie her?

MONSA. She was untied already.

ANNA. I thought it was the little boy who was untied.

MONSA. So it was. But that was after, child.

ANNA. After what?

MONSA. After they untied him. If you don't pay attention, Anna, I won't tell you another word of the story.

ANNA. Haven't I been paying attention, Monsa?

MONSA. Not a bit of it. And you've fought all day long with Filomena.

ANNA. Because you asked her to help you. I tell you nobody is going to fight on the days you ask me to help.

MONSA. Except you and Filomena.

ANNA. Yes; I know. Untied who, Monsa?

MONSA. Untied who? [*Catching herself*] How can I tell, Anna? You ask so many questions. You've got me all mixed up in the story.

ANNA. [*Running up to the doll, which is lying in a chair*] Oh, the poor dear! The poor dear! Look, Monsa, look! Here, take her. And here's the stuff for her dress.

MONSA. Bring it to me, Anna. Poor thing, she'll catch cold.   [*She takes the doll.*

ANNA. She will catch cold.

MONSA. Shall we make her coat, Anna?

ANNA. Yes! A great big coat, because she's so big herself. Here's the scissors; and let's make her slippers, too.

MONSA. [*Busy cutting*] Of course! A pair of slippers.

ANNA. And we'll get her married, Monsa. Who will we have her marry, though? Dearie me! Who will we have her marry?

MONSA. That will be for her to say.

ANNA. For her? Oh, she never says anything! She'd marry anybody. Monsa, why won't you let me take her to school?

MONSA. School is no place for dolls.

ANNA. I'll tell you who she'll marry, Monsa. [*Clapping her hands*] That little kid of Andrew's; that little kid on the hill!

MONSA. No!

ANNA. What a pair they'd make! But he's littler than she is, Monsa, not half so big.

MONSA. He won't be able to hurt her then.

ANNA. Oh, he's lots too little to buck.—Monsa, don't you ever mean to get married?

MONSA. Mean to get married? What nonsense you do talk!

ANNA. [*To the doll*] You do talk such nonsense, child! Monsa . . .

MONSA. [*Counting the stitches*] Wait, I have only four more stitches.

ANNA. [*To the doll*] Wait, you chatterbox! Monsa!

MONSA. What is it?

ANNA. Haven't you ever been married, Monsa?

MONSA. Never.

ANNA. What? Never?

MONSA. Never.

ANNA. Get married then. Get married, Monsa. [MONSA *laughs*] Why haven't you ever been married, Monsa?

MONSA. I—I— Anna, how can I tell?

VALENTINE *enters by the outer door and goes upstairs.*
MONSA *begins to sew a pocket on the dress.*

ANNA. [*Seizing the dress*] No, no! I don't want a pocket. No!

MONSA. Yes, child, yes; she must have a pocket.

ANNA. No. Because she's a lady, a real lady, Monsa. She wouldn't like it.

MONSA. Child, let go.   [ANNA *tries to take the doll.*

ANNA. It'll make her mad!

MONSA. Mercy, how you pull!

ANNA. I don't want a pocket! I won't have a pocket.

          [*She takes the doll.* VALENTINE *comes downstairs.*

MONSA. Valentine, where have you been? Your face is all flushed.

VALENTINE. Eh? Down by the gate, Monsa, making a *duro.* I never saw such a bright one before.

MONSA. A *duro?* A whole *duro?*

VALENTINE. A whole *duro.* Uy! See it shine. A lady gave it to me.

MONSA. [*Going on with her sewing*] Who gave it to you?

VALENTINE. How do I know who it was? Ramón told me to go down to Pujal and look after the sheep. The first thing I knew, two ladies got out of a carriage . . .

MONSA. A carriage? [*Surprised*]

VALENTINE. Yes, I just told you—a carriage. When I got there, there was a carriage at the end of the street and two ladies were just getting out of it. And the handsomest of them called to me and asked me where I came from, and when I told her from Ramón Anglada's, she began to clap her hands and laugh—yes, laugh and call out, "A boy from Ramón's! A boy from Ramón's!" as if she'd gone clean crazy.

MONSA. [*Startled*] Suppose it should be Daniela?

ANNA. Who's Daniela?

[MONSA *gathers up the doll's clothes.*

VALENTINE. Hm! Daniela is poor, and this lady gave me a *duro* for nothing. Now I'm not going back to Pujal to look after the sheep.

[*Exit* VALENTINE *at the rear. Enter* ANTONIA.

ANTONIA. What's the matter with Valentine?

MONSA. Antonia, two strange ladies have just come to the village.

ANTONIA. Two ladies? What do you mean?

MONSA. If we thought she'd really started, it might be, Antonia . . .

ANTONIA. *Santísima!* You don't mean it, Monsa!

MONSA. But if she hasn't left Paris . . .

ANTONIA. No, no; it's she; it is she, Monsa. She's right here. That Frenchman said so.

MONSA. If it should only be!

ANTONIA. If she comes here, Ramón won't have her. God help us!

MONSA. If it should only be! It must be, it must be, Antonia! She asked for Ramón immediately.

ANTONIA. Monsa!

ANNA. [*At the door*] Mamma! Mamma! Two ladies are coming up the road.

MONSA. I'd better go, Antonia.

ANTONIA. No, don't leave me, Monsa. [ANNA *starts to run away*] Anna! Don't you go.

MONSA. She always loved me because I was lonely like herself.   [*Meanwhile* ANNA *has gone back to the door.*

ANTONIA. Anna!

ANNA. Here they are! Mamma, here they are! They're coming in!

MONSA. [*By the door*] It is she. What a lady she has grown to be!

          [*She makes a movement to go, but is detained by* ANTONIA.

ANTONIA. Don't leave me, Monsa. Ramón . . .

MONSA. Shall I tell them not to come in?

          The LADIES *are heard talking, without, however, being seen.*

ANTONIA. For mercy's sake, not before me! Say nothing.

MONSA. I wouldn't have known her. How good it is to see her back!

ANTONIA. Hush! They're here.

          ANTONIA *draws* MONSA *to the right, away from the door.*
          ANNA *remains where she is, further to the front.*
          Enter DANIELA *and* JEANNE.

DANIELA. No, I don't know. I can't say for certain. . . . It looks just the same as it used to outside, except that everything seems so much smaller. [*Abruptly, with pleasure*] Ah! Yes! This is the place. Yes, yes! One day I fell down those stairs. I remember it as if it had been yesterday. Ramón's father, my uncle, used to thump down them so slowly—one step at a time—pam, pam, pam! It took Ramón just four leaps, and then we would be off together, in rooms and out again, all over the house. Ah! How good it feels to be back again! But what a dreadful journey! [ANNA *bursts out laughing*] Who is this child laughing? [*She notices the others also*] Ah!

MONSA. Good—good-afternoon.

ANTONIA. Good-afternoon, lady.

DANIELA. Good-afternoon. Do you know I wouldn't let anybody show me the way? We left the carriage at the head of the street. I said, see if you can find the house yourself, and I did find it myself. Didn't I find it, Jeanne?

JEANNE. You did, Madam.

DANIELA. But I know that it has grown smaller. Why, it used to be so big there never was any end to it! Where is Ramón?

ANTONIA. He's coming, lady.

[*She speaks with* MONSA, *uneasily.*

DANIELA. [*To* JEANNE] You didn't think that it would look like this, did you? But there is health here. [*Looking about and breathing deeply*] Health in every breath!

ANTONIA. Anna, run and call your father.

[ANNA *stands as transfixed, looking at* DANIELA.

DANIELA. [*Raising her voice*] Ramón! Ramón! [*To* ANTONIA *and* MONSA] You can't imagine how good it feels to call that name again.—Ramón!

MONSA. We didn't know, Señora . . .

DANIELA. That I was coming? No, of course not. [*To* JEANNE] My heart just leaps within me. Why, I can remember a thousand things that happened when I was so high!

ANTONIA. [*To* MONSA] I'm going out.   [*Exit* ANTONIA.

DANIELA. [*To* JEANNE] I lived here many years. [*Laughing*] Who ever would have thought it? I never could have died happy without coming here again.—Look! See her standing there. [*To* ANNA] Come here, child!

MONSA. Go and speak to the lady.

[ANNA *goes up to* DANIELA.

DANIELA. She is well brought up.

ANNA. Yes, ma'am.

DANIELA. What is your name, little girl?

ANNA. I'm Anna. [*Evidently astonished that there is any one who does not know her*]

DANIELA. [*Laughing*] Anna! [*To* JEANNE] She says she's Anna.

MONSA. She's Ramón's daughter.

DANIELA. Ah? Has he so old a child? He is married, then?

MONSA. Yes.

DANIELA. And you—you are his wife?

MONSA. Oh, no! I'm—don't you remember me? I'm Monsa—at the school . . .

DANIELA. [*Trying to recollect*] Monsa, Monsa—Ah! I have such a memory!

MONSA. [*Disappointed*] You don't remember?

DANIELA. No. As a child were you always very pert, very precocious?

MONSA. No, I was always very poor. But I used to think a great deal of you, a very great deal. You don't remember?

[ANNA *makes a sign, asking permission to show her doll.*]

DANIELA. Yes, of course. Bring it here. [*Laughing*] If it doesn't look just like a person! Anna, I am going to buy you a fine doll, a very fine doll. [*To* JEANNE, *smiling*] She's Anna! [*Then seriously*] But it doesn't seem that it can be. Here I am again happy, and yet I can scarcely keep from bursting into tears. So many years passed when I never once thought of this place, and now it seems to me that if I don't see Ramón directly something will happen to me.

MONSA. Sit down.—Here's a chair.

DANIELA. Jeanne, quick, quick!

JEANNE *gives* DANIELA *a bottle of salts, which she takes from a bag which she carries with her. Enter* ANTONIA.

ANTONIA. He's coming, Monsa; they've told him.

[*She is much agitated.*

MONSA. Does he know she's rich?

ANTONIA. He'll send her away.

MONSA. He couldn't do it!

[*A voice at the door.* MONSA *pauses.*

ANTONIA. Here he is.

MONSA. I'd better go.

DANIELA. Eh? Ramón? [*They nod their heads*] Is it Ramón? Happiness at last! [*Breathing heavily*]

    Enter RAMON.

RAMON. Where is she? Where? . . .

DANIELA. Ramón! [*Throwing her arms about his neck and giving him a kiss*] Ramón of my soul! Ramón!

RAMON. [*Throwing her off*] What is this? God!

[MONSA *prevents* DANIELA *from falling, supporting her.*

DANIELA. Oh!

MONSA. [*Aside*] The brute!

ANTONIA. Ramón! What have you done?

RAMON. Now she remembers her home—now, when there's no place for her in it!

MONSA. [*To* JEANNE] Help her—help her here. The brute! Let her sit down.

[ANTONIA *also goes to help* DANIELA.

DANIELA. He pushed me away! He threw me off! What did I ever do to him? It cannot be Ramón; no, for he loved me, and when they used to vex me he would defend me; yes, and he would cry with rage himself! Jeanne, why didn't I stay in France to die? You told me not to come here—no one would want me here. And they do not want me! No, no! [*With desperation*] No, I'll not die here. Out, out! I must leave this house! Into the free, the open air! . . . [*She drops back, falling into the chair*] I cannot; I am too weak! I cannot.

MONSA. [*Aside*] Has the man no heart?

ANTONIA. [*To* MONSA] Speak to him, Monsa.

> MONSA *continues helping* DANIELA, *without hearing* ANTONIA. ANTONIA *turns to* RAMON *and endeavors to dissuade him from sending* DANIELA *away.*

DANIELA. [*To* MONSA] Are you crying, too? What makes you cry?

MONSA. They hurt you so.

DANIELA. Look at me now; look at me straight in the eye.

MONSA. Poor Daniela!

DANIELA. Now I know you—when you cry I know you. You were always crying in the old days when you used to help me. Monsa! Monsa!   [*They embrace, weeping.*

ANNA. [*Speaking lowly*] Papa!

MONSA. Yes, yes. It is I! It is I!

DANIELA. Monsa! Monsa!

ANNA. Papa! Don't let that lady go away; she's going to buy me a new doll.

ANTONIA. [*To* RAMON] You see how weak she is; let her stay a little while.

> [RAMON *is seated; his features are rigid.*

MONSA. [*Going up to* RAMON] Ramón, Ramón! [*He does not move*] Listen, Ramón!

ANNA. [*To* ANTONIA] She's not going away?

ANTONIA. [*To* RAMON] For pity's sake, Ramón, don't behave like this. Say something to comfort the poor woman.

RAMON. Abandoned woman!

> ANTONIA *tries to divert* DANIELA *so that she may not hear the words of* RAMON.

MONSA. Hush!

RAMON. [*To* MONSA] Abandoned—yes! You'll never know the havoc she has wrought with me. No, nor will she ever know!

> DANIELA *leaves the chair, supported by* JEANNE. ANTONIA *endeavors to console her.*

Monsa. But she's ill, she's faint, Ramón. [Ramon *shrugs his shoulders*] Let her stay a little while! Till tomorrow!

Ramon. You don't know what you are asking, Monsa. Better she were dead!

Monsa. Have you no feeling, man?

Ramon. How do you know what I feel?

Monsa. Think of your children, the love that you bear them . . .

Ramon. My children? Ay! You don't know what you are saying, Monsa. Let her go! Let her go!

> *As he finishes speaking, in a low voice, his eyes meet those of* Daniela, *who is approaching him.*

Daniela. Say nothing more to him, Monsa. I am going away. [*To* Ramon] But before I go, I must have one look at you, for it is fourteen years since I have seen you. [*He is about to speak, but she prevents him*] Yes—it was my fault, I know it; all the fault was mine. I do not wish to excuse myself. All those years after I had left you I knew that I did not deserve to have you take me back. And now you need not take me back.

Ramon. But woman!

Daniela. Woman? Yes, woman,—say it,—say the worst! I do not care. But do not turn your eyes away to insult me. Look at me; for I like to have you look at me, for then I know it is the old Ramón! Yes, you—you, the Ramón that was a boy with me! [Ramon *makes a gesture of dissent and seats himself, turning his face away, scarcely conscious that he does so*] The old Ramón of former years with whom I used to play, and who used to run and romp with me, and tumble over and over until we had to stop for want of breath, and lie there exhausted, laughing, on the ground. How I used to call you when you came home past the aloes from the wood! Ramón! Just like that—Ramón!

> Ramon *makes a gesture as if the old affection were reborn.*

MONSA. [*Fearing that he is about to strike* DANIELA] For pity's sake!

DANIELA. And then, when he came, that old Ramón, how I always ran to meet him! Ramón, how many violets I have picked with you! Ramón, what cherries from the trees! And then I always made them sweeter by first tasting them myself. And then—the partridge nest! Ramón! The partridge nest! How the little birds ran out, splashing in the water down the stream, and how we used to skip after them, poor little things, to catch them through the tall marsh grass! And when we caught them, Ramón, do you remember?— we always let them go again, to play there, happy, underneath the trees. And then, and then—one day, there came a time when I too ran out and fled down the stream as they. And it seemed to me that I had wings—and I soared I know not where! And at last I felt myself wounded, crippled and sore and sad, and then, Ramón, like them I turned, and flew back home again to my nest, as they would have done— home again to my nest—straight, straight home!

RAMON. Straight home? There came a time when you ceased to care for your home, or for my father, or to respect yourself. And now, when misfortune overtakes you, back you come. Through all these years you never so much as once thought of this house—no, not once! Don't look at me like that; that is the way you used to look at me before you went away! [*Growing excited*] Daniela! Unhappy woman! Ungrateful, unkind! [*He goes up to her as if to strike her.*

DANIELA. Don't say that! Don't abuse me; no, Ramón. No, I am going away, I am going now. You will never see me any more. Be happy—happy as you always were!

MONSA. [*Going up to her*] Daniela!

DANIELA. Jeanne, take me back to the train—to Paris. Take me back to Paris! For Ramón will have it. He turns me away; he will have it so!

ANNA [*To* ANTONIA] And my doll?

MONSA. Ramón!—He is crying!

RAMON. [*To* MONSA] Let her stay, but don't tell Antonia that I told you so.   [MONSA *runs to tell* DANIELA.

ANTONIA. [*Going up to* RAMON] She can stay?

RAMON. [*To* ANTONIA] I don't know. Settle it among yourselves. But at most until tomorrow; only till tomorrow.

DANIELA. [*To* MONSA] Ay, *Madre mía!* But I am glad to hear it!—Where is Ramón?

MONSA. Say nothing to him now.

> *Enter* VALENTINE.

VALENTINE. The sheep are here.

RAMON. The sheep? Good!—Antonia, where's the boy? I haven't seen him.

> [*He covers his face with his hands, as though dazed.*

ANTONIA. This is the way that a man falls in love. [*Aside.*

> [*Exeunt* RAMON *and* ANTONIA *to the room on the right.*

DANIELA. Ah! I am so happy! Jeanne, where are the trunks? The trunks ought to be here.

> JEANNE *disappears at the back, returning a few minutes later.* TOMASETA, PONA, ANDREW *and other village people enter.*

TOMASETA. Ay! Is this the lady, Monsa?

MONSA. Yes. Don't say a word; she's rich.

ANDREW [*To* MONSA] Hm, I thought so—she must be very rich. There's a whole cart-load of boxes at the door.

PONA. [*To* DANIELA] God keep you, Señora.

> [DANIELA *returns a formal bow.*

TOMASETA. Good-afternoon.

DANIELA. [*To* MONSA] It seems I was expected.

MONSA. A strange gentleman brought word that you were coming. He was here with the Doctor this afternoon.

DANIELA. Gracious! But what has become of him? I have not seen him anywhere.

> *Two men enter, carrying a large trunk. The townspeople comment to one another upon the luggage as it is brought in, moving hither and thither examining the boxes and bags, always with the greatest curiosity.* MONSA *endeavors to restrain them.*

PONA. [*To* MONSA] If we can do anything for the Señora . . .

MONSA. No, nothing.

> M. ALBERT *enters.*

M. ALBERT. Thank heaven! I have found her at last!

DANIELA. [*Reproving him*] So, you are here, are you? Do I send you ahead so that you will leave everything for me to do? You attend to nothing. Why were you not at the station?

M. ALBERT. I did not think that you would be on that train.

TOMASETA. [*To* DANIELA, *who takes no notice of her*] If we can do anything . . .

DANIELA. [*To* M. ALBERT] You never think, you never act, you never accomplish anything.

> [*More trunks are carried in.*

M. ALBERT. Pardon. But I saw the physician . . .

DANIELA. What do I care about the physician? I am here now. Dismiss the carriage, go to your lodgings and bring me Frou-Frou immediately; yes, bring me Frou-Frou. I was homesick for her the whole journey.

ANDREW. If you should happen to need a large house . . .

TOMASETA. Or one just whitewashed today, Señora, till it looks like new . . .

> DANIELA *draws out some banknotes which she hands to* M. ALBERT.

DANIELA. Here, take these, and see that everybody is paid. I shall remain where I am for the present myself. Later I mean to build a chalet near by; I noticed a splendid site on the road from the station. "Villa Daniela!" [*Addressing the company, much pleased*] How does that sound to you? "Villa Daniela!" Tomorrow I shall see an architect, for we must make haste. We have no time to lose. [*Everybody approves of the plan*] On the day it is completed the whole village shall be there. Ay, but we shall have a festival! [*She pauses, seeing* RAMON *at the door on the left, to which he has come looking for* MONSA] We shan't be enemies? No, Ramón?

[*Coaxingly to* RAMON.

RAMON. [*Much moved*] No.

DANIELA. But friends?

RAMON. Yes, friends.

DANIELA. Forever. Friends forever? Yes?

[*Still pleadingly.*

RAMON. Yes—yes. Forever.

Enter ANTONIA *from the room on the right. She goes straight up to* RAMON *and* DANIELA.

RAMON. This is my wife—Antonia; the mother of . . .

[*He points to* ANNA *and to the room where the cradle is.*

DANIELA. [*To* ANTONIA, *deeply moved*] We shall be friends, I know.

ANTONIA. [*Also much affected*] I only want to please Ramón.

MONSA *goes up to* DANIELA. ANTONIA *opens the door of the room at the back and directs* JEANNE *to have the trunks carried in.*

RAMON. [*To* VALENTINE] What was that you told me about the sheep?   [*Looking straight at* DANIELA.

VALENTINE. The sheep are here. Shall I send them to the pens?

RAMON. Yes, to the pens. Good, good! Monsa! Monsa!

MONSA. What is it, Ramón?

Great confusion at the back while the boxes are being carried into the other room. Much curiosity on the part of all.

RAMON. [*To* MONSA] God grant that no harm may come of it—of Daniela's being in the house, I mean.

DANIELA. [*Taking leave of* M. ALBERT] Above everything, remember Frou-Frou, for I must have her; remember, I must have her.   [M. ALBERT *goes out.*

MONSA. [*Surprised*] Why, Ramón!

RAMON. You're a good woman, an angel, Monsa! [*Enjoining silence*] I loved Daniela.

MONSA. But that was a long time ago.

RAMON. I loved her! I loved her! I tell you I loved her!

MONSA. [*Horrified*] Ramón!

RAMON. [*Rushing up to* DANIELA] Daniela! What do you want, Daniela? What is it you desire?

DANIELA. [*Surrounded by the people*] I have come home to stay. We will sit together at dinner. [*Radiantly happy*] It will be a feast day for us all!

MONSA. [*Apart*] But he loves Antonia. I know he loves Antonia!

> As the curtain is about to fall, a man enters by the outer door, carrying a trunk that stands as high as his shoulder. Above the chatter of the people rise the excited tones of RAMON and the happy voice of DANIELA.

Curtain.

ACT II

The same. The cradle stands to the right with the child sleeping in it. It is late afternoon. ANTONIA is seated beside the cradle, sewing. Presently MONSA enters from the rear. When DANIELA is heard speaking, it is from the porch, outside upon the left, without, however, being seen. As the curtain rises a number of workmen may be heard at a distance, busily cutting stone. MONSA hesitates a moment after entering before presenting herself.

MONSA. Why do you let the baby sleep all day, Antonia? He'll surely keep you awake tonight.

ANTONIA. Yes, I'm afraid he will.

MONSA. Of course he will.

ANTONIA. Yesterday Ramón told me the same thing.

MONSA. Whenever a man finds something interfering with his sleep, it doesn't take him long to complain about it.

ANTONIA. It isn't that, Monsa; Ramón never complains about anything any more.

MONSA. Don't you believe it, Antonia; it's because he's so taken up with the new house. He's had to tend to everything himself; that's what makes you think so. No wonder, either, with Daniela so impatient to get into it!

ANTONIA. Humph! Maybe. Is school over yet?

MONSA. Yes, for today. I just finished taking the little children home, and now I'm done till tomorrow. Where's Anna? I didn't see her at all this afternoon.

ANTONIA. Oh! She's busy with Daniela and Ramón. I told her I wanted her to stay with me, too. I never saw any-

223

thing like it, Monsa—that woman runs away with everything that comes near her—absolutely everything.

MONSA. The men are working in double shifts. How have they ever been able to get through so much in such a little while? It's only a month today.

The click of the stone-cutting becomes less frequent and presently dies away.

ANTONIA. Only a month? They have done a good deal.

MONSA. Daniela wants to hire everybody. By the way, she told me when I came in to tell you they were at supper; they're waiting for you.

ANTONIA. [*Significantly*] Yes, now we have supper in broad daylight, and out on the porch, because she wants it there, so as to be able, she says, to see the sun set! Every meal is a party.

MONSA. She's certainly a good deal better.

ANTONIA. I dare say you're not so sorry for her now, Monsa.

MONSA. I'll always be sorry for Daniela, not because she's rich, but on account of all the trouble that she's had to go through.

ANTONIA. And aren't you sorry for me, Monsa?

[*Bursting into tears.*

MONSA. For you? Why should I be sorry for you?

ANTONIA. Because I am the unhappiest woman in the world, Monsa! Because Ramón is no longer the same to me —he's another man. That woman has stolen him away— like a thief!

MONSA. For pity's sake, Antonia!

ANTONIA. No, I don't know Ramón any more. He was always hasty, he had a temper, but he was kind to me; but now he never even looks at me, he never speaks to me, he doesn't care for anything in all this house—except that woman! That woman! She is all he thinks about.

MONSA. Nonsense, Antonia! But it isn't so. He only wants to finish the house so that she can get away to live in it.

ANTONIA. You're trying to console me, Monsa. No, it is so. You don't like the way Ramón behaves any better than I do.

DANIELA. [*Calling outside*] Antonia! Come to supper!

MONSA. There! She's calling you. Go along.

ANTONIA. Let her call. I don't mean to go. I can't be pleasant to that woman any longer.

MONSA. That's not the way to talk.

ANTONIA. I'm going to tell Ramón that he's got to send her away, or I'll take the children and go back to my father's. I'm tired of pretending to be nice. To think that we should have all this trouble because she's staying in the house!

[*Crying bitterly.*

MONSA. Whatever else you do, don't be foolish enough to say anything to Ramón about it. Sleep on it till tomorrow. It won't seem so serious then after all.

ANTONIA. Are you trying to defend Ramón?

MONSA. [*Offended*] Pshaw! I'm only trying to prevent you from making yourself unhappy. Go on out to supper.

ANTONIA. But Monsa, what have you to say about her?

MONSA. A good deal that I don't mean to tell you. But remember this; she never knew how to deceive, and if she loved Ramón, poor thing, she'd be quite capable of saying so—before everybody! You've hurt her so many times.

ANTONIA. Poor thing, eh? Now I see! I understand. Because she's rich . . .

MONSA. And I haven't anything? Now you hurt me, Antonia. You must be very unhappy to talk like that.

ANTONIA. I am unhappy, Monsa! Very, very unhappy! So unhappy that I want to die, to kill myself!

MONSA. Stop crying—some one is coming. The Doctor!

ANTONIA *endeavors to control herself. Enter* DON JOAQUIM.

DON JOAQUIM. [*Sympathetically*] What's the matter with Antonia?

ANTONIA. Good-afternoon, Doctor.

DON JOAQUIM. When I found that you weren't at supper with the others, I made up my mind that I'd stop in and say how do you do to you.

ANTONIA. Thanks, Doctor.

DON JOAQUIM. But what's the matter? What are you crying for?

ANTONIA. Nothing, Doctor.

MONSA. How did you find Daniela? Does she seem better today?

DON JOAQUIM. She seems much happier, and certainly that is something. She would be the happiest woman in the world, I think, if you would all only help a little.

MONSA. You don't think she's better then?

DON JOAQUIM. Better? Oh, dear, no! Poor woman!—far from it. What she needs is rest. We must be careful to keep her from every sort of worry or excitement—she must not be disturbed or crossed in anything. That is absolutely essential. Do you understand, Antonia?

ANTONIA. Yes, Doctor.

MONSA. But you don't mean that she is seriously ill?

DON JOAQUIM. I do. Very, very seriously. I may as well tell you. Daniela can never be cured. The day after her arrival I received a second letter from Paris, from her physician, in which he informed me that her malady was mortal, and, as I have since discovered for myself, that she was even then in a most critical condition.

MONSA. *María Santísima!* Doctor, what is to be done? What is the trouble with her?

DON JOAQUIM. What is to be done? It's a question of her heart; I don't know how to explain it. When a person has a heart like hers . . .

MONSA. Cure her, Doctor, cure her!

DON JOAQUIM. My dear woman, you might as well say to me, turn young again, Señor Doctor, turn young!

ANTONIA. That French doctor says this to make himself appear important.

DON JOAQUIM. No, Antonia. I have studied her case myself, and I say so too. But not a word of this to any one. If she should hear of it . . .

MONSA. Not a word.

DON JOAQUIM. Remember! She is not to be excited or disturbed. I cannot impress that upon you too strongly. Above all, Antonia, I must caution you.

ANTONIA. Me? Why me more than the others?

DON JOAQUIM. Don't be offended; it is the advice of a physician.

ANTONIA. Very well.

DON JOAQUIM. [Laying his hand on her shoulder as he takes leave of MONSA] Ah, Monsa! You're a lamb of God's flock! A lamb of the true flock!

MONSA. Oh, Doctor!

DON JOAQUIM. And you're one too, Antonia, though sometimes you mayn't show it. But remember, I want you to be careful! Be very careful what you do. [He turns to go.

ANTONIA. But, Doctor—this that you've told me—have you spoken to Ramón about it?

DON JOAQUIM. I have, and he asked me to speak to you.

ANTONIA. He did? To speak to me?

DON JOAQUIM. That's the reason that I have talked so plainly. Now remember you have promised to be good.

ANTONIA. Yes.

MONSA. Good-afternoon, Don Joaquím.

Don Joaquim. [*Aside, going*] Adios! I have still three calls to make.   [*Exit to the rear.*

Antonia. Now, I see. She isn't sick nor anything else.

Monsa. She isn't sick?

Antonia. Of course she isn't! Don't you see? Ramón has been talking to the Doctor. They want to have me eat my heart out, to die with grief.

Monsa. But didn't you hear what the French doctor said?

Antonia. The French doctor! Yes, Ramón wants me to wait on her and be her maid. That's the reason that they tell me that she's sick. What right has he to talk about me to the Doctor, and have him tell me that I have no heart?

Monsa. He didn't say that.

Antonia. And that you're better than I am? And that I must make Daniela happy!

Monsa. Listen, Antonia . . .

Antonia. And that my husband, the wretch, wants me to nurse her and take care of her, and all the time with them here, right before my face—the fools!

> Daniela *is heard laughing outside. Presently another laugh, in which* Daniela *and* Anna *join.*

Monsa. Hush! She's coming.

Antonia. I won't have her see me crying; she shan't have that satisfaction, anyhow.

Monsa. Not another word, do you hear?—for your own sake and for everybody's!

Antonia. No, no, I'll be cheerful now. I can laugh just as well as she can. [*She laughs*] Why shouldn't I laugh?

Monsa. Hush! Of course! [Antonia *resumes her sewing.*

> Daniela *and* Anna *enter from the rear.* Anna *is carrying a large new doll. As they enter,* Monsa *picks up a part of the baby's dress and pretends to busy herself with it.*

DANIELA. We waited for you as long as we could, Antonia. I do believe now I couldn't hold another thing.

MONSA. Supper in broad daylight!

ANNA. Oh, mamma, we had such funny things to eat.

DANIELA. Everything is new to her.

ANTONIA. Anna, come here to me. Didn't I tell you that I wanted you today? Why didn't you go to school?

ANNA. Oh! I was with father.

DANIELA. It was all my fault.

ANTONIA. Your place is here with me, child—do you hear? Here with me and the baby.

MONSA. Antonia, do be careful; you'll prick her with your needle.

ANNA. Ah, do be careful, mamma, you'll prick the doll!

DANIELA. Did they tell you, Monsa? I had to send Jeanne away.

MONSA. No!   [ANNA *tries to take* DANIELA's *parasol.*

ANNA. Let me have it! I'll run and put it in your room.

    ANTONIA *makes a gesture so as to prevent her from taking the parasol.*

ANTONIA. Anna!

    As soon as ANNA *hears her mother call she runs off and puts the parasol in* DANIELA's *room, returning immediately. It is evident that she prefers to be with* DANIELA *rather than with her mother.* DANIELA *is patently in high spirits.*

DANIELA. Yes, I had to send her away. She was always fretting and crying—and you know I don't want to have anybody crying about me. I want to see everybody happy. Light, Monsa, light! I must have that to be satisfied. There isn't anybody in the world who can bear a grudge against me—I never did anybody any harm. If people would only show me a little love and a little kindness, Monsa —for I am so hungry for love, and so jealous of it when I see it anywhere! [*As she speaks to* Monsa *she directs her remarks at* Antonia] I wanted you all to love me here in a different way, not as they did in Paris, but dear me, I don't know why it is, you all seem to find so many faults in me! [*She steps back to look at the boy in the cradle*] Ah! he's asleep; the boy's asleep. How beautiful he is! A second Ramón— Ramón all over again. Ah, Monsa! Look! Look! He's asleep, fast asleep. And there now, he's going to turn over. He's waking up! He's waking up! [*She rocks the cradle gently*] Ah! Ah! Ah!

Antonia. [*Running toward her*] No, don't wake him up.

[Monsa *detains* Antonia.

Daniela. Yes, yes! [*Laughing*] Don't make a sound.

Monsa. Let her alone, Antonia.

Antonia. [*To* Daniela, *controlling herself*] Let the child alone, he doesn't know you. [Daniela *leaves the cradle.*

Daniela. [*To* Monsa] How I love to run my hands under the quilt! He feels so nice and warm. Look at Antonia! [*Aside, under her breath*] Look at her! How I envy her; how I envy Antonia! [*Then to* Monsa] Look at her now. How happy she is with that child!

Daniela *and* Monsa *stand for a moment apart, looking at the cradle without speaking a word.*

Monsa. She's very, very happy—because it is her child.

Antonia. [*By the cradle*] Go to sleep, little boy, go to sleep! Oh! Oh! Oh! Go to sleep, go to sleep!—He's asleep.

Monsa. [*Aside to* Daniela] How good it must be to be a mother!

Daniela. A mother!—Pshaw! How should I know? I shall never know!

[*With a shudder she turns away from the cradle to* Monsa.

Anna [*To* Daniela, *placing the doll in her hands*] Here! Take her! Put her to sleep!

DANIELA. The years nave fled by and I feel that I am old. And there is nothing in the world that I can call mine!

The doll is about to fall without DANIELA's *being conscious of it.*

ANNA. Ay! But you'll kill her! The poor dear!

[MONSA, *also pensive, remains silent.*

MONSA. [*Sighing deeply, then rousing herself*] Ah! Daniela, how about the chalet? Don't you think they've been working fast?

DANIELA. Fast? I don't think so. It seems to me they don't do anything at all. I wanted—you know—to have it ready for the fiesta. But . . .

[*Her attention wanders back to the cradle.*

MONSA. They'll have to hurry to get it ready for the fiesta.

DANIELA. That's what makes me angry! It's first one stone, then another, while I have to wait—I who have always done everything myself—at once—like that!

She accompanies the sentence with an emphatic gesture.
Meanwhile ANTONIA *has resumed her sewing.*

MONSA. But it's only a month since you came.

DANIELA. Only a month? [*Brightening up*] So it is! Tell me, Monsa, don't you think I am quite another person? [*Much moved and nervous*] Sometimes it seems to me that I never went away, and then sometimes, when I think of those days, all at once a pain comes over me. . . . When I took the train to come here I thought I should go mad with joy, and would you believe it, in half an hour I was wanting to turn back again?

MONSA. No?

DANIELA. Yes, I was.—I thought I ought to have waited till tomorrow or the next day. Yes, I did! And then I missed Frou-Frou. Oh, I couldn't bear the thought of losing Frou-

Frou! Poor thing! And then Richard and Huguette and the others had to console me. [*Laughing*]

MONSA. Who did you say they were?

DANIELA. Of course you don't know. [*Laughing because* MONSA *does not understand her*] Why, they were the players in my company—the people who used to act with me. I told you that they came on the same train. On their way back to Paris they promised to stop off and see me, but, Monsa, they are such flyaways! You can't believe one word they say. They never remember promises at all. The poor dog wouldn't have left me, though. I thought that if they didn't bring her immediately I should die of grief. [*She laughs at herself*] And now, just think of it, I've had a letter that they've lost her, and I have scarcely shed a tear.

MONSA. Poor Frou-Frou!   [ANTONIA *laughs sarcastically.*

DANIELA. [*To* MONSA] But don't think that I am heartless. [*Laughing*] I did cry for a minute. Antonia doesn't seem to think that I cried.

ANTONIA. I think . . .

MONSA. Of course she thinks you cried.

ANTONIA. I think that when you left this house you cried —for the man you left in it! [*Laughing*] That time you ran away!

MONSA. Why, Antonia!

DANIELA. [*After a pause*] Yes, I did cry when I left this house. [*Emphatically*] And I shall leave it again before you make me cry again. Yes, I shall leave it immediately! [AN-TONIA *laughs*] I shall go away! [*Much overcome*]

MONSA. Antonia!

DANIELA. I went before because Ramón's father struck me. [ANTONIA *laughs*] I know it—and because I was half mad in those days.

ANTONIA. Only in those days?

DANIELA. No, not only in those days; but I was half mad then, and I know now that I am not like the rest of you. No, for sometimes I change, and what pleases me today I hate—I hate tomorrow. But that doesn't give you the right to dislike me, Antonia. You ought to respect me and try to help me, because I want to change.

ANTONIA. Want to?

MONSA. [Aside] Holy Mother!

DANIELA. [With decision] No, not want to, for I have changed. I am like the rest of you now. I only want to live here in peace and to be happy with those I love and who love me, and who have learned to respect me. And then I want—and I mean to do it too—I want to dress like the rest of you, and wear the same clothes that you do, and have some work to do myself, like you.

[She wanders back to the cradle.

ANTONIA. Poor Frou-Frou!

DANIELA. Don't say that, Antonia. No, it isn't true. I have a heart. Oh, I cry sometimes! I cried a great deal when I was coming home—a very great deal. And then what did I do? I began to laugh and talk and forget myself when I saw you, until I was alone again; and then I cried again. Oh, how many times I've thought of coming back and it was always so! And then my courage failed me, and at last I passed years without ever allowing myself to think of this place at all. [Burying her face in her hands] And then, then sometimes, I—I . . .

MONSA. [Wishing to divert her] Yes, yes, Daniela, no wonder. No wonder. But you're better now; you're much better.

DANIELA. Yes! When no one is unkind to me. Then I became worse, very much worse. But now I have the medicines I brought with me from Paris, and Don Joaquím comes every day to see me, and you're here with me too, Monsa.

So I am better. [*To* ANTONIA] What are you going to do, Antonia?

ANTONIA. [*Takes a baby's dress from a drawer*] Nothing; dress the boy.

DANIELA. What fun! Let me dress him, Antonia.

ANTONIA. Ah, no!

DANIELA. I'll show you. You'll see if I don't know how. Give me the dress. Look, Monsa! Look! Isn't that the way?

[ANTONIA *goes on preparing to dress the child.*

MONSA. That's it. Let her do it, Antonia.

DANIELA. [*Seated*] Bring him to me. Do! Quick, Antonia! Hurry!

As ANTONIA *passes in front of her to reach the cradle,* DANIELA *catches hold of her skirt.*

ANTONIA. Let go! Woman, let go, I say.

DANIELA. No, no; I want to dress the boy. Do let me have him, Antonia, and then I'll rock him to sleep in the cradle.

ANTONIA. Let go, I tell you.

DANIELA. What makes you talk to me like that? Let go, woman, let go! [*Laughing*] Then I'll take him anyhow. See now what I am going to do.

[*Running up to the cradle.*

ANTONIA. [*Trying to push her off*] Go away!

DANIELA. I am here first. [*Laughing softly*] You'll see now if he knows me.

ANTONIA. [*Pushing her away*] Go away, he's mine! This child has a father and mother. He doesn't know you. Get somebody else's to nurse—your own, if you have one!

DANIELA. Ah, how she hurts me!

[*She lays her hand on her heart, overcome.*

MONSA. Take care, Daniela!

DANIELA. Yes, Monsa, yes. She is right—it is her child. But she ought not to have hurt me so.

MONSA. Come away. [*Diverting her attention.* ANNA, *who has gone out through the door on the right with her doll, has re-entered a moment before*]

ANTONIA. Here, you, Anna. [ANNA *does not hear*] Come help me. Take hold of the cradle. By the foot—by the foot, I tell you! [ANNA *lays the doll across the foot of the cradle*] Drag it into the other room. Quick! Go along, go along!

> *Exeunt* ANTONIA *and* ANNA, *dragging out the cradle through the door on the right. When* ANTONIA *disappears she is pushing the cradle from behind. Her last words are said behind the scene.*

DANIELA. [*To* MONSA] My heart goes out with that child.

MONSA. Poor Daniela!

> *She passes her hand through* DANIELA's *hair, holding her in half embrace.*

DANIELA. She's very bitter against me.

MONSA. No.

DANIELA. [*Impetuously*] I am going to ask her why she treats me so.

MONSA. [*Detaining her*] Don't do that.

DANIELA. It's because she doesn't want me to touch her child. [*Sadly*] Ay, how she hurts me, Monsa! But Ramón has a great heart.

MONSA. Come, we've got so many things to talk about.

DANIELA. Have we, Monsa? Monsa, tell me! Why do you take such an interest in me?

MONSA. Pshaw! I've always had it. That's the way I'm made.

DANIELA. [*After a pause*] As I am made—not like the rest! But that woman will kill me, Monsa. She can't even bear to see me in the house. What harm would I do to her boy? I should like to know that. Listen, Monsa. [*Turning abruptly to her*] Didn't you ever have a lover?

MONSA. A lover?

DANIELA. Yes.

MONSA. A lover? Oh, yes! One.

DANIELA. One? I thought so. Tell me about him. Some one who promised he would marry you and to whom you gave your love, and who afterward flew away—like the birds?

MONSA. [*Laughing sadly*] Oh, no, no! Nothing like that. It was nothing like that.

DANIELA. Monsa, never believe in any man. Men do not love, you know—they do not love! Where is he now?

MONSA. In another village—far away.

DANIELA. And how was it that you didn't marry him?

MONSA. He wanted me to marry him and I loved him dearly; but one day I found that he had deceived another girl, and that she had had a child by him, and then—I didn't want—well, I wanted him to marry her.

DANIELA. You did? And you?

MONSA. I was alone and poor, and I remained alone and poor as before. And then I began to teach the children, so now I pick up a crumb here and there like the birds. But sometimes it is cold and I have nothing for fire; and sometimes I am discouraged and downhearted, and then the children come and they run up to me and kiss me and hug me, and then, before I know it, I look up, and I find that all the bitterness is gone.

DANIELA. You do? But what did you say to each other when you found it out?

MONSA. Adios, Manuel. Adios, Monsa.—That was all.

DANIELA. Why don't you marry some other man?

MONSA. Oh, no, never another! I shall never love again.

DANIELA. [*Incredulously*] Never again, never again? [*She bows her head in shame; then, after a moment, she throws her arms around* MONSA's *neck and imprints a kiss on her forehead*] Monsa! You are an angel! An angel, Monsa! You are just my age, and it seems to me that I have kissed a child. But

I am old myself.   I see now that I have grown old.   [*A pause*]
Pst!   [*Looking straight at* ANTONIA's *room*] She has done me
a great wrong.

MONSA. A wrong?   I?   Daniela!

DANIELA. Antonia first and you afterward—but you more
than she, poor Monsa!   I am going away.

MONSA. Going away?

DANIELA. Yes, I am going away.   I ought never to have
come back to my home.

MONSA. Don't say that!

DANIELA. Yes, I must go.   To Paris, back to Paris!   My
mind is made up.

MONSA. What is the matter?

DANIELA. I don't want to be old, I don't want to be sad;
I want to put it all behind me.   I have only made myself unhappy by coming here again.   Here I am a hated thing, and
there I was still beautiful and young!

MONSA. But the chalet?

DANIELA. Don't remind me of the chalet!   I can't bear
to think of it—now that it's going up so fast!   The porch
is almost done.

> RAMON *and* VALENTINE *enter.   The latter carries a*
> *roll of plans and a small book under his arm.*

RAMON. They'll put the balustrade on the porch tomorrow.

DANIELA. [*Happy at once*] The balustrade?   On the porch?
The middle one?

RAMON. I have a letter from the mason.   [*He has the letter*
in his hand] It is ready now.

DANIELA. Are they going to put it up tomorrow?

RAMON. Tomorrow.   [*Implying that he means to attend to it.*]

DANIELA. Then can we use it immediately?   [RAMON *as-*
sents] Ramón, we'll go out on it tomorrow, and we'll invite
all those dreadful old people who never give us a minute's
peace, to see it; and we'll have them all stand below in rows

and clap their hands, and then we'll bow and smile and call out: Thanks, thanks, slanderers and backbiters! Thanks, thanks, you tongues of scorpions, thanks! [*She laughs*]

RAMON. [*Laughing also*] Yes; indeed we will! [*To* VALENTINE] Put down the papers; that's all for today.

> *Making a sign to* VALENTINE, *who leaves the papers on the table and then goes out.*

DANIELA. [*Laughing*] Now, Monsa, I am not going away.

MONSA. Daniela!

RAMON. [*Before the table*] We've got a good deal to do this afternoon.

MONSA. [*To* DANIELA] I want to speak to you about Antonia—and about him—soon.

DANIELA. What? Tell me now, tell me now.

RAMON. Is that Monsa here yet?

MONSA. When we're alone. Good-bye.

DANIELA. Yes, afterward.

MONSA. Don't be long. [*Exit* MONSA.

RAMON. [*Busily engaged with the papers*] Come, come. You've got to have your say about these things.

DANIELA. Now I am yours. You're a good boy, Ramón.

RAMON. Look at that carefully.

> [*Showing her a drawing of the façade of the chalet.*

DANIELA. I am looking at it.

RAMON. Señor Felip wants to know whether you want the tower like this, or whether you'd rather have it finished. . . . Wait! I have it here. [*Unrolling another paper*]

DANIELA. Higher, higher! I want it a great deal higher. [*Speaking of the first plan*]

RAMON. Wait till I show you. [*He finishes unrolling the second paper*] Here it is. What do you think of that?

DANIELA. Let me see it . . . [*Measuring the drawing*] One palm and a half. Now let me see the other. Hold the paper open—wider open. [DANIELA *gives* RAMON *a pat on the head.*

*He starts involuntarily, and she bursts out laughing; he remains
quite serious*] Oh, higher, higher! We must have a higher
tower. What does Señor Felip have to say?

RAMON. Higher? Then it will be almost as high as the
church tower.

DANIELA. Do you mean to tell me that my tower won't
be as high as the church tower? Pshaw! [*Striking the paper
with her fist*] Take it away! Tell them to draw me another;
I want to look down on the church tower. I'll show you.
See! A white tower with gilded tiles like that, 'way up there,
and the church tower 'way down below here, all huddled up
and black, just as if it were the child of my tower and pro-
tected by it. [*Laughing*] There! What do you think of that?

RAMON. I don't know. People will talk. [*Rolling up the
paper*] But Señor Felip will do as you please, and let them
talk.

DANIELA. What do you mean?

RAMON. Let them talk. Everybody seems to think that
they have a right to mix themselves up in it.

DANIELA. In what?

RAMON. Nothing. Let's go on to something else.

DANIELA. No, I want to know.

RAMON. Why, it's this way then.—The priest says that
he doesn't intend to have the tower of your house taller
than the church tower, so that it will be cast into the shade.

DANIELA. He doesn't intend to have it? I'd like to know
if he thinks that he owns the air? Maybe he's afraid that by
mounting up higher, I am going to get away from him.

RAMON. I wouldn't laugh about it; it's not a laughing
matter.

DANIELA. Oh, dear!

RAMON. I told him that the tower, its height . . . but never
mind about the tower. We've talked too much about it
already. It's none of his business. If he hadn't been who

he is, and I hadn't had to respect him, I'd have knocked him down.

DANIELA. For talking about me?

RAMON. Yes—and other things.

DANIELA. Maybe he'd like to see me go away too? So you defended me to the priest? Eh, Ramón? Don't defend me. Believe me, don't defend me. It isn't worth the trouble.

RAMON. Well, never mind. Let's go on to something else. I paid the bills today. Here they are. [*Producing several papers, also some money*] This is what is left over—a good deal too. Take it.

DANIELA. No, keep it yourself; you'll need it soon.

RAMON. No, no, take it.

DANIELA. What did the priest say to you that makes you not want to take it?

RAMON. [*In a low voice*] I would have respected myself more if I had never touched a penny.

DANIELA. [*Taking it herself*] Poor Ramón! You—who used to think so much of me!

RAMON. Yes, I did. [*He rises*] And I still think much of you.   [*He moves off.*

DANIELA. Still? What do you mean by still? Señor Cousin, come here! Come right here! I want you to explain yourself. Still? You don't bear a grudge against me any more?

RAMON. I? A grudge? I am nobody, Daniela.

DANIELA. [*Affectionately*] Imperious always since you were a boy! The bristles ought to be sticking out all over you, Ramón; you are just like a hedgehog, and have been all your life. Why, when I first came home I ran up to you and threw my arms about your neck, laughing, because I was so glad to be back again, and you drooped your head and turned your face away until I thought that you were going to assassinate me—yes, with a look from your eye! Just

like that, now! Ouf! What's the matter with you, man?
Are you afraid?

RAMON. Do you dare to say that? [*Aside*] I am no longer
afraid.

DANIELA. We were to be friends, Ramón, friends, as we
always used to be. [*Tenderly*]

RAMON. Yes.

DANIELA. And we always must be friends. Let us understand each other. Promise me, Ramón, that you'll never
abuse me again, as you did that day?

RAMON. [*Interrupting her*] Never! I promise. And you
will promise me that you'll never go away?

DANIELA. I promise; never! I'll never go away.

RAMON. Thanks, Daniela, thanks. Daniela ... [*He pauses
a moment*] Thanks, thanks.

DANIELA. What is it? [RAMON *remains silent, not wishing
to speak*] No, no, what is it?

RAMON. Nothing. Your word—that's enough.

DANIELA. You didn't mean to say that. No, no! Tell me
at once; what is it?

RAMON. Well, I didn't mean to say that. But that is all
that I mean to say.

DANIELA. Why? Is it something unpleasant? [RAMON
shrugs his shoulders] No, I want you to tell me.

RAMON. I can't tell you, Daniela. When we were young,
I—I couldn't have told you, and I can't tell you now. [*She
draws back, serious*] Come! Let's go out. [*He gathers up the
plans*] We've finished our business.

DANIELA. Then I'll run over and see Monsa.

RAMON. [*Dropping the plans*] No, not yet, wait here—a
minute longer. [*Nervously*] I've still some things left to do,
and, meanwhile, we can talk.

DANIELA. [*Very seriously*] About what?

RAMON. Oh—about what you please. [*He sits down*] Don't

go away. [*Springing up violently*] I don't want you to go away.

DANIELA. But we were not going to talk about that any more.

RAMON. [*Violently*] I don't want you to go, I say. [*Pleadingly*] For if you do, I know this time you never will come back. [*Beside himself*] You shall not go!

DANIELA. [*Looking at him for a moment*] Ramón! [*He strides in front of her without speaking*] I want to ask you a question. [*She pauses*] When I went away, it cannot be that you were in love with me? Answer me, Ramón.

RAMON. I—I in love with you? What makes you say that?

DANIELA. I don't know. It occurred to me. I'd be very sorry to think it had been so. Then I should never have come back.   [*Daylight is fading from the sky.*

RAMON. You'd be sorry? Why?

DANIELA. Oh! For no reason. Let's talk of something else.

RAMON. For no reason? Humph! I thought so. You'd not be sorry, then.

DANIELA. Yes, Ramón, I would be sorry. I would be very, very sorry, because if you had loved me, it might have been that I would have loved you, and then we should have grown up together, and I should never have gone away. We should have been married then, Ramón, and Anna and this boy would have been our children—our children, Ramón, yours and mine! But now they are not mine, no, and they do not want to have them love me. What a pity!

> She speaks with the deepest feeling, but without any outward manifestation of love for RAMON.

RAMON. What a pity! Yes, what a pity and a shame! I can no longer keep it from you, Daniela—I loved you! And when I missed you first, a great flame shot through my brain, a wild burning to find you out wherever you might be the whole world through, to kill you perhaps, to kiss you, to seize you, embrace you, to die or to live with you —I don't know which, nor what, nor how! And then I left this house, and like a lightning flash my heart flew after you along the rails to France. But I had no money. I could not follow you—I was too poor; and with the little that I had, I set myself to play, to get more money for the journey. And I lost. Then I fell, for to play more one night I forced open the drawer of my father's desk with a knife, and took what I wanted there; and with the little that I took, I returned to play, and again I lost. Then I returned again to the desk, each time more disgraced! At last, one day, in the gray of the early morning, my father surprised me as I was forcing open the drawer—for you, Daniela, for it was for you; and do you know what he did? He put the key into my hands and said to me, smiling sadly: "Why do you take it like that, my boy? For, see, it is all yours!" And then he left me, and I saw that he was crying. And I flung the key down on the desk, and the veil fell from my eyes, and with all my soul I cursed you!

DANIELA. Oh! [*She stands looking at him, bewildered*] And you never told me this before?

RAMON. I didn't know it. I didn't know how! I didn't know it myself!

DANIELA. [*Laughing sadly*] In love with me and silent so many years? Who would have thought it! And others who never really loved me, have told me, oh, so quickly! What, Ramón? Wait fourteen years to say it!

RAMON. [*Offended because she laughs*] Pshaw! I was right to wait. [*She laughs again*] I was right. For you—you never deserved it.

[*He goes straight to the door at the back to go out.*]

DANIELA. [*Offended*] I never deserved it? Will you tell me why not?

RAMON. [*Bitterly*] Because you were — what you were. And now when I tell you my disgrace, you laugh at me!

DANIELA. I laugh at you? Ramón! And doesn't it make your heart bleed to see how I laugh?

RAMON. Bleed? No. Why should it? Does your heart bleed? You never bled for anything. [*Again she laughs sadly; again* RAMON *is disturbed by her laughing*] I was a fool to pity you. Go! Go where you please, Daniela! If we had been married, it would have been the same—you would have left me some day to follow the glad life, and laugh at me; and no wonder—for we are what we are! No wonder that you laugh.

    She begins to tear up the plans of the house, one by one, very deliberately.

DANIELA. No wonder that I laugh. No wonder! I see it all now. The priest was right. I see it all. We are what we are. No woman ought ever to be what I have been, but after she has been, all the avenues are closed; it is impossible for her to turn back—ever, ever to turn back!

RAMON. What are you doing, Daniela? Those are the plans.

DANIELA. The priest was right. I give everything to you, Ramón—the house, everything. Pull down what has been finished and let them build the church tower as high as they please. I wanted to raise myself into the air, but it is not to be. I must return again to the ground—to grovel again on the ground!

RAMON. Why do you say that?

DANIELA. Because I am alone in the world—alone and without a home! Where I come I only bring disgrace. I despise myself, and I have made you despise me.

    [*It grows darker.*

RAMON. Daniela, do you think that I despise you?

DANIELA. Yes, I think so, and I always want to think so —you hate me, you despise me. Hate! Disgust!

RAMON. But I don't despise you. I . . .

DANIELA. You think you pity me.

RAMON. Not pity. No, Daniela, no; not pity. I don't mean that. When I speak with you . . .

DANIELA. [*Quickly*] Not another word!

RAMON. When I speak with you . . .

DANIELA. [*Stopping her ears*] I won't hear you, Ramón. No, no, I tell you I won't hear you! No, no, Ramón! [*With decision*] Ramón!

RAMON. [*Also with decision*] Very well. But I won't let you go away.

DANIELA. Not another word, or this minute, just as I am, I walk out of this house! I see it all now. In one minute you have made me understand it all. I am in the way, you do not believe in me. And I who have lived that life . . . [*He is about to protest*] Yes, for I have lived it—I may be as repentant as you please, but I have lived it—I came here to be a good woman, in so far as I could, but you will not let me be one, and I cannot bear the disgrace! I wanted to find repose, to be received like a mother, like an elder sister, burdened with years and kind, and to be respected . . . [RAMON *again endeavors to speak*] Yes, to be respected by you and your wife and by the children, more than all; and to cleanse myself— but it was not to be! I have not deserved it.

RAMON. Daniela, don't say that.

DANIELA. I have not deserved it. For you have hurt me, Ramón, more than all the others—you have hurt me more than all the other men I have ever known. For I came here to seek oblivion and healing, and to rise and build my tower, and you have only seen in me the woman that I was, and that I do not want to be.

RAMON. The woman that you were? No, no, Daniela— the reverse. I don't know how it happened—the reverse, I didn't mean to say that.

DANIELA. I don't want to be it!

RAMON. Have I hurt you, Daniela?

DANIELA. I don't want to be it! I don't mean to be it!

[*She is about to go.*

RAMON. [*Seizing her by the arm*] Stay! Stay here, I tell you! You promised not to go away.

DANIELA. It cannot be, Ramón. It cannot be.

RAMON. Why not? We will never speak of this again.

DANIELA. I know what we are, Ramón, better than you do.

RAMON. I know myself.

DANIELA. And I too know myself—and you would be lost! Poor Ramón! You would be lost!

RAMON. [*Firmly*] Lost? Well, let me be! . . .

DANIELA. Be still!

[*A light is seen approaching from the room on the right.*

RAMON. I would be lost!

DANIELA. [*In a whisper*] Look! Look!

Enter ANTONIA *from the right, a light in her hand.*

ANTONIA. Ramón!

DANIELA. Antonia!

ANTONIA. Daniela, eh? If I disturb you . . .

[*She stops short with the light in her hand.*

DANIELA. No, no, Antonia . . .

RAMON. [*Striking the table*] Set down the light.

[ANTONIA *sets the light on the table.*

ANTONIA. [*To* RAMON] Have you forgotten the market at Vallclara tomorrow?

RAMON. No.

ANTONIA. If you're going you'd better answer that letter of your friend Guillemas; he's expecting you . . .

RAMON. I'm not going to Vallclara; I don't mean to go.

ANTONIA. I wanted to speak to you about it, because I'm thinking myself of going for a few days to my father's. You haven't been doing anything all the month . . .

RAMON. Ha?

ANTONIA. You know my father hasn't been well for some time . . .

RAMON. No. Go if you like. Who'll look after the boy?

ANTONIA. Oh! I'm going to take the children with me.

RAMON. No, you're not. The children will stay here with me. They fret you, Antonia. You know you'd find them a trouble on the journey.

ANTONIA. A trouble? To me?—the children? You've no right to talk like that, Ramón.

RAMON. Then I'll take the right. The children shall not leave this house.

DANIELA. [*Impetuously*] Antonia, I've something to say to you—to you alone.

ANTONIA. To me? Tell Ramón, woman, what you want to say to me.

RAMON. No, Antonia, there are no secrets between us. Daniela, sit down. Aren't you better now?

DANIELA. Much better. [*Going up to* ANTONIA] Antonia, don't go away. [RAMON *taps the table nervously with his fist.*

ANTONIA. No! I won't go away. What? Leave my children? With him? A mother never leaves her children, no! But a father . . .

RAMON. A father? What nonsense! They love me better than they do you.

DANIELA. Ramón!

RAMON. I'll not have it said that my children don't love me. She is wearing out my patience with her sour face. It's a perfect hell in the house all day.

ANTONIA. I am the mother of your children, Ramón! I— I—and no one else is their mother!

[*The last remark she directs at* DANIELA.

RAMON. What is the use of saying that?

DANIELA. Antonia! Antonia! Listen, Antonia!

[ANTONIA *bursts into tears, hearing nothing.*

RAMON. [*Aside*] But she is right! They are her children.

DANIELA. I have made up my mind. I am going away. Listen, Antonia! [RAMON *is about to interrupt;* DANIELA *turns upon him*] I am going away, [*To* ANTONIA] but before I go I want to ask you not to hate me, for you have no right to hate me.

ANTONIA. Pst!

DANIELA. No, for I have been a good woman here. I have been your friend. I have lived here just as you have done. Yes, better than you have done, because it has cost you nothing. And now you drive me out of the house, and it may be that it is just as well!

[*She says this with the implication that she might revenge herself upon* ANTONIA.

RAMON. She drives you out?

DANIELA. Yes.

RAMON. She does? It is not I, is it? I do not drive you out?

DANIELA. [*To* RAMON] Yes, and you, too! You more than Antonia. You drive me out.

[ANTONIA *shrinks away from* DANIELA.

RAMON. I'll not have it! I . . .

[*He stops short,* ANTONIA *coming up to him.*

ANTONIA. Who, you? You'll not have it? See if you dare to say it? No, you don't dare to say it! But even if you don't, you don't deceive me. And she doesn't deceive me either. [*Laughing*] For I know her!

RAMON. [*Enraged*] Stop!

DANIELA. Let her talk.

ANTONIA. You're the one who's deceived—you! For she's inflamed you! Like a boy, she's inflamed you. Wanton!

RAMON. [*Furious*] Antonia!

ANTONIA. Wanton!

DANIELA. No, no, Ramón! Ramón! It's true!

ANTONIA. [*Laughing*] She knows herself. She's had experience!

DANIELA. Experience?—I, the woman of the world, who never once thought of this place when she was well and all the sky was bright!

ANTONIA. [*Laughing sarcastically*] No, no! Not once!

DANIELA. And now that I am sick and old, I come back here to rob you of Ramón? Eh?

ANTONIA. Yes, because you're a thief!

RAMON. Antonia!

DANIELA. [*Indignantly to* ANTONIA] And don't you see anything in me that is good? No honorable thought, nothing that pleases you?

ANTONIA. What should I see in you that pleases me? Get out of my house!

DANIELA. Ah—yes, yes! [*Resigned*]

RAMON. [*To* ANTONIA, *furious*] You! You to your room!

ANTONIA. [*Without moving*] Get out of my house!

RAMON. In, into your room, I tell you!

ANTONIA. Strike me! Kill me! I have borne too much.

RAMON. [*To* DANIELA] I'll not let you go. [*To* ANTONIA, *who is about to speak*] Another word, and I will kill you.

> [*Threatening her with his clenched fist.*

DANIELA. No! Ramon!

ANTONIA. Don't you defend me! Don't you dare! Get out of my house! Wanton! Thief!

DANIELA. I am going, I am going now. [*She turns to the door.*

RAMON. [*Detaining her*] Daniela!

ANTONIA. [*Laughing*] You're going now? Ha, ha! He can't do without a woman, and he'll not soon get such another!

DANIELA. [*To* RAMON] No, let me go, for if I don't, I shall revenge myself on her! Then, alas! for her.

> [*Menacing her with her fist.*

RAMON. [*To* DANIELA] No!

> [DANIELA *sinks back into a chair.*

ANTONIA. [*Furious*] She threatens me! Me!

DANIELA. [*Rising and advancing upon* ANTONIA] Yes, I threaten you—because I can bear no more!

> *Enter* VALENTINE *from the rear.*

VALENTINE. Here's some company for Daniela. Some people who want to see her.

RAMON. [*Seeking to drive him out*] Out of the door! Get out! [*A number of voices are heard approaching outside.*

VALENTINE. [*Going*] Here they are. They're coming in.

MAX. [*Without, almost voiceless*] Where is Daniela?

HUGUETTE. [*Without*] Daniela! Daniela!

DANIELA. [*Composing herself*] Oh, they're the players! Let them come in, Valentine! Valentine! Let them come in.

ANTONIA. [*Going to her room*] They shall not take my children from me! I'll not let them take them from me!

> *Exit* ANTONIA *to the right. Exit* VALENTINE. MAX *enters.*

MAX. Ah! Here's Daniela!

> *Enter* HUGUETTE.

HUGUETTE. Here she is! Our Daniela!

DANIELA. How glad I am to see you! Come in! Come in! [*Seeing* RICHARD *enter*] And Richard too!

> *Enter* RICHARD.

RICHARD. [*Laughing*] Ah! Your hand, Mademoiselle! How are you? [*Great chatter and rejoicing among the players.*

DANIELA. Splendid, Richard, splendid! Thank you so much for coming.

HUGUETTE. But you have turned brown. It is the country.

DANIELA. [*Frantically*] Yes, I never felt so well—never in all my life.

> *Meanwhile* RAMON *is nervously gathering up the papers on the table.*

RAMON. [*Aside*] She shall not go away. I'll see to it that she shall not.   [*Exit* RAMON *by the back.*

MAX. We have done famously everywhere, my dear. At Barcelona, at Valencia, at Madrid—everywhere the same. The applause was stupendous! And now, you see, we are going home.

HUGUETTE. We said to ourselves, we must stop off and keep our promise to Daniela.

DANIELA. You who all love me!

MAX. Tell me, how do you think I am? In excellent voice, eh?

DANIELA. Oh, excellent!

HUGUETTE. He sings like a nightingale, and he has more notes, too, when he sings.

MAX. We took the mail train, so we have four hours to wait for the express.

DANIELA. You can't imagine how glad I am to see you! [*She drops her eyes for fear that they will see that she has been crying*] Now that everything is over with me! That it is the end—I say the end! [*Laughing*] Eh? What do you think of that?   [*General surprise.*

MAX. Why—what is this? If it is inconvenient . . .

DANIELA. No, not in the least! No! Most opportune, most opportune—if you only knew it!

HUGUETTE. Be frank with us, Daniela.

              [DANIELA *laughs, forcing herself to appear gay.*

RICHARD. [*Rising*] No, no, let us go.

DANIELA. For God's sake, don't leave me now!

MAX. If you are in trouble . . .

DANIELA. I have nobody, nobody but you in all the world; you know that. And you are all my family.

                    [*With great feeling.*

HUGUETTE. Do calm yourself, Daniela. You don't know how excited you are.

DANIELA. You find me in great trouble—in very great trouble—I don't know how to tell you.

MAX. [*Confidentially*] Are you out of money?

HUGUETTE. [*Confidentially*] I hope that you haven't fallen in love?

DANIELA. Oh, dear, no! I came here to rest quietly—to be myself again, and now I find—I find that I have only brought disgrace upon this house, because they see in me— well, what they have never seen before.

HUGUETTE. The hypocrites! And so they want to drive you out?

MAX. Just take my advice, Daniela. Return to Paris and live again. If they had begun to tire of you there, and to give you the cold shoulder, I should say, of course, stay here, and if you happen to have money, seek out some man who hasn't any, and who doesn't concern himself much about history, settle down, and get married.

DANIELA. [*Weeping*] But it isn't that way!

HUGUETTE. [*Interrupting*] Ah, no, Max! [*To* DANIELA] If you get married, marry for love, for without love there is no happiness. [*Retrospectively*] I've always found it so myself.

RICHARD. Invariably, as you might say.

HUGUETTE. But a country fellow! Oh, my dear! I wouldn't think of it! For what is yours then will be his, as it has been with all the others. Some day you'll be wanting to travel to Italy or some other place, like little Fanny Mairi who married the Marquis of Rigolat. Poor fellow! He was so poor that he hadn't a *sou* to his name. And then what do you think he told her? That he intended to travel no further than up the fifth flight where they lived! And what help was there then for poor Fanny Mairi? Next year she ran off with somebody else.

DANIELA. You don't understand me.

MAX. Richard, what would you do if you were in Daniela's place?

RICHARD. Before everything else, Mademoiselle, I should do whatever came into my head. For you are sovereign, supreme! [*To* DANIELA] What is the question? Look! Throw a *louis* into the air. As it falls, it is impossible to tell how it is coming down. Is it to be heads or is it to be tails? But it is no matter—it is all the same. Chance ordains, my dear, that some of us shall live this life wearing the veil, our eyes raised up in prayer to heaven; and some of us shall live it on the stage, our toes raised up, without the veil, toward the ceiling.

DANIELA. I am not that way, Richard. I reflect.

RICHARD. Yes, the moment the *louis* is in the air!

[RAMON *appears at the door, watching* DANIELA.

DANIELA. [*After seeing* RAMON] No! It is not that way. I have decided. I am going back to Paris.

RICHARD. Ah, heads, heads! The coin is on the floor.

[*They all laugh except* DANIELA.

HUGUETTE. Good! Back to Paris!

MAX. And I will find you a manager.

DANIELA. Oh, I have always had more managers than I knew what to do with! When they hear that I am in town, you will see them come.

She takes her position on the right, tapping the floor
proudly with her foot, because she sees RAMON outside.

RICHARD. The war-horse hears the trumpet! See how she spurns the ground at the scent of battle in the air! Brava! Brava! [*All talk to her at the same time*] But let me tell you something.—Eh, shall I tell her? [*Turning to the others. All say "yes."* DANIELA *laughs wearily*] You are going away, my dear—because you are afraid of falling in love!

[DANIELA *makes a sign to him to be silent.*

HUGUETTE. [*Laughing loudly*] What! Daniela in love?

MAX. [*To* DANIELA] You in love?   Oh, oh!

DANIELA. It isn't true! [*They make a great noise*] Do be quiet.   Hush!

> As she says this, RAMON decides to enter with VALEN-
> TINE.   The players continue to laugh hilariously.

RAMON. [*To* VALENTINE] You must be tired.   Go to bed; I'll lock up.

VALENTINE. Good.   Good-night.

> VALENTINE goes upstairs.   RAMON, after closing the
> door of ANTONIA's room, takes his place by the table,
> while DANIELA leads the others a little way off, en-
> deavoring to make them speak lower.   They follow,
> laughing among themselves, quite unconscious of
> RAMON's presence.   DANIELA continues to watch
> RAMON.

MAX. But what do you mean, Richard?   Explain yourself, my boy.

RICHARD. Oh, I am an old fox, I am!

> [RAMON *seats himself at the table.*

HUGUETTE. [*To* DANIELA] Tell me about it.

DANIELA. But it isn't true!   To prove it, listen to me. [*Leading* MAX *to one side*] I am going straight back with you to Paris now.   Tonight! [*General satisfaction*]

MAX. Tonight? [*She assents*]

HUGUETTE. There is decision for you.   As you are?

DANIELA. Say nothing.—How did you come?

> RAMON throws himself into a chair, absorbed in his
> own thoughts, not hearing what they say.   RICHARD,
> smiling, separates himself from the others and ap-
> proaches RAMON.

MAX. In a carriage from the station.

DANIELA. Is it waiting outside?

> RAMON springs up violently and then sits down again,
> oblivious of the others.

MAX. At the door. The express leaves at midnight.

                    [DANIELA continues to talk with MAX.

HUGUETTE. [*To* RICHARD] I'd like to see the lover.

RICHARD. Would you like to see him? Look over there.

HUGUETTE. [*Laughing*] A country fellow? Oh!

DANIELA. [*To* MAX] When you are ready, I will go with you to the station.

MAX. Good! We are ready now.

    RICHARD *draws nearer to* HUGUETTE. *They stand behind* RAMON.

RICHARD. [*To* HUGUETTE] Leave him to me. I'll show you. [*Raising his voice so that* RAMON *may hear, but speaking as if he were carrying on a conversation with* HUGUETTE] Daniela is very wise to go back with us to Paris.

    RAMON *strikes the table a blow and turns sharply upon them.*

RAMON. What? That's a lie!

                [*Astonishment on the part of every one.*

RICHARD. I beg your pardon. I didn't mean to disturb you.

DANIELA. What's the matter?

RAMON. Nothing. I thought I heard him—nothing—these papers . . . I've got some things to do—about the building. We have to see how we stand, you and I.

DANIELA. [*Coldly*] There is no hurry. The papers can wait. I have my friends with me.

RAMON. Very well, then. We'll wait.

DANIELA. Yes, they are going now. [*To the players*] I'll see you to the carriage. When I come back, I shall have time for you. [*To* RAMON]

RAMON. No, for I am going too. And since the night is dark, maybe you'll have need of this.

    He takes a revolver from the drawer and places it upon the table.

HUGUETTE. Ay! A revolver! [*Frightened*]

DANIELA. No, no, put up the revolver and wait here. [*Very significantly*] I am not afraid.

RAMON. I'll not wait here. There! It's in the drawer. [*Returning the pistol to the drawer*] I have strength enough in my arms. [*Laughing fiercely*] In my arms that have tossed you in the air so many times, like a bird, before you knew how to fly! [*To* HUGUETTE] And you, lady, do not be afraid; I shall not harm you nor these gentlemen.

[DANIELA *sinks into a chair.*

MAX. Harm us? Of course not! [*Laughing and feigning the bravo*] We are two to one.

HUGUETTE. [*Laughing*] Look at Max! Max is brave.

RAMON. Brave? You? Why, you are pale with the light of the stage. But here the winds sweep down on us from the mountains; no fox nor wolf can make us turn pale. You slay and are slain to cause a smile—the roar of a cannon is the pop of a gun. The curtain falls, the dead rise up, throw off their shrouds, and live again.

RICHARD. Capital! I like this fellow.

HUGUETTE. [*Forcing a laugh*] He frightens me. [*Aloud*] Come! let us go.

RAMON. Yes, as soon as you like. [*Taking down a lantern —without lighting it, however*] I'll give you a light. And you, Daniela, don't leave the room. [*She rises*] The night is cold. [*With great violence*] The night is cold, I tell you.

[DANIELA *tries to speak, but* RICHARD *prevents her.*

RICHARD. Must we wait at the station? We shall be bored to death.

DANIELA. No, no, for I am going too. This has lasted too long.

RAMON. What has lasted too long?

DANIELA. Everything—everything between us has lasted too long. I am going to leave this house.

[HUGUETTE *turns to go.* RICHARD *detains her.*

RICHARD. We have plenty of time.

RAMON. Now, gentlemen, you see what this woman is. Before God, she has had the grace not to attempt to feign before you. [*To* DANIELA] But you shan't go away this time! By heaven, you shall not go this time!

DANIELA. Ramón, there is nothing for me to do but to go.

RAMON. That is a lie! You shall not go because you have deceived me, because you told me that you had changed your life, but now, at the sight of these, you become what you were again.

DANIELA. No, Ramón.

RAMON. Yes, at the sight of these. Confess. For you have lived in the world, and now the world passes before you and calls you again. Confess it! Confess it! And I'll let you go —yes, and by the Lord, I'll see that you go quickly!

[DANIELA *looks toward the door of* ANTONIA'S *room.*

DANIELA. Yes, I confess it. I am what I am, and I mean to remain so! I want to live, to enjoy myself, to die among my people! Among you, my friends! Take me away! Take me away in your arms.

[*Embracing* MAX *and* HUGUETTE.

MAX. Come on.

RICHARD. [*Enjoying himself*] Wait—the curtain!

RAMON. Now I see! Now I know you! That is the smile you wore when you went away the other time. And I—I believed that you . . . [*Laughing hysterically*]

DANIELA. That I was a viper? A viper more infamous— than I am?

RAMON. No, Daniela, for you are another person; since you have been here, you have been another person.

DANIELA. [*Indignantly*] Another person! Reformed? By you? [*To the others*] And do you know how he meant to reform, to regenerate me? By making me his mistress— here, in the face of his wife! Reformed! Reformed!

RAMON. No, no!

> *He keeps repeating the words while* DANIELA *is speaking. The others laugh, discreetly.*

DANIELA. Yes! Reformed! That is the way he would have reformed, have regenerated me!

RICHARD. Is this mountain honor?

> [*With pretended indignation.*

RAMON. How can you know what is passing in my soul?

HUGUETTE. [*To* MAX, *laughing*] Oh, the scandals of Paris!

RAMON. You have no hearts. You cannot feel. You cannot sympathize with my disgrace!

> [DANIELA *sinks into a chair.*

RICHARD. [*With mock concern*] What will the priest say to this?

RAMON. I don't care what the priest says. A curse has fallen on me—a curse that this woman has brought!

RICHARD. [*Laying his hand on* RAMON's *shoulder*] Calm yourself, calm yourself!

HUGUETTE. This is the love of a tiger, Daniela.

RAMON. [*To* RICHARD] You don't know how long I have waited for her!

RICHARD. I don't wonder you complain.

RAMON. For fifteen years I have lived only for this woman. She has been sacred to me!

RICHARD. Sacred! That interests me.

> MAX *follows* RAMON *at a distance, containing himself, but smiling at the doleful appearance of* RICHARD.

RAMON. I respected her like a saint from heaven! I worshipped, I adored her, and to see her happy I would have given up my life, the blood of my veins, my very soul itself!

> DANIELA *has risen and stands with her arm about* HUGUETTE, *who can scarcely keep from laughing at* RICHARD, *who pretends to weep sympathetically.* MAX *is unable to restrain his laughter.*

MAX. [*Aside*] Oh, oh, this mountain honor!

RICHARD. [*To* RAMON] It's a shame!

RAMON. And now you see, she has no heart! For, gentlemen, this woman has no heart. [*He weeps with rage*] And if I let her go, my life will surge out after her, because I will kill myself. I will die with despair, for I am dying with grief and despair.

> RICHARD *begins to weep, and the other players break out laughing.* DANIELA, *much affected, remains in the background because of the situation of* RAMON, *who falls back also, without comprehending the reason for the laughter.*

MAX. There could be nothing finer than this.

HUGUETTE. It is exquisite.

RICHARD. [*Wiping his eyes*] It will break my heart.— Bravo! Bravo!

DANIELA. [*Rising and coming forward indignantly*] What do you mean? Are you laughing at him? What right have you to laugh at this man? [RAMON *stands as one dazed.* RICHARD *begins to weep again. The others laugh*] Don't you see that all that he says is true? Fools!

RICHARD. [*To* DANIELA] Brava! Brava!

> [*Clapping his hands.*

DANIELA. Don't you see that it is torn from the very bottom of his soul?

RAMON. For you! It is for you. [*Beside himself*] Take care! I can bear no more.

> [*Like a beast he makes a leap toward them.*

DANIELA. [*Interposing*] Fools! Fools! [*They go on laughing*] Don't laugh any more!

RAMON. [*About to throw himself upon them*] I must kill some one! I want blood!

HUGUETTE. Ah!

> *With a cry, she takes refuge behind* MAX. DANIELA *endeavors to restrain* RAMON.

DANIELA. Ramón, Ramón!

RAMON. Blood! Blood! [*He opens the drawer for the revolver*]

DANIELA. No, no!

> RAMON *thrusts the revolver back into the drawer. The others approach the door slowly, still laughing, but now from fear.*

RICHARD. Curtain! Curtain!

DANIELA. Get out of the house!

RAMON. Oh, what disgrace!

MAX. [*Still laughing*] But Daniela . . .

DANIELA. Fools! Get out!

HUGUETTE. [*To* DANIELA, *laughing*] But I didn't laugh!

RAMON. I can bear no more.

> *Burying his face between his arms on the table; then he jumps up again, wildly.*

DANIELA. [*To* HUGUETTE] You go, too. You are no better than the rest!   [*They are already at the door.*

HUGUETTE. [*Brazenly*] Nor than you.

DANIELA. Go! Go!

RICHARD. [*Going out last*] We are all the same.

> [*He bows ceremoniously.*

MAX. [*Already outside*] We beg your pardon.

> [*With a great laugh.*

DANIELA. Away!

HUGUETTE. [*Without, while* DANIELA *closes the door*] Remember us when he fires the shot!

> [*They are heard laughing as they disappear.*

DANIELA. [*Turning to* RAMON] There! I stay!

RAMON. Thanks, Daniela, thanks.

DANIELA. I stay because I pity you. You have what you want; I pity you.

> *She is much exhausted and supports herself with the aid of the table, breathing with great difficulty.*

RAMON. Yes, Daniela, and I thank you for it. I am mad with joy. See, all is still about—there is no sound. They are gone, Daniela, gone! And we find ourselves alone—after so many years of waiting!

DANIELA. What? [*Falling back*] No, Ramón no! Good-night, good-night!   [*She staggers toward her own room.*

RAMON. [*Seizing her and holding her fast*] Daniela! Daniela, listen!

DANIELA. [*Turning*] No, not one word! I know now that I have to die. My hours are numbered. My life has ebbed today.

RAMON. No! Ah, no!

DANIELA. And I must die alone.

RAMON. You are going to fall. Lean on me.

DANIELA. Let go!   [*She is about to fall.*

RAMON. I'll hold you up. [*He catches her*] See! Now I hold you up.

DANIELA. Let go! Let go!

RAMON. [*Carrying her to her room*] I love you! I love you!

DANIELA. [*Repulsing him*] Your wife! Your children!

RAMON. Be still!

DANIELA. Ramón!—God! [*Indignantly*]

RAMON. I do not hear! I am mad! I do not hear!

> They reach the door of DANIELA's room. As they do,
> holding her in his arms, he is about to give her a kiss.

DANIELA. [*Avoiding him furiously*] I won't have it! I won't have it!

RAMON. [*After having kissed her*] In! In!

DANIELA. [*Breaking away from him*] No! No! Help! Help!   [*Running toward ANTONIA's room.*

RAMON. [*Running after her*] Be still! Be still!

DANIELA. Help!

> She throws open the door of ANTONIA's room. ANTONIA
> is heard singing:

"Mother of God, a little child
    Is laid upon thy breast."

RAMON. Oh, God!
    In a voice of agony, but stifled for fear that ANTONIA *will
    hear.*
DANIELA. In there! [*Pointing to the room.   He hesitates an
    instant*] In, into your own!
RAMON. Ah! Wretch that I am!
                        [*He rushes headlong into the room.*
DANIELA. To suffocate! To die! [*Moving away*] To die!
To die! To die—alone!
    *She staggers across the stage into her own room and
    closes the door behind her.* ANTONIA *continues her
    song.*

            Curtain.

ACT III

The same. It is a cloudy morning. The door of DANIELA'S *room is closed;* ANTONIA'S *room stands open. The cradle occupies the same position as in the previous act, but without the child.*

When the curtain rises the stage is empty. Presently a number of little girls pass at the back, talking. Other children follow, who stop at the door; and later, other children, who stop also.

FIRST CHILD. Hurry up, it's late!

SECOND CHILD. I'm not going to run.

THIRD CHILD. [*Calling from the door*] Anna! Anna!

FOURTH CHILD. What's the matter with Anna?

THIRD CHILD. What will Monsa say to you, Anna?

FOURTH CHILD. Anna, are you asleep?

ANNA. [*Within*] I'm coming as soon as I finish my chocolate.

CHILDREN. Anna, Anna! . . . Monsa will fix you, Anna! . . . Wait and see!

   ANNA *enters.*

ANNA. I've just swallowed my chocolate. For goodness' sake!

CHILDREN. Here she is! Here she is! Anna's just got up! She's just got up!

ANNA. No, I haven't either. Shame on you! [*Enter* ANTONIA] Mamma, oughtn't they to be ashamed of themselves?

ANTONIA. Come here and get your 'kerchief. What a child!

263

ANNA. I'm coming! I'm coming! In a minute!
To the children who are jumping up and down at the door.

ANTONIA. [*Adjusting the 'kerchief*] Can't you stand still?
Some of the girls run away from the door, others promptly take their places. There is constant bustle among the children who are playing, jumping up and down, nibbling at candy, romping and striking one another, but always with the utmost good-nature.

THIRD CHILD. [*To* ANNA] I dressed myself and fixed my hair all by myself.   [*Other children say the same.*

ANNA. You did? Now my hair-ribbon.

ANTONIA. Can't you keep still?

ANNA. They're trying to tease me, mamma! Hurry up!

ANTONIA. There! Now give me a kiss.

ANNA. And one for the baby!   [*Running up to the cradle.*

ANTONIA. The baby isn't there.

ANNA. Where is he?   [*Running to the door of the room.*

ANTONIA. No, child, he's at your aunt's.

ANNA. [*Stamping*] At my aunt's? [*Running out*] I'm coming, I'm coming!

CHILDREN. Here she is! Here she is! She's ready now!

ANNA. I had two cups of chocolate. Mamma didn't want me to have them either!
The children rush up to her and form a ring, circling about and singing as they disappear. Gradually their voices die away in the distance. TOMASETA *enters with a basket on her arm.*

TOMASETA. Good-morning, Antonia! I am late today. I should have gotten out before this.

ANTONIA. Good-morning.

TOMASETA. I'm going down to the village, and I thought I might stop in and see if there was anything you wanted me to do.

ANTONIA. No, nothing this morning, Tomaseta. I was at the village day before yesterday, and tended to everything myself.

TOMASETA. I suppose you did. You have to lay in such lots of stuff for Daniela. I daresay, though, she pays for everything herself.

ANTONIA. You'll have to ask Ramón about that.

TOMASETA. It takes my breath away to think of so much money being spent at every meal.—Do you suppose Daniela wants anything this morning?

ANTONIA. She isn't up yet.

TOMASETA. She isn't up? Perhaps I'd better wait and see.

ANTONIA. Yes, wait as long as you like.

        Enter ANDREW.

ANDREW. Antonia, where's Ramón?

ANTONIA. He's up at the house, working.

ANDREW. Oh! Never mind then. I've just finished breakfast and thought I'd drop in. Hello! Who's here?

TOMASETA. When you are supposed to be busy, what you are really doing is gossiping with the neighbors.

ANDREW. It began to rain as I was coming along the road.

TOMASETA. What? And I haven't been to the village.

ANDREW. The masons finished the porch this morning.

TOMASETA. I hear you had company yesterday—actors.

ANTONIA. Yes, I think they were; something of the sort.

TOMASETA. What did they have to say?

ANTONIA. Nothing.

ANDREW. [*Laughing*] Oh, they had something to say!

        PONA *enters, carrying a basket of cherries.*

PONA. Good-morning. Your wife's looking for you, Andrew.—I'm all wet through.

ANDREW. My wife? Where is she?

PONA. Didn't you hear her call?

ANDREW. She can wait. Don't tell her I was here, Antonia.

TOMASETA. Why not?

ANDREW. You know. She's jealous!

[*Pointing to* DANIELA'S *room. They all begin to laugh.*

PONA. You're a perfect devil, Andrew! [*To* ANTONIA, *showing the cherries*] Aren't they fine cherries? I made up my mind I'd better get them off the trees before it began to rain. Perhaps Daniela would like some.

ANTONIA. I'll ask her when she gets up.

PONA. What? Isn't she up yet?

ANDREW. Oh, that's the French of it; they turn day into night. [*To* PONA] Don't you want to look and see if my wife's there? [PONA *goes to the door to look.*

TOMASETA. I must go on to the village.

ANTONIA. Call her if you like.

TOMASETA. No, I'll wait . . . [*To* ANTONIA] Caramba! Those actors! [*Laughing*]

[ANTONIA *moves away from* TOMASETA, *uneasily.*

PONA. [*To* ANDREW] She's sitting down by the gate, sewing. [*Looking out of the door*]

ANDREW. Well, I haven't done anything anyway. [*He puts down a shoe which he had taken up*] She might sew up her tongue.

TOMASETA. [*To* ANTONIA] Do you think Daniela is going to get well?

ANTONIA. How should I know?

PONA. She's building a house.

TOMASETA. That shows she likes it here.

PONA. Yes. But I seem to be wasting my time.

ANDREW. [*To* PONA] Will you do me a favor when you go?

PONA. What is it?

ANDREW. When you pass my wife, stand in front of her so that I can slip out.

PONA. Go along, holy man.

TOMASETA. I'm going to tell her you're here.

ANDREW. I'll get even with you if you do.

ANTONIA. [*Surprised*] What's the matter?

> *Returning from her room into which she has stepped for a moment.*

PONA. He's afraid his wife will find him out.

ANDREW. I'm afraid of her? The trouble is that she's afraid of me.

PONA. I'm going to call Daniela. [*To* ANTONIA] We can't wait any longer.

ANTONIA. Yes, call her.

PONA. [*Going up to the door*] Daniela! Get up, Daniela! I've brought you a basket of cherries from the garden. [*Leaving the door*] Now she'll get up.

TOMASETA. What time is it?

ANDREW. It must be eight o'clock.

PONA. A quarter to nine. [*Going back to the door*] Daniela! Daniela! [*Coming away again*] I've got a day's work to do—and two boys who don't do a thing but wear out their shoes.

ANDREW. Thank God I haven't got any girls!

PONA. Do you hear what he is thanking God for?

> [TOMASETA *goes up to* DANIELA'S *door and listens.*

TOMASETA. I can't hear anything; she must be asleep. Daniela, don't you want anything from the village? [*Listening at the door*] If you want anything from the village, it's I—I, Tomaseta.

> [*Making a sign to the others that she doesn't hear anything.*

ANDREW. There—now!

TOMASETA. No—not a sound.

PONA. See if she'll hear me. Daniela! Daniela! [*Knocking loudly*] Daniela!

TOMASETA. [*At some distance from the door*] Wait a minute . . .

ANDREW. Keep still!

> [PONA *lays her ear against the door, listening.*

ANTONIA. What can the matter be?

PONA. Something must have happened. [*She knocks again.*
> *The children can be heard in the distance, singing at*
> *school.*

ANDREW. She can't be in bed. She must have gone out.

TOMASETA. Oh, of course!

ANTONIA. She always gets up late.

PONA. Monsa will be sure to know. [*Exit* PONA, *running.*

TOMASETA. Come right back, Pona.

ANDREW. Now I know where she is—where she spends all
her time. Up at the house with Ramón!

TOMASETA. To be sure! She told me to come up there
this morning and see her, and since it's raining she is afraid
to come down. Why didn't we think of that before?

> [*The children have stopped singing.* PONA *re-enters.*

PONA. Monsa says she hasn't seen her pass.

ANDREW. Why should Monsa see everything?

> *Enter* MONSA.

MONSA. No, Daniela hasn't gone out.

TOMASETA. Then she'd be in her room, and she isn't there.

MONSA. I don't know what to make of it. Let's see if she
isn't there. [*After looking through the keyhole*] Daniela!

> *The others converse among themselves.* MONSA *listens*
> *after having called.*

PONA. It's very strange.

ANTONIA. Pona! [*So as to be able to hear*]

MONSA. [*Again looking through the keyhole*] Everything is
dark. If she'd gone out, she'd have opened the windows.

PONA. But if she hadn't, she'd be in there, and then she'd
answer.

ANDREW. And she doesn't. That's what makes all the
trouble.

MONSA. Daniela! Daniela!—What has happened? [*She runs her finger into the keyhole*] The door's locked and the key's inside. Daniela's in there!

ANTONIA. Holy Mother!

PONA. How are we ever going to get in?

MONSA. Get some tools—a hammer and chisel, quick!

ANTONIA. And call Ramón.

PONA. Hurry!

[*Exit* TOMASETA *at the back.*

MONSA. [*Banging on the door*] Daniela!

Re-enter TOMASETA *with* RAMON.

RAMON. What's the matter?

TOMASETA. Daniela hasn't opened the door. She doesn't answer.

MONSA. Daniela's in there and doesn't answer.

RAMON. Have you called her? Out loud?

ANTONIA *draws a little to one side at the entrance of*
        RAMON.

MONSA. Yes. [*Shaking the door*] It's locked on the inside.

RAMON. Daniela! Daniela!

[*Throwing himself against the door.*

MONSA. Bring a hammer, an ax!

RAMON. No, no—I'm here.

*Thrusting his shoulder against the door, preparatory to
        forcing it open.* ANDREW *comes to help him.*

MONSA. Now both together! Push!

TOMASETA. [*To* ANTONIA] Poor Daniela!

ANTONIA. Yes.

MONSA. Push! Now! [*By the door*]

RAMON. Wait! Now push, man. There!

[*The door opens with a crash.*

MONSA. Daniela! [*Entering first*]

ANTONIA. No, me!—let me go first.

She runs in before PONA *and* TOMASETA, *who follow her.*
RAMON *starts to enter, but falls back. The women are
heard talking within the room.*

ANDREW. [*To* RAMON] Maybe she's . . .

RAMON. [*Trying to listen*] Don't talk to me!

MONSA. [*From the room*] Daniela!

ANTONIA. Lift up her head.

MONSA. Hold her. Hold her—so.

TOMASETA. Daniela!

RAMON. Oh, Andrew! [*Anxiously*]

MONSA. She doesn't answer. She doesn t speak a word.

PONA. Don't let her fall.

[RAMON, *greatly distressed, is about to enter the room.*

ANTONIA. [*Confronting him at the door*] No, Ramón!

RAMON. How is she? [*Wishing to know if she is dead*]

ANTONIA. [*Sympathetically*] She's alive! She has opened her
eyes. I came out to tell you. [RAMON *falls back*] The Doctor!

RAMON. [*To* ANDREW] Run for the Doctor—and Valentine,
too. Hurry! [*Exit* ANDREW.

PONA. [*To* ANTONIA, *coming out of the room*] Quick, Antonia! Salts—have you any salts?

ANTONIA. They are on the table in my room.

ANTONIA *re-enters* DANIELA'S *room;* PONA *runs into*
ANTONIA'S.

RAMON. [*Going up to the door of* DANIELA'S *room*] I must
see her.

[*To* MONSA, *who appears, waiting for the return of* PONA.

MONSA. [*Severely*] You can't come in. Why doesn't she
hurry? [*Impatiently*]

RAMON. [*To* MONSA] If you let her die! . . .

PONA. [*Re-entering with the bottle*] Here they are.

MONSA. Give them to me.

[*She takes the bottle and runs back into* DANIELA'S *room.*

PONA. [*To* RAMON] We were sitting here all the while just

as calmly as you please. Who would ever have believed that
she was in there like that?

> RAMON *moves away so as not to hear her; she disappears
> into* DANIELA'S *room.*

MONSA. [*In the room*] It's I, I—Daniela.

PONA. Now she knows us.

MONSA. [*Laughing*] Yes, we're all your friends. Yes, this
is Antonia; she loves you, too.   [RAMON *starts.*

TOMASETA. [*Re-entering; to* RAMON] She's better now.

PONA. [*Re-entering*] Why do people have to suffer so? I'm
all a-tremble.

TOMASETA. [*To* RAMON] Perhaps you'd better take something—and Antonia too. We'd all better take something
on account of the shock.

> *Enter* VALENTINE, *carrying an umbrella.*

VALENTINE. Here he is!

RAMON. At last!

TOMASETA. But I am glad!

> *Enter* ANDREW, *also with an umbrella.*

ANDREW. He's here! The Doctor!

PONA. I'll run and tell them. [*Exit into* DANIELA'S *room.*

TOMASETA. Not too much noise! [*Exit, running after her.*

RAMON. [*To* VALENTINE] Wait by the door; let nobody in.

> *Exit* VALENTINE. DON JOAQUIM *enters with an um-
> brella.*

RAMON. Don Joaquím, Daniela is dying.

DON JOAQUIM. So soon? You surprise me.

RAMON. For God's sake, Doctor, hurry! If she should
die . . .

DON JOAQUIM. How? [*Surprised at his manner of speaking.*

RAMON. You mustn't let her die!

DON JOAQUIM. [*Pausing*] Why, Ramón! What is this?

RAMON. Quick, quick!

TOMASETA. Ay, Señor Doctor! [*Within*]

Don Joaquim. I'm coming. I'm coming.

[*He goes into* Daniela's *room.*

Pona. [*Coming out as the doctor enters*] She's resting more quietly.

Andrew. [*To* Tomaseta, *who is at the door*] How do you think she is, Tomaseta?

Tomaseta. Much better. She's trying to raise herself up.

Pona. Now we'll see what the Doctor will do to her.

Andrew. Humph! Doctors always come too late. The patient's either dead or well already.

Tomaseta. Now he'll try to make us believe he's cured her.

Pona. If I hadn't stopped in with the cherries . . .

Tomaseta. If I hadn't called Ramón to break down the door . . .

Andrew. If I hadn't helped him break it down . . .

[Ramon *paces anxiously to and fro across the room.*

Tomaseta. [*To* Ramon] I wonder what could have given Daniela such a shock?

Ramon. Leave me alone! Don't you see how I feel? . . . [Tomaseta *endeavors to interrupt him*] That's right—stand there and stare! Amuse yourselves with our misfortunes. You've always amused yourselves with the misfortunes of this house. [*He turns away from them and continues talking to himself*] Why was I ever born? To suffer? Never to be happy from one year's end to the next—hating and despising myself, like one lost! For I am lost, damned utterly, through this world and the next! I care for no man! My hand is against them all! [*To* Andrew, *who is following him*] Yes, talk! That's right—talk!

Tomaseta. Ay, Ramón!

Pona. But we . . .

Andrew. I . . .

Ramon. I tell you, I am not myself. But I've got to know

what is going on in that room.   If she's going to die I've got
to know it.

> *He rushes up to the door, but halts at the entrance of*
> MONSA. *They all surround her, excepting only*
> RAMON, *who draws back for fear of bad news.*

MONSA. She's talking alone with the Doctor—as if she
wanted to confess.

PONA. How is she?

MONSA. Better, I told you.

TOMASETA. [*To* PONA] Of course she's better.

MONSA. [*To* TOMASETA] Go and look after the children.
There is nobody to take care of the school.

TOMASETA. I'll see to them.

> MONSA *returns to the room.* TOMASETA *prepares to
> leave.*

ANDREW. [*To* TOMASETA] Take my wife with you, do you
hear?

TOMASETA. Get out!   [*Exit.*

ANDREW. That's it.   I can't get out!

PONA. Here comes the Doctor.

RAMON. [*Aside*] What will he say now? [*Enter* DON
JOAQUIM] What is it, Doctor?   How is she?

DON JOAQUIM. [*Reserved*] Resting quietly.

PONA. She's not in any danger, Doctor?

DON JOAQUIM. No! [*Forbidding them to speak*] I tell you no!

RAMON. Thanks, Don Joaquím!   Thanks!   You don't
know how glad I am to hear you say so.

DON JOAQUIM. Not so fast. [*To the others*] I must ask you
all to leave—to leave immediately.   It is absolutely essential.
[*To* RAMON] Let no one else in.   There has been far too much
confusion already.

RAMON. No one shall come in, I promise you.

PONA. Very well, Doctor. [*To* RAMON] If we can do anything . . .

RAMON. Thanks.

ANDREW. [*To* DON JOAQUIM] Must I go too?

DON JOAQUIM. Certainly.

ANDREW. Wait, Pona!

PONA. What's the matter?

> [*She is already outside the door.*

ANDREW. Stay on this side.

PONA. On this side?

ANDREW. And don't run too fast.

> [PONA *and* ANDREW *retire.*

DON JOAQUIM. [*To* RAMON] Why didn't you go into the room with me?

RAMON. Because—Doctor, I cannot go into her room— I am not the man you think. You do not understand. I am not myself. I . . . [*With desperation*]

DON JOAQUIM. Yes, I understand. You're a . . .

> [*He is about to use a disagreeable word.*

RAMON. A wild man, Don Joaquím! A beast! Disgraced!

DON JOAQUIM. No, you are a man whose heart is evil. I wouldn't have believed it possible that you could have changed like this. One finger of that woman's hand is worth more than your whole body.

RAMON. I am disgraced.

DON JOAQUIM. She has shown more feeling than you have, more sense of right. It is not she who has wished to dishonor this house. Can you deny it?

RAMON. No.

DON JOAQUIM. You have persecuted her, you have humiliated her. You have done everything in your power, both you and your wife, to make it impossible for her to enjoy that peace of which she stood so sorely in need. You have killed her.

RAMON. Killed her, Don Joaquím? Daniela?

DON JOAQUIM. You have killed her. She is as dead as the

dead in their graves already. Remember, I charged you a hundred times, and Antonia too, not to excite her, not to cross her in anything. In any case death would have ensued before long—the French doctor predicted it and I foresaw it clearly, but it lay in your power to prolong her life a little, and to render her days happy and peaceful at the close.

Re-enter MONSA *and* ANTONIA.

MONSA. How is she, Doctor?

DON JOAQUIM. Dead, unless for a miracle.

[ANTONIA *looks at* RAMON.

MONSA. Don Joaquím!

DON JOAQUIM. And you must not expect me to work miracles.

MONSA. But, Doctor, she's sleeping quietly . . .

DON JOAQUIM. It makes no matter. Oh, if I only had it to do over again!

RAMON. What would you do?

DON JOAQUIM. When they wrote to me that they were going to send her here, I ought to have forbidden it. Her stay in this village was sure to prove fatal. I felt it from the beginning. With your narrow-mindedness she was certain to be hounded to death.

ANTONIA. Doctor, but I—I thought . . .

DON JOAQUIM. You thought? Have you ever once thought of showing a kind heart? You have persecuted her with insults—I have seen it myself repeatedly. And when I took you to task for it, you imagined that I was conspiring against you.

MONSA. Doctor!

DON JOAQUIM. Poor woman, you are the only one who has not considered yourself, who has had the grace to be true. I don't know what we'd do without you, either.

ANTONIA. [*Weeping*] But, Doctor, I was a stranger in my own house, and I'm Ramón's wife, and she . . .

DON JOAQUIM. She? What did she ever do to you? She has respected you. Another woman—I should have liked to see it—another woman in her place might not have returned good for evil; she might have revenged herself.

MONSA. Shall we wake her for the medicines?

DON JOAQUIM. No, let her sleep while she is able. And don't let these people disturb her! *[He is about to go.*

ANTONIA. Doctor, I'll never disturb her.

DON JOAQUIM. I'll call again this afternoon; meanwhile continue with the medicines as before.

MONSA. Don't delay, Don Joaquím.

DON JOAQUIM. I repeat, don't let these people disturb her.

ANTONIA. I'll lock the door. *[Standing beside it.*

RAMON. *[Drawing near the door]* Do you mean to tell me, Doctor, that there is no hope—cost what it may?

[DANIELA appears at the door of her room.

DON JOAQUIM. I have just told you—she is as good as dead already. And you are the cause of her death—you and your wife!

RAMON. But if we want a consultation?

DON JOAQUIM. A consultation!

MONSA. Suppose she tries to get up?

DON JOAQUIM. It makes no difference. In the end it will be the same.

RAMON. *[Going out with the doctor]* But, Doctor, a consultation . . . *[They are already outside.*

DON JOAQUIM. *[Without]* She is dead, I tell you. She is dead already! *[MONSA closes the door behind them.*

ANTONIA. Daniela!

MONSA. *[Running up to her]* What did you get up for?

DANIELA. Because I wanted air and light. Because I want to live. *[They help her to a chair.*

MONSA. You're better now, Daniela, much better. It was only an attack of weakness. The Doctor said so.

DANIELA. Yes, I am much better.

> [*She turns around to look for* RAMON.

MONSA. What is it? What do you want?

DANIELA. I want . . . [*Looking at* ANTONIA] Nothing, nothing.

MONSA. Are you more comfortable now?

DANIELA. Yes, yes, more comfortable—now. I passed a horrible night.

MONSA. Why didn't you call?

DANIELA. Call? Whom? [*With desperation*]

MONSA. Anybody.

DANIELA. [*To* MONSA, *aside*] Hush! [*Then aloud*] I—I heard you when you knocked on the door—but I wasn't able to open my lips and reply. Daniela! Daniela! And I was lying there in bed not able to move, not even to open my eyes. Maybe when death comes I shall be lying there, all wide awake and still, and I will hear you call, Daniela, Daniela!—and not be able to reply. Will you kiss me, Monsa, when I die?—My Monsa since I was a child! Will you kiss me when I die?

MONSA. But you are better. You are not going to die.

DANIELA. [*Irritated, like a child*] No, don't tell me that. Will you kiss me when I die?

MONSA. Yes, yes. Of course.

DANIELA. And Antonia—will you still hate me, after I am gone?

ANTONIA. [*Much affected*] No, Daniela! No.

DANIELA. Will you treat me the same then? Will you still call me what you've called me so many times?

ANTONIA. No, no! Never again!

DANIELA. Wanton, eh?

MONSA. You must be quiet, Daniela.

ANTONIA. No, Daniela, I don't wish you any harm; I want you to get well. [*Weeping*]

DANIELA. Will you kiss me then, Antonia?

ANTONIA. Yes, just like Monsa! Just the same as she.

DANIELA. When I am dead, eh? But not the same as she!
It will not be the same. For Monsa will kiss me as she used
to do when we were girls together, and she will try to shield
me now from death because she wants to have me live. But
you will kiss me because I have to die, and they are coming
to make the cross upon me—the cross upon the dead!

MONSA. No, no, you mustn't talk like that, Daniela. The
Doctor wants you to be quiet.

ANTONIA. Yes.

DANIELA. Everybody will forgive me after I am gone. My
sins will be washed out; I shall be white as snow. And
since I have to die without confession . . . [*They try to speak,
but she prevents them*] . . . you think you'll pardon me a little
in advance, and let me know beforehand that I'll be forgiven
and absolved. [*She looks at* ANTONIA]

MONSA. [*Forcing herself to laugh*] But, Daniela, you're not
going to die.

DANIELA. I am going to die. The Doctor said so.

ANTONIA. He didn't say so.

MONSA. He said just the opposite.

DANIELA. Oh, no, no! I was there, and I heard him say
so. [*Pointing to the door of the room*] And when he said so,
[*To* ANTONIA] I looked at you—and you looked at Ramón,
and you smiled.

ANTONIA. No! That would have been a mortal sin.

DANIELA. [*Laughing*] You didn't see that you smiled, but I
saw! I saw!

MONSA. [*Compassionately*] You're so weak, Daniela.

DANIELA. [*Overcome*] Yes! I am dying. In all the world
there is no help for me. [*With sudden resolution*] But all men
have pity on the dying, and now you have to pity me, because
I can do no one any harm. Like a broken, withered branch,

I am clinging to the tree. [*She rises from the chair, supported by the women*] I'll not do you any harm. [*Sadly, to* ANTONIA] Be happy with your children. Lay your boy in the cradle and rock him to sleep. I'll not be here to come near you nor disturb you nor to kiss your boy. I'll let you be. I am alone in the world, and I must go alone.   [*Pointing to the sky.*

MONSA. Nonsense, Daniela.

ANTONIA. Daniela, you mustn't treat me so. I hated you because I believed what wasn't true—I was afraid. Ramón hated me. You would have done the same in my place. You would have done the same.

The children are heard singing at school; only DANIELA
notices the song.

DANIELA. They are singing—singing! You live in them, in the children, Monsa! Listen, listen! You've a corner in the heart of every one. Listen! Ah! It's like a great choir!

ANTONIA. [*Pleadingly*] Daniela! Daniela!

DANIELA. Don't speak to me,—I hear them singing. I am breathing in their song! Their life fills my breast. Ah! [*To* ANTONIA] Leave me, leave me! For now I envy you. For you are going to live on in the world and be happy, afloat on an ocean of joy! [*She looks at her*] But for me there is nothing—nothing! No laughter nor smiles any more, for I am dying of thirst, and look!—there is so much water everywhere.

ANTONIA. Daniela!

MONSA. Leave her, Antonia.

DANIELA. But I know where there is water for me, and I mean to have it. I mean to drink. [*She laughs hysterically*] Yes, I mean to drink. I will have it, too! [*Aside, to* MONSA] Send her away! Monsa, send her away!

MONSA. Leave us for a little while.

ANTONIA. If you think best.

MONSA. I'll calm her; then you can come back.

ANTONIA. I'll run after the boy.

MONSA. Do.

> *Exit* ANTONIA *to the rear.* MONSA *follows her to the door and closes it behind her.*

DANIELA. [*Aside*] Now to be happy! I must be happy, too!

MONSA. [*Returning*] You must be quiet, Daniela, very, very quiet. I want to tell you about the house.

DANIELA. The house? I give it to you for the school. It shall be yours.

MONSA. No. [*Wishing to change the subject*]

DANIELA. Yours and the children's. And everything I have shall be yours—and the children's. With it, you will be so much richer than I! [MONSA *weeps*] Has Antonia gone?

MONSA. Yes.

DANIELA. Then call Ramón. Quick! For I want my share of happiness, my hour of life! All ought not to be for others.

> *Through the scenes which follow,* DANIELA *becomes delirious from time to time, in greater or less degree, as is apparent from her manner and speech.*

MONSA. What do you say?

DANIELA. Ramón! I want Ramón! Call him.

MONSA. He's coming, Daniela.

DANIELA. [*Becoming impatient*] But I've no time to lose. I want Ramón!

MONSA. Listen to me!

DANIELA. Ramón!

MONSA. But he's coming, I tell you.

DANIELA. Ramón! Ramón!

MONSA. Ay, but he'll soon be here!

> [*Not knowing what to do.*

DANIELA. Ramón! Ramón! I want Ramón!

> [*Enter* RAMON.

RAMON. Daniela!   [*He closes the door.*

DANIELA. Ah, he's here! You heard me call?

RAMON. Yes, I heard you.

DANIELA. My Ramón! Ramón of the old days! Ramón
that used to be a boy with me!

RAMON. Yes, it is I! I—your Ramón, who will never leave
you any more!

DANIELA. Never! . . .

RAMON. Daniela, how are you? Courage! See, the tower
of the chalet is mounting higher and higher, and the church
tower will soon be left far below.

DANIELA. Yes. But I must make haste. I must make
haste!   [*Breathing with great difficulty.*

MONSA. You'd better let me get you something.

DANIELA. No, I want to talk to Ramón. I want to tell
him so many things about my journey; for I am going.
Leave us, leave us, Monsa! I'll call you, Monsa! Monsetta!
                         [*Throwing her arms about her neck.*

MONSA. Daniela. Daniela!   [*Embracing her.*

DANIELA. Thanks for everything! Thanks!

MONSA. [*To* RAMON] I'll be with the children when you
want me.

RAMON. I'll call you soon.

                    [*Exit* MONSA. RAMON *closes the door.*

DANIELA. Ramón, Ramón, Ramón! [RAMON *turns to her*]
Ah! [*With satisfaction*] Listen!

RAMON. What is it, Daniela?

DANIELA. You have never left this village? You have
never traveled very far?

RAMON. No. Why?

DANIELA. Suppose that I should say to you, Ramón, that
there is still one way left to save my life—one way, and only
one: to carry me away, and let me live.

RAMON. Then I would do it. Anything to save your

life. I have been acting for so many years. All the while I yearned to come to you—I said to myself to kill you, but I knew it was not so. I was only trying to deceive myself, to find an excuse to go. For I was always yours, and I would have ended at your side, your slave. How many times your voice has called to me, yet at the moment that I most longed to go my heart held back; I could not. On the brink my head turned, I sickened with disgust. I don't know how. But if I would have gone with you then, Daniela, how much more would I go with you now—now, to save your life!

DANIELA. It is the brink. Do you know, it is the brink? And the deeper the chasm the louder it calls, and the more surely it sucks us down. Ramón, what is there left to me of life, if I should want to live?

RAMON. You must live. I want you to.

DANIELA. Then let us fly together.

RAMON. Fly? You say, let us fly together?

DANIELA. Yes, for as I am now, no one would deny me anything—no more than they would a condemned man.

RAMON. But you are not ill, Daniela.

DANIELA. No—no. [*Firmly*] Listen! What difference does it make to you? If I am ill—out of my head, mad, what of it? You said that you loved me and wanted to make me happy. Then let me be happy. Let me be happy, then, with you! [*With delirious excitement*] Come! Let us fly far away—to Paris!—to live, to intoxicate ourselves with life! For here something gnaws at my heart, and with every look you revenge yourself on me.

RAMON. I revenge myself?

DANIELA. Yes, you assassinate me! But quickly, Ramón, quickly, while we may. Throw me over your shoulder when I cannot walk, catch me up in your arms, fling me about your neck—I do not care—snatch me away from death! We will fly with our heads bowed to the ground like the criminal faster, faster, through the dark, speaking to no man. And it may be that we can hide from death, and that he will come and look for us, and look in vain, and that we will laugh at him because he cannot find us!

RAMON. Daniela, be calm! Daniela, I want what you want. When I am with you, there is nothing else in all the world for me. There is nothing else but you. I would give everything I have to save your life.

DANIELA. Then fly—fly with me from death. Look! Look! [*She moves backward, with a hoarse cry, seeming to avoid the apparition of death*] Fly, fly!

> *Terrified, she embraces* RAMON. *Her delirium seems to communicate itself to him.*

RAMON. Fly? Ah! I give my word. Nothing shall hold me back. I swear it.

DANIELA. Then it must be quickly. Now! My time is growing short.

RAMON. [*Distracted*] What? Now, Daniela?

DANIELA. Yes, now, for unless we cheat death, he will not let us go, and *she* will prevent you! [*Meaning* ANTONIA]

RAMON. She will prevent me! You are right. [*Wildly*] It must be now.

DANIELA. Now!

RAMON. Come on! Ah!—wait. [*Looking around*] No! I can't allow myself to think. [*Running to the door and calling*] Valentine!

DANIELA. They'll stop us!

RAMON. Not now! Come on.

> VALENTINE *enters.* RAMON *leaves* DANIELA. *She retires into her room.*

VALENTINE. Did you call?

RAMON. Fetch the tartana—like lightning. Quick! Do you hear?

VALENTINE. Yes.

RAMON. And let no one come in. Daniela's well again. [*Exit* VALENTINE] I'll send back word from the village— I can't write now, not now! Daniela! Where are you? Daniela!

> DANIELA *re-enters from her room carrying a wrap, but without having put it on.*

DANIELA. [*Aside*] Here! This will do. [*Aloud*] I am ready. I have everything.

RAMON. And so have I—everything. At last we are together! My money—ah, no money! [*Ransacking his pockets and examining his papers*] I can get it at the village. I can get what I need there. [DANIELA *meanwhile tries to put on the wrap*] Let me help you. [*Assisting her. Both are greatly excited*] We have to wait for the tartana.

DANIELA. [*Impatiently*] Ah, this delay!

RAMON. [*Frenzied*] Don't think, I say! I am ready now for anything, and if they try to hold us back, I'll kill them. By the Lord, I'll kill them! [*Looking out*] The tartana is here. Quick! Quick!

DANIELA. Yes, yes; I am coming. [*Gasping*] But—wait! Wait a moment! Wait!   [*Falling into a chair.*

RAMON. [*Running up to her*] What's the matter?

DANIELA. Nothing, it's nothing. It's the joy of taking you with me!

RAMON. [*Much affected*] Yes, it's the joy! The joy! . . .

DANIELA. The past will fly behind us, like an evil thing. And all the world will fly, fly far behind, and call out to us as we pass, abandoned, wanton, lost! I hate you!

> RAMON *wrings his hands; his voice is choked with anguish.*

RAMON. Yes, the past will remain behind. And all the world will remain behind. All, all will remain behind!

> [*The children are heard singing at school.*

DANIELA. Ah! That song! That wretched song! . . . [*Stop-*

ping RAMON's *ears with her hands*] Don't hear it, Ramón.
Come away! Come away!

RAMON. Courage! Courage!

[*She rises,* RAMON *supporting her.*

DANIELA. Help me with the wrap. Ah! I can do it—so.
No, help me! [*Then, referring to the children*] They are singing, still singing . . . [*She speaks very loudly so that the children may not be heard*] There, that's it—so! That way!

RAMON. Quick! [*Running to look out of the door*] There's
no one here. [*At the door*] Come! Come!

[*Wiping his face to hide a tear.*

DANIELA. I'm coming! I'm coming!

[*Unable to move from where she stands.*

RAMON. Don't delay! Quick, I say!

*Without looking at her, so that she may not see how
    much moved he is.*

DANIELA. Yes, yes—I'm coming—now!

RAMON. But—what is this?

DANIELA. [*Bursting into tears*] Ay, Ramón, I cannot! [*He
runs up to her*] Help me! Help me!

RAMON. Great God!

DANIELA. Carry me, Ramón! Carry me in your arms!

RAMON. I am mad!

DANIELA. I am cold as the grave.

RAMON. I am mad!

*He bundles her into her wrap as best he may. It falls to
    her feet. What with dragging her behind him and lifting
    her in his arms, they reach the outer door together.*

DANIELA. I want to live! I want to live!

RAMON. [*Like a wild man*] You are mine! Mine! I claim
you now!

DANIELA. Life! Life! To live! To live! I will not die!

The children have stopped singing. Enter MONSA.
She pauses in the doorway.

MONSA. What's this? Where are you going?

RAMON. Out of my way!

MONSA. Daniela!

DANIELA. We are going away.

MONSA. Going away? Where are you going?

RAMON. Stand back!

> *Meanwhile* DANIELA *has slipped from* RAMON'S *arms, supporting herself with difficulty against the wall.*

MONSA. [*Placing a hand on each jamb of the door*] No! Where are you going? . . .

RAMON. Come, Daniela!

DANIELA. To be happy with him, like the woman I am! I have not been able to become like you.

MONSA. I am happy in another way.

DANIELA. Out of my sight! Ramón, take her out of my sight!

RAMON. [*To* MONSA] Out! Out!

MONSA. Let go; I'll call!

DANIELA. Ramón! Ramón!

> RAMON *leaves* MONSA *and runs up to* DANIELA *to carry her away.*

RAMON. Come! Come!

MONSA. You shall not go! [*To* DANIELA] You shall not go!

RAMON. Because you are too good?

[*He struggles with* MONSA, *trying to seize her by the throat.*

MONSA. No, no—you'll strangle me!

DANIELA. Ramón, no, no!

[RAMON *has thrown* MONSA *to the floor.*

MONSA. Don't go! Don't go!

[*She catches* RAMON *about the knees so that he cannot go.*

RAMON. Come! Be quick!

[DANIELA, *meanwhile, has staggered to the door.*

MONSA. Not though you kill me!

RAMON. [*Infuriated*] Fool! I see blood!

[*With his hands at* MONSA's *throat.*

MONSA. [*Loosening his grip*] Anna!

DANIELA. [*To* MONSA] No, for God's sake!

RAMON. [*Falling back*] Hush, hush, I say!

MONSA. [*Getting up*] Anna! Anna!

Enter ANNA.

ANNA. What's the matter?

RAMON. [*To* MONSA] Be still!

MONSA. Your father's running away! Hold him, Anna!

ANNA. Father! Where are you going, father?

[*Bursting into tears.*

MONSA. [*To* DANIELA] Better you had died!

DANIELA *lays her hands upon her heart, apparently suffering great pain.*

RAMON. [*To* ANNA, *wildly*] Let go! Let go!

MONSA. No, Anna, hold him tight! They're taking your father away!

RAMON. Monsa! [*Seeking to quiet her.*]

ANNA. Father!

MONSA. Hold him tight! Hold him tight! Don't let him go!

ANNA. Father! Father! [*Throwing her arms about his neck.*

RAMON. My child! My child!

[*Pressing her to his heart and bursting into tears.*

MONSA. [*To* DANIELA] Now take him away—if you are able.

DANIELA. I?—I?—I must go . . . [RAMON *makes a movement toward her*] Alone! [*She takes a step toward the door and comes face to face with* ANTONIA] Antonia! [DANIELA *pauses.*

ANTONIA. What is this? [*All are silent. To* DANIELA] Where are you going? Alone!

ANNA, *still in her father's arms, hugs him convulsively.*

DANIELA. To find a home in the earth that is warm, for I

am chilled to the bone.   A home in the heart of the earth—
my mother!

ANTONIA. But what's the matter?

> *To the others, seeing that no one helps her. DANIELA is
> about to fall. ANTONIA runs to catch her; MONSA
> comes up at the same time.*

MONSA. Daniela!

DANIELA. Nothing, it s no matter—it's no matter if I fall.
I am dying!

ANTONIA. Dying? God!

> *Enter TOMASETA, PONA, ANDREW, VALENTINE and
> others from the village, both men and women, followed
> also by the children. They enter slowly, a few at a
> time, and stand about the door. The children, as they
> appear, distribute themselves among the older people.*

MONSA. The Doctor! Quick!

DANIELA. No, no—no doctor! Lord—our—God! Forgive!

MONSA. Quick! Quick!

> *Several standing near the door run out. Others, however,
> enter, scarcely daring to come forward.*

DANIELA. Take me out in the road to die!

ANTONIA. No!   She doesn't know what she is saying.

DANIELA. [*Continuing*] Yes, I must go.   Help me . . .

MONSA. What do you want, Daniela?

DANIELA. To go! [*Aside to* MONSA] I am the stain, the
stain upon this house.

MONSA. Ah, no, no! [*To the children*] Come!   Stand around
her. [*The children approach* DANIELA, *forming a half-circle
about her*] You don't want her to go away? You don't, do
you?   [*The children say "no," very sadly.*

DANIELA. [*With her arms about them*] Ah!   I am happy—
now! I am happy now! [*To* ANTONIA, *pleadingly*] And Anna?

ANTONIA. [*Calling her*] Anna! Anna!

DANIELA. Come! Come! Anna! [ANTONIA *places* ANNA *in* DANIELA's *arms*] She has saved us all. Thanks, Antonia. [*To* ANNA] Poor Anna! *Looking at* ANTONIA] *My girl, my girl!* [*Aside to* ANNA] Anna! Your father, Anna—take him to your mother. Yes—yes! Anna! [ANNA *takes her father by the hand and leads him to* ANTONIA, *who is standing near*] Ah! I am happy now!

[DANIELA *motions to the children to come nearer.*

ANNA. [*Returning to* DANIELA] Aren't you going to stay? Aren't you going to be ours?

DANIELA. Yes, yes! I am yours! Yours!—How cold I am! [*The children press about her more closely*] Yes, yes! Nearer! Nearer! All! All!

MONSA. [*Aside*] Poor Daniela!

DANIELA. And the sun will make all bright again. [*The shower has passed; little by little the sky has been growing lighter*] Monsa, you can pull down the tower.

A CHILD. Closer! Poor dear, she's cold!

OTHER CHILDREN. Aren't you going to stay?

DANIELA. I'll never go away. I shall be here always—always!

> *A number of children have appeared in the street. They join hands and begin to sing, as at the beginning of the act. The workmen at the house can be heard cutting stone.*

MONSA. They're at work again.

DANIELA. [*Looking at the cradle*] Show me the boy! [*With a convulsive effort she gets up*] I'm going to the boy . . . I'm going to the boy·

> *She advances to the cradle, assisted by* MONSA *and* ANTONIA, *and followed by the children. The two women are scarcely able to support her. When she reaches the cradle she slips out of their arms, sinking on her knees beside it.*

DANIELA. [*As she falls upon her knees*] Little boy! Little boy!

MONSA. [*Aside*] The cradle's empty! Oh!

RAMON. Don't touch her!

DANIELA. [*Singing, her voice stifled*] "Mother—of—God"...

MONSA. [*Aside*] She is singing.

DANIELA. "Of God—of God" . . .

So saying, she lays her cheek on the cradle. It tilts to one side under her weight.

MONSA. [*Looking up to heaven*] Forgive!

DANIELA. "God—God" . . .

She drops dead, lying on the floor at the foot of the cradle. The children fall back in terror, weeping softly.

MONSA. Dead!

ANTONIA. Ramón!

RAMON, sobbing, embraces ANTONIA. ANNA hides herself in the folds of her mother's skirt. MONSA kneels and imprints a kiss on the brow of DANIELA. The cradle, freed from her weight, is still rocking. In the street the children continue to sing. The workmen go on cutting stone.

Curtain.   (2)

051671